Activism on the Web

Activism on the Web examines the everyday tensions that political activists face as they come to terms with the increasingly commercialized nature of web technologies and sheds light on an important, yet under-investigated dimension of the relationship between contemporary forms of social protest and internet technologies.

Drawing on anthropological and ethnographic research among three very different political groups in the UK, Italy, and Spain, the book argues that activists' everyday internet uses are largely defined by processes of negotiation with digital capitalism. These processes of negotiation are giving rise to a series of collective experiences defined by the tension between activists' democratic needs on one side and the cultural processes reinforced by digital capitalism on the other. In looking at the encounter between activist cultures and digital capitalism, the book focuses in particular on the tension created by self-centered communication processes and networked individualism, by corporate surveillance and data-mining, and by fast capitalism and the temporality of immediacy.

Activism on the Web suggests that if we want to understand how new technologies are affecting political participation and democratic processes, we should not focus on disruption and novelty, but we should instead explore the complex dialectics between digital discourses and digital practices; between the technical and the social; between the political economy of the web and its lived critique.

Veronica Barassi is Lecturer in the Media and Communications Department at Goldsmiths, University of London, UK.

Routledge New Developments in Communication and Society Research

Series Editor: James Curran, *Goldsmiths, University of London*

Activism on the Web

Everyday Struggles against
Digital Capitalism

Veronica Barassi

Routledge
Taylor & Francis Group

LONDON AND NEW YORK

First published 2015
by Routledge

2 Park Square, Milton Park, Abingdon, Oxfordshire OX14 4RN
711 Third Avenue, New York, NY 10017

Routledge is an imprint of the Taylor & Francis Group, an informa business

First issued in paperback 2017

Library of Congress Cataloging in Publication Data

Barassi, Veronica.
Activism on the web : everyday struggles against digital capitalism / by Veronica Barassi.
   pages cm. — (Routledge new developments in communication and society research ; 4)
Includes bibliographical references and index.
   1. Information technology—Social aspects. 2. Information technology—Political aspects.
   3. Capitalism—Social aspects. 4. Political participation. 5. Social action. I. Title.
HM851.B364 2015
306.2—dc23   2015000689

ISBN: 978-0-415-71791-5 (hbk)
ISBN: 978-1-138-57569-1 (pbk)

Typeset in Sabon
by codeMantra

Contents

Acknowledgments

First of all, I would like to thank those who have made this book possible, by teaching me that there are multiple and complex ways in which we can fight for social justice. I would like to thank all the people of the *Cuba Solidarity Campaign*, for their stories, understandings, and insights. In particular, I would like to show my gratitude to Rob Miller, Trish Meehan, Natasha Hickman, Matt Willgress, and Frank Liddiard for having made the everyday context of my fieldwork so lively and fascinating. A special thanks goes to Dean Weston, for his friendship, complicity, and support.

I also would like to thank all the activists of *Ecologistas en Acción*. In particular I would like to thank José Vincente Barcia for having inspired this book with his critical insights and in-depth knowledge of social and environmental injustices. A special thanks goes also to Luis Gozález, Javier Martín, Mariola Olcina Alvarado, and Rodrigo Calvo Lepez for their help and support with my research.

Last but not least, my immense gratitude goes to all the activists involved with the *Corsari* and ZAM whom I had the pleasure to meet during my fieldwork. Growing up in Italy, I am deeply connected to their cause. A very special thanks goes to my very good friend Davide Furia, who has always believed in me, despite his criticism, and has made my research possible. I also would like to thank Silvia Martorana, Carlotta Cossutta, Nicoló Garufi, Alice Monguzzi, Giacomo Belolli, Edoardo Todeschini, Elia Rosati, and Claudio Bonavera.

My immense gratitude goes to the Arts and Humanities Research Council (AHRC) and to the British Academy Small Research Grants scheme, which have made this research possible. I am equally grateful to the Anthropology and Media and Communications Departments at Goldsmiths, University of London, and to iCES (Institute of Contemporary European Studies) at Regent's University for having believed in my project and having enabled me to strengthen my cross-disciplinary research.

In the years of my research, I met a variety of scholars who have mentored and inspired me. First of all, I am particularly indebted to Natalie Fenton. Throughout the years, her expertise, vast knowledge, and critical reflections have been the source of constant motivation and support. I doubt that I will ever be able to convey my appreciation fully, but I owe her all my gratitude. Another person who has been crucial to my development as a researcher and teacher is Nick Couldry. His passion for social theory with his in-depth knowledge and ability to see people for what they are has not only inspired me but has also enabled me to pursue my dream. There are no ways in which I can thank him appropriately.

I also would like to address a special thanks to James Curran for having believed in my research and having supported me in my personal development. Another special thanks goes to David Graeber, for reading my doctoral thesis, on which part of this book is based, and providing me with many inspirational comments and advice. I am also equally indebted to Àngels Trias i Valls and Michael Scriven.

I would have not been able to complete my research without the academic and emotional support of my fellow colleagues and friends. Our discussions enriched my understanding of the importance of critical theory in the study of digital activism. In particular I would like to thank Emiliano Treré, Alice Mattoni, Gholam Khiabany, Des Freedman, Mirca Madianou, Victoria Goddard, Elisenda Ardèvol, John Postill, Mila Steele, and many others who have strengthened not only my critical skills but also my belief in the importance of the ethnographic method.

There are no words to express how deeply grateful I am to my family. I am particularly indebted to my sister Brada for her complicity and unconditional support and to my parents Patrizia and Gianni without whose inspiration, care, and encouragement I would have never come so far. Finally, I would like to thank Paul and my daughter Lea for being my source of love, enthusiasm, and inspiration and for making my everyday life so special and exciting.

Introduction
Activist Cultures, the Web, and Digital Capitalism

The early months of 2011 were months of social and political discontent in Spain: The effects of the financial crisis and the austerity measures imposed by the Socialist government of Zapatero were impacting everyday life. In March 2011 – as the platform of Democracia Real Ya[1] was being developed, giving rise to one of the largest mass mobilizations Spain had seen since the end of the dictatorship – I had the pleasure to sit down for an interview with Barcia.

Jose Vincente Barcia, known by everyone as Barcia within *Ecologistas en Acción* – one of the three organizations I studied for the research presented in this book – was born in 1969 in Galicia but grew up in Madrid. He had been involved in environmental activism from the age of 13 and throughout his life he was an active participant in a variety of radical left social movements. He participated in the democratic movements that followed the fall of Franco's dictatorship in the 1980s; he took part in the global justice movements of the late 1990s; and he demonstrated in the streets of Madrid during the 15M movements in May 2011.

In the interview Barcia talked about his life, about his political commitment, and about his perspectives on new and old media technologies. He also talked about capitalism. At the age of 42, after almost 25 years of involvement in environmental and political activism, he had a lot to say about capitalism. When I interviewed Barcia, I had been doing ethnographic work among activists for more than four years, studying how three very different political organizations used internet technologies as tools of political action. The interview with Barcia was one of my last interviews, and what he had to say about capitalism inspired this book.

B: Capitalism is not a power outside of me, but within me. I am capitalism. [...] Now for me recognizing that I am capitalism, and that I am part of the problem, it means that I am also recognizing that I am part of the solution.

Barcia's comment really surprised and inspired me. I was struck by a fundamental contradiction. In fact, as a trained anthropologist, I had to come to terms with trying to make sense of the fact that a political activist, who had dedicated his life to the *ecologismo social* (social environmentalism) – an ideology that is based on a profound critique of capitalism by combining environmental politics with radical left understandings – would see capitalism as a personal process.

As I was listening to what Barcia had to say, I thought about all the research work I had done on activist organizations and suddenly realized that his statement was in fact really not surprising at all. In his life as a political activist Barcia had to come to terms with some fundamental transformations in the capitalist modes of production and exploitation, which impacted his everyday practices and life. These transformations were largely fueled by the extension of computer mediated communication and information technologies. Thus, it is not surprising that – as he was discussing the relationship between internet technologies and social movements – Barcia talked about capitalism not only as a deeply unfair system but also as a personal process, as something that he was part of as a political activist.

He explained that he saw capitalism as an "organism" that was able to survive because of two different strategies. The first is defined by capitalism's ability to constantly re-invent and adapt itself to a given time or culture. The second strategy is represented by the fact that capitalism is able to transform everything and empty it of meaning by relying on people's short-term goals. According to Barcia, we are all part of capitalism as we try to fulfill our short-term desires. However, we can all become politically aware of this and take part in social movements with the intent of criticizing capitalism from within and reminding the "organism that if it continues like this it will die."

Barcia's analysis of the relationship between social movements and capitalism made me think about Boltanski and Chiapello's (2007) theory on the *New Spirit of Capitalism*. The scholars argued that capitalism manages to survive because of its ability to cyclically renew its 'spirit' when forces of indignation challenge its moral justification.[2] Their theory shares many lines of similarities with Barcia's argument, first because they talk about capitalism's ability to renew itself, and second because they argue that transformation within society occurs through *a dialectical relationship between forces of domination and forces of resistance*, between capitalism and social movements.

This book is based on the understanding that the dialectical tension between capitalism and forces of indignation represents a key aspect of the relationship between social movements and internet technologies. However, within communication research there is little exploration of such complex dialectics. On the one hand, political economy scholars are eager to highlight that internet technologies and especially web 2.0 technologies are supporting a new type of capitalist domination, which is based on a politics of dispossession of personal data (Jakobsson and Stiernstedt, 2010; Van Dijck and Nieborg, 2009, Bauwens, 2008), on corporate surveillance (Andrejevic, 2003, 2009, 2013; Jarrett, 2008), and the exploitation of immaterial labor (Terranova, 2000, 2013; Huws, 2003; Fuchs, 2007, 2014; Scholz, 2013).

On the other hand, scholars interested in social movements are highlighting how new web technologies are used to mobilize collective action and promote social change (Juris, 2008; Lievrouw, 2011; Hands, 2010; Gerbaudo, 2012; Mattoni, 2012; Cammaerts et al., 2013; Wolfson, 2014).

In this framework we have little data available on how activists understand and negotiate with digital capitalism. This book focuses on the everyday life of three political groups in Europe and discusses how they negotiate with the *ethnographic tensions* that emerge in the encounter between *digital capitalism* and their activist cultures. The aim of this book is to demonstrate that it is in the way in which people imagine and negotiate with social and technological structures that social change happens. It argues that if we want to comprehend how new technologies are affecting political participation and democratic processes, we should not focus on disruption and novelty, but we should instead explore the complex dialectics between transformation and continuity; between the technical and the social; between the political economy of the web and its lived critique.

DIGITAL CAPITALISM AND THE WEB

Internet Technologies, Globalization, and Digital Capitalism

We cannot fully comprehend the notion of *digital capitalism* without looking back at the 'globalization' literature and the early 1990s. At the time different scholars highlighted the fact that there was a bound relationship between the extension of new computer and satellite technologies and the emergence of new capitalist modes of production and consumption. David Harvey ([1989] 1991) and Anthony Giddens (1991) suggested that new satellite technologies were shrinking the world, so that space and time could no longer be considered as direct constraints for the organization of human experience. Despite having theoretical differences, both scholars believe that since the 1970s the world has gone through key social and political transformations triggered by the saturation of national markets and, subsequently, the increased over-taxation from governments, leading to the emergence of more disembedded institutions and a networked economy that has strongly relied on new information technologies (Harvey, 1991:141–172; Giddens, 1991:79).

By the mid-nineties, with the extension of internet technologies, the processes described by Harvey (1991) and Giddens (1991) accelerated, and capitalism consolidated its new global character. In this framework, the work of Manuel Castells (1996) was well-timed and particularly important. Castells (1996), in a similar manner to Harvey and Giddens, understood globalization as an economic and technological process that started to emerge at the end of the 1970s. However, following a more techno-deterministic stance, Castells (1996) placed a particular emphasis on the 'information technology revolution' and suggested that the global re-structuring of capitalism was greatly facilitated by new information and communication technologies. In this framework, he argued that the technological revolution did not originate and diffuse by accident or as a consequence of the re-structuring of capitalism. On the contrary, according to his perspective, new technologies made the re-structuring possible, since they provided the indispensable material basis for such a new economy to develop (Castells, 1996:66).

Throughout the1990s, the techno-historical transformations described by scholars such as Harvey, Giddens, and Castells affected a great majority of social contexts across the world. Following the fall of the Soviet bloc, different countries embraced the neo-liberal model promoted by Thatcher and Regan, which stressed free trade, privatization, and the deterritorialization of corporate power and technological dependency. In this context, discussions started to arise as to whether scholars could understand global transformations in terms of a Wallersteinian (1980) model of 'core versus periphery' and if the local was being replaced by global homogeneity. Research demonstrated that in fact a dual process of homogenization and heterogenization defined globalization and that the 'local' existed in a dialectical interaction with the global (Appadurai, 1996; Anderson, 2002; Friedman, 2000; Gupta and Ferguson, 1992; Kearney, 1995; Tomlinson, 1991). In this framework the globalization of markets, media, and information technologies was seen as a dynamic process of 'disjuncture' and 'difference' (Appadurai, 1990) rather than as a process of imposition from 'above' or from a global center.

Even if scholars were able to demonstrate that local cultures did not disappear in a vortex of global homogeneity, the literature of the 1990s started to highlight the fact that the rapid growth in usage and extension of internet technologies was supporting new forms of capitalist production and exploitation, with clear implications for social and political organization. The Autonomous Marxists were the most influential scholars who – drawing on a critical re-reading of Marx – argued that digital technologies facilitated a new emerging type of capitalism, a capitalism that was based on new forms of immaterial labor (Hardt and Negri, 2000; Lazzarato, 2006; Dyer-Whiteford, 1999; Terranova, 2004). They argued that industrial modes of material production were being replaced by immaterial modes of production and contended that scholars needed to consider those areas of labor that are involved in the production of 'the informational and cultural content of the commodity' (Lazzarato, 2006:133). In this book, I will highlight some of the weaknesses of the work of the Autonomous Marxists; here, however, I want to focus on the that, despite their weaknesses, the Autonomous Marxists highlighted the fact that there was a bound relationship between internet technologies and new forms of capitalist accumulation and exploitation.

Such an understanding was widely shared by political economy scholars within communication research and gave rise to many different important contributions in the field. At the turn of the century we saw the emergence of a variety of works, which used concepts such as *digital capitalism* (Schiller, 2000), *cybercapitalism* (Mosco and Schiller, 2001), *virtual capitalism* (Dawson and Bellamy Foster, 2000), *technocapitalism* (Kellner, 2002), and *informational capitalism* (Castells, 1996) to address the social complexities and nuances of the relationship between new technologies and capitalism. Although I am aware of these social complexities and of the fact that the relationship between capitalism and new technologies encompasses different political economic aspects and can be approached from a variety of socio-political perspectives (e.g. Kellner and the 'spectacle'), in this book I decided to draw in particular on the earlier work of Schiller (2000) and refer to the notion of *digital capitalism*. In his book Schiller (2000) demonstrated that under the pressure of the neo-liberal logic of Western governments (in particular the U.S. government) the internet began a political economic transition in order to support "an ever growing range of intracorporate and intercorporate business processes [...]" (2000:1). This transformation, according to Schiller, has led to the establishment of a communication infrastructure network that is highly shaped by the neo-liberal logic. Such an understanding, as Curran (2012) and McChesney (2013) have shown, is particularly important for the analysis of what the internet has become today and for a critical reflection of the democratic challenges that we are facing. In my opinion, Schiller's work is particularly interesting also because it shows that the establishment and strengthening of digital capitalism were tightly linked to the refashioning of the World Wide Web as a consumer medium (Schiller, 2000:89–142). This understanding lies at the very heart of the reasoning behind this book.

The Web as 'User Interface' and Digital Capitalism

The creation of the World Wide Web, as Curran (2012) argued, was a turning point in the history of the internet (2012:35) that radically transformed and influenced the way information on the internet was accessed, shared, and organized worldwide. Drawing on Curran (2012), I understand the web in very simple terms, namely as the construction and establishment of a "user-interface that provides a convenient method of organizing and accessing distributed data across computer networks" (2012:35). Therefore, the advent of the World Wide Web was crucial in the definition of our understanding of the internet simply because it defined not only our experience of it but also the way in which we understand it and imagine it.

As it is well known, the creator of the World Wide Web, Tim Berners-Lee, has always been committed to values of public welfare and imagined the web as an 'universal medium' for sharing information; a medium that was not primarily defined by commercial interest (Berners-Lee, 2005; Curran, 2012:41). However, throughout the 1990s, Berners-Lee's original project was subverted and undermined by an aggressive commercialization of the web (Curran, 2012), which strengthened corporate control over content, as well as new practices of corporate surveillance and exploitation. The increased commercialization of the web was made possible through a series of technological advances and web developments, such as the establishment of the Google monopoly in research browsers, the transformation in mobile communications, and the emergence of web 2.0 technologies.

In 2004, Tim O'Reilly announced that the early 2000s had seen the development of a different type of web, the web 2.0. According to O'Reilly (2005), the new web, in contrast to the web 1.0, differentiated itself because it was no longer based on a network of hypertexts but was instead defined by co-production of information, social networking, and the harnessing of the collective intelligence of crowds to create value. 'Participation,' 'interactivity,' 'user-generated content' became the buzzwords used within business circles, the popular press, and academia to define the new developments in web technologies.

Since its introduction, the term *web 2.0* has become extremely popular, to the point that at the end of 2005 it had 9.5 million citations on Google (O'Reilly, 2005). Within academic circles, some scholars jumped to a quick conclusion on the so-called potentials of new technologies and argued that the new web, for its interactive features, was offering unprecedented possibilities for user engagement, creativity, and cooperation (Gillmor, 2006; Jenkins, 2006; Reynolds, 2007; Shirky, 2008; Tapscott and Williams, 2007; Castells, 2009). Such uncritical and techno-optimistic understandings have been quickly deconstructed by those who have instead highlighted the fact that far from being democratic, web 2.0 technologies were in fact strengthening new forms of capitalist exploitation and corporate surveillance (Mosco, 2004; Hidman, 2008; Fuchs, 2007; Fisher, 2010; Morozov, 2011; Lovink, 2011; Curran, 2012; McChesney, 2013). Particularly interesting is the work of Fisher (2010), which draws on the theory of Boltanski and Chiapello (2007) to argue that the digital discourse around web 2.0 works as a form of capitalist justification and legitimation and reinforces the 'new spirit of capitalism' today. His analysis is both poignant and interesting.

In this book, therefore, I am particularly interested in the relationship between web technologies and capitalism, and using the term *digital capitalism* I want to explore the relationship between web platforms and new forms of capitalist discourse and practice. In particular I want to focus on some of the cultural, social, and political tensions that digital capitalism creates. In fact, in contrast to Schiller (2000) whose notion of digital capitalism is grounded on a 'monolithic' perspective (Wheeler, 2000), I understand digital capitalism as *an economic, cultural, and political process,* which is radically transforming the design of web platforms with clear consequences for the relationship between democratic processes and internet technologies. Therefore, I am not interested in mapping structures of digital capitalism, but rather I am concerned with the social tensions that arise in people's *encounter with digital capitalism* in their everyday internet uses.

One problematic aspect that emerges from contemporary communication research is the fact that political economic scholars often do not consider how people are experiencing and negotiating with *technological structures*. The aim of this book is to investigate these processes of negotiation by departing from the ethnographic contexts of political activism and to explore how anti-capitalist activist cultures deal with their encounter with digital capitalism through their everyday web uses. Although in this book I am focusing on the concept of digital capitalism, and on the social and cultural tensions that digital capitalism creates especially in the context of political activism, I certainly believe that "cultural experiences witnessed on web platforms cannot be 'simply dismissed as yet another form of corporate control over culture, or Orwellian dataveillant machine'" (Langlois et al., 2009:1). However, in this book I want to focus on the cultural experiences created by digital capitalism, because I feel that we have little data available on how activist cultures that have been fighting for years against capitalism are dealing and negotiating with the bound relationship between digital technologies and emerging forms of capitalist accumulation and exploitation. This book argues that activists' critical awareness of changing technological structures and capitalist exploitation on the web provides us with important insights on the social complexity of contemporary web practices and on the relationship between digital capitalism and everyday political critique.

ACTIVISM ON THE WEB

Internet Technologies and the Changing Repertoires of Political Action

The history of the internet, as Curran (2012) has argued, is defined by four different yet complementary cultural tensions: military science, academic circles, countercultural communities, and the European walferist tradition. Thus, when approaching the study of web technologies, we must bear in mind that the historical development of the internet in the West needs to be understood as 'chronicle of contradictions' (2012:48). During the 1990s and early 2000s while internet technologies were becoming the material support of new forms of networked capitalist exploitation and accumulation (Castells, 1996, 2009 ; Hardt and Negri, 2000; Terranova, 2004; Boltanski and Chiapello, 2007) among social movements, they became the material support for the construction of un-hierarchical and affinity-based relationships, based on notions of 'autonomy' and 'solidarity' that challenged the globalization of capitalism (Castells, 1997; McCaughey and Ayers, 2003; Meikle, 2003; Atton, 2004).

In 1994, a small collective of artists and activists in Europe and the U.S. – known as the Critical Art Ensemble – argued for the importance of creating networks of 'electronic disturbance.' Drawing from the theories of Deleuze and Guattari ([1987] 2004), the collective of artists contended that power was liquid and that its networks extended through the means of communication. Therefore, according to them, political and cultural resistance had to be fought in cyberspace (Critical Art Ensemble, 1994:12, 23, 57–58). The same year as the Critical Art Ensemble called for constructing electronic civil disobedience, in the far southeast of Mexico, a guerrilla army of indigenous Mayan peasants – the Zapatista Army of National Liberation (EZLN) – rose up in rebellion against neo-liberal capitalism and in particular against the North American Free Trade Agreement (NAFTA).

Since the very beginning, the Zapatista struggle distinguished itself from other political movements for two main reasons. In the first place, the *guerrilleros* led by the Subcomandante Marcos showed a disinterest in state power or hierarchical structures and instead emphasized autonomy, direct democracy, and relationships of affinity (Day, 2005; Graeber, 2002; Holloway, 2002; Khasnabish, 2008; Tarrow, 1998). These political ideologies have moved beyond the Mexican borders and have had a profound 'resonance'[3] on political activists across the world (Khasnabish, 2008). In fact, it was within the movement for the liberation of Chiapas that the People's Global Action (PGA) network was created, which in turn led to the 1999 Seattle demonstrations and the rise of the networked movements for global justice (Klein, 2001; Graeber, 2002).

In the second place, the Zapatistas were one of the first social movements to use the internet to agitate, enact their autonomy, create a collective identity, and construct worldwide support and networks (Castells, 1997; Ribeiro, 1998; Slater, 1998; Kowal, 2002; Atton, 2004). It is for this reason that Castells defines their struggle as the first form of "informational guerrilla activism" (Castells, 1997:79). Khasnabish (2008) has argued that in understanding the pervasiveness of internet technologies within Zapatismo, scholars have often romanticized the situation and have not addressed the problem that in actuality Zapatista communities lacked electricity and running water, let alone internet technologies (2008:18–20). Without romanticizing, however, the conflict in Chiapas brought about an important variation in the repertoires of political action across the globe. Indeed, following the Zapatista insurrection and the creation of the People's Global Action network, political groups across the world started to turn to internet technologies because they saw them not only as tools of social and political organization but also as 'weapons' of resistance that enabled them to simultaneously challenge political, media, and corporate power (Melucci, 1996; Della Porta and Diani, 1999; Della Porta and Tarrow, 2004; Juris, 2008).

The development of mobile technologies and web 2.0 platforms has marked a new and complex transformation of the repertoires of mediated political action. In the last few years, countless examples have emerged of mass protests that relied on social media in order to mobilize and organize collective action (Hands, 2011; Lievrouw, 2011; Gerbaudo, 2012;

Cammaerts et al., 2013; Barassi and Treré, 2012; Castells, 2012; Wolfson, 2014; Postill, 2014). This is especially true if we consider the historical developments and 'revolutions' that have affected the North African and Middle Eastern regions (Bayat, 2009; Sreberney and Khiabany, 2010), as well as the 15M movements in Spain or the Occupy movements in the United States (Gerbaudo, 2012; Postill, 2014; Castells, 2012; Juris, 2012). As Sreberney and Khiabany (2010) have argued with reference to the 2009 Iranian Revolution, although it is important to maintain a critical understanding about the use of web 2.0 technologies in the region, scholars need to realize that the internet is changing things in ways that neither governments nor social movements can anticipate.

A Critique of Techno-Determinism, and the Importance of the 'Media as Practice' Approach

In understanding the new political imaginations that have affected social movements in the last decades and their relationship to new technologies, different scholars have emphasized the 'power of networks,' especially internet networks, and relied on generalized concepts such swarms/multitude (Hardt and Negri, 2000; Virno, 2004), 'mobs' (Rheingold, 2003), and 'networked-individualism' (Castells, 2001, 2009). According to Castells (2012), for instance, the mass uprising of 2011 began on social networking sites and spread by contagion in a world of wireless communication, mobile media, and the viral exchange of images and content. He argued that social media networks created a 'space of autonomy' for the exchange of information and the sharing of feelings of collective outrage and hope. He thus reached the conclusion that web technologies have become the material support of a new type of political participation, a participation that is based on horizontal networks, political autonomy, and leaderless organization.

In contrast to the implicit techno-determinism of scholars like Castells (2012), in recent years we have seen the emergence of a variety of studies that, drawing from the understanding of 'media as practice' (Couldry, 2004; Brauchler and Postill, 2010), have provided us with a variety of great scholarship on activists' uses of web technologies (McCurdy, 2011; Gerbaudo, 2012; Mattoni, 2012; Barassi and Treré, 2012; Cammaerts et al., 2013; Feingenbaum et al., 2013). Current research on social movements' media practices is insightful and necessary. This is because it challenges techno-deterministic assumptions on the pervasiveness and agency of internet technologies in the everyday life of social movements by considering the tension between 'old' and 'new' media and by highlighting the complex relationship between media structures, practices, and beliefs. What seems to be emerging within this body of literature is that we need to move away from the debate between the techno-optimists (Shirky, 2008; Castells, 2009, 2012) and the techno-pessimists (Morozov, 2011) and to critically consider how internet technologies have become a tool of opportunity and challenge for social movements.

Despite being insightful in highlighting the multi-faceted complexities of social movements' engagement with different forms of media, much of contemporary scholarship on media and social movements focuses on how new technologies enable the emergence of new modes of political and social organization but does not systematically explore the problematic tensions between activist cultures and digital capitalism. The aim of this book is to contribute to the existing literature on movements' media practices by exploring the tension between activists' democratic needs on the one hand and structures of digital capitalism on the other. In doing so, and in contrast to current approaches, I draw heavily on the anthropology media. Current approaches on movements' media practices are defined by a lack of engagement with anthropological theories, which is somehow surprising given the fact that anthropologists have long been involved in the analysis of the human and social complexities involved in cultural practices (Sahlins, 2005).

The research presented in this book draws from the theories and methodologies of Anthropology and Media Studies and aims to demonstrate that – although disciplines are 'systems of meaning' with their own codes and signifiers (Peterson, 2003) – a careful deconstruction of academic boundaries and the cross-fertilization among disciplines create the basis for the emergence of new possibilities for social research. *Activism on the Web* is the product of this cross-disciplinary effort.

DIGITAL CAPITALISM AND ACTIVIST CULTURES

A Media Anthropological Approach

Anthropological contributions to the understanding of media practices date back to the work of the Lynds on community media in the United States (1924 in Peterson, 2003) or to Powdermaker's (1950) ethnography on Hollywood filmmakers. However, it was only during the 1990s that the field of 'media anthropology'[4] started to emerge. One of the first to initiate the debate was Ginsburg (1994) who wrote an essay, titled 'Culture/Media: A Mild Polemic,' where she argued that people's engagement with media images and technologies needed to be a matter of ethnographic enquiry as were other cultural practices. Another seminal essay is the one of Spitulnik (1993), titled 'Anthropology and Mass Media,' which explored the many different ways that anthropologists could study the media.

While anthropologists at the beginning of the 1990s started to really push forward the importance of developing a branch of the discipline that looked at media, during the late 1980s and beginning of the 1990s, in media studies different media scholars started to turn their attention toward anthropological methods, theories, and concepts. Carey (1992) was one of the first to use the anthropological notion of 'ritual' in order to argue that communication scholars had to move away from the understanding of communication as a unidirectional process (sender/medium/receiver) and instead consider the cultural practices around communication. Another example is represented by audience research, where scholars like Morley (1992) and Ang (1995) argued for the development of an approach that relied on the ethnographic method and considered how audiences were not passive receivers but actively responded to media texts, according to cultural and social specific understandings.

Therefore, the field of media anthropology – as Coman (2005) argued – was created by two different yet complementary tensions in anthropology and media studies. On the one hand, there was a 'cultural turn' in media studies, where communication scholars started to focus on the media as social and cultural processes. On the other hand, there was 'the reflexive turn' in anthropology, which brought the understanding that anthropologists were neglecting an important dimension of social life, like the media. It was thanks to these debates and tensions that the field of media anthropology was finally established in the decade of the 2000s. Between 2002 and 2006, three different readers and influential books in anthropology of the media were published (Ginsburg, 2002; Askew and Wilk, 2002; Peterson, 2003; Rothenbulher and Coman, 2005). In 2004 the EASA Media Anthropology Network was established. Since then we have seen the growth of different areas of research in media anthropology, from the study of 'media as practice' (Couldry, 2004; Postill and Brauchler, 2010) to the study of 'journalism' (Hannerz, 2004; Bird, 2009) to the analysis of internet technologies and digital cultures (Horst, 2012; Boellstorff, 2010; Miller, 2011; Coleman, 2012; Gómez Cruz and Ardèvol, 2013; Roig and San Cornelio, 2013).

The developments in the field of the last years have proven the richness of the media anthropological approach, which distinguishes itself for three main reasons. In the first place it draws on the ethnography of media to understand how people negotiate with communication technologies. In the second place it is defined by scholars' commitment to theorize and understand media as everyday practices and as social processes (not merely as text, technologies, or organizational structures). In the third place it challenges ethno-centric and techno-deterministic understandings of media's social impacts by looking at cultural variation. Askew (2002), I believe, provides us with the most illuminating and comprehensive definition of what it means to apply a media anthropological approach, when she argued that such an approach is an "Ethnographically informed, historically grounded and context-sensitive analysis of the ways in which people use and make sense of media technologies" (Askew, 2002:3).

The research presented in this book was largely based on the principles and beliefs of media anthropology. In fact, not only has the book been inspired by in-depth ethnographic research among activists, but it draws extensively on anthropological theories to explore the 'encounter' between activist cultures and digital capitalism as well. Anthropologists have long been interested in the way that local cultures negotiate with colonial or state powers; during my research, I used my anthropological knowledge in order to understand the way that activists negotiate with digital capitalism.

Furthermore, my research was inspired by the anthropological belief that, in the study of media technologies, researchers need to be committed to 'cultural relativism' (Horst, 2012). Miller and Slater's (2000) early study in Trinidad was groundbreaking in the anthropology of the internet, because they argued that the internet was invested with cultural meanings and understandings. A similar approach was used by Miller (2008) in his latest work on Facebook. The understanding behind these works is that cultures and humans negotiate with the structural constraints of technologies in different ways through a process of cultural translation and adaptation. This book is based on a similar theoretical standpoint and, thus, on the understanding that if we want to explore how web technologies are transforming political participation, we have to explore how different political groups, which are grounded on completely different political cultures, understand internet technologies according to context-specific political imaginations.

In the last decade different communication scholars have highlighted the importance of adopting a comparative perspective in the understanding of media systems, cultures, and practices (Hallin and Mancini, 2004; Couldry and Hepp, 2009). However, as Livingstone (2003) has argued, comparative media research can present profound methodological and theoretical problems. One of these problems is the fact that often researchers depart from the biased assumption that nations and cultures can be understood as units and therefore be compared. Following Livingstone's (2003) important criticism of cross-national and comparative research, and her quest to locate one's own research assumption, I locate myself among those researchers who believe that a comparative analysis between cultures, nations, and groups is impossible because they are not comparable units. However, although I believe that it is impossible to come to conclusions by relating one culture to another, I strongly believe that a cross-cultural approach can enable scholars to understand media processes for their social and cultural specificities (Livingstone, 2003:12–14). As the next part of the chapter will show, this understanding lies at the very heart of the research project presented in this book.

A Cross-Cultural Ethnographic Project

This book is based on a research project that aimed to ethnographically explore the way in which the activists involved in three very different organizations in Europe reacted to the web developments of the last years and the growing commercialization of the internet. The three organizations were chosen because they differed largely in political cultures and ideologies. The first organization is the *Cuba Solidarity Campaign*, a British international campaigning group that was created in 1978 and is attached to the political ideologies of the British Trade Union Movement. The second organization is *Ecologistas en Acción*, an environmental activist group that was funded in 1998 during the global justice movements and is based on a political culture that combines radical left ideals with environmental awareness. The third organization is called the *Corsari*. Created in 2008, it is embedded in the Italian autonomous movement, which is based on political culture that highlights the importance of self-management, political autonomy, and direct action.

Activism on the Web will show that the three groups, despite being based on different political cultures and despite being embedded in very different social, economic, and cultural contexts, have to engage with similar techno-social transformations brought about by digital capitalism. It critically assesses the way in which these transformations are impacting the internal politics, everyday practices, and understandings of collective action. The book argues that activists' everyday internet uses are constantly defined by complex processes of negotiation with the social, cultural, and economic constraints created by the corporate logic of web technologies. These processes of negotiation, it will be shown, are giving rise to a series of different 'ethnographic tensions' or, in other words, a series of collective experiences, which is defined by the tension between activists' democratic needs and digital capitalism.

This book will therefore explore three main ethnographic tensions faced by activists when using web technologies as tools of political action: the tension created by self-centered communication processes and **networked individualism**; the tension created by the exploitation of user-generated data and **digital labor**; and the tension created by the hegemonic temporal context of immediacy. Each chapter of the book therefore will not draw on a comparative analysis of the three different groups but will explore these ethnographic tensions by looking at the ethnographic contexts in which these themes have emerged.

Chapter One will introduce the ethnographic context of the three organizations. It will introduce the concept of *'media imaginary'* and will argue that it is impossible to fully appreciate the organization of activists' media practices without an in-depth knowledge of their political cultures. In doing so the chapter will argue that one of the main weaknesses and limitations of contemporary studies on digital activism is represented by a lack of ethnographic engagement and thus by a clear understanding of the relationship between activists' media usages and their political projects.

Chapter Two combines a thick description of the changing communication strategies of the three groups with extracts of the life histories of the people involved, which discuss how web developments have changed their experience of political activism. The chapter will argue that activists are critically aware of the fact that the web has become a space of corporate surveillance and exploitation. It will propose a theoretical framework that can enable us to understand the tension between activist cultures and digital capitalism. In order to develop this theoretical framework, the chapter will try to re-frame current debates on technological agency by looking at the relationship between technological discourses and everyday practices (De Certeau, 1984; Orlikowski, 2000; Couldry, 2004; Brauchler and Postill, 2010) and by showing how the web has become a contested space of imagination and practice (Kelty, 2012).

Chapter Three will explore the first ethnographic tension experienced by activists in their everyday use of web 2.0 technologies and especially social media: the problem of mass-self communication (Castells, 2009, 2012). It will argue that, in contrast to those who advocate the rise of mass self-communication as positive for social movements (Castells, 2009, 2012), activists are critical about the individually centered networks of social media and believe that there is a strong connection between online self-communication, individualism, and the capitalist discourse. Drawing from some of the insights of the anthropology of the person and the self (Mauss, 1985; Cohen, 1994; Morris, 1994), the chapter will argue that the relationship between social media and political activism is embedded in a tension between the notion of political autonomy as promoted by activists and the 'individualistic' autonomy promoted by social media platforms. Therefore, the chapter contends that activists' everyday social media uses are defined by an ongoing process of negotiation with the 'self-centered' logic of these web 2.0 technologies. This process of negotiation, it will be shown, varies from context to context, as it is often defined by activists' *media imaginaries* or, in other words, by the need to shape their social media practices with reference to their own political cultures and projects.

The understanding that people adapt the uses of internet technologies according to cultural and context-specific political projects raises fundamental questions on the way that people actually negotiate with corporate exploitation on the web. *Chapter Four* will focus on the issue of *digital labor*. The extensive use of web 2.0 platforms and social networking sites has triggered a growing concern among scholars on the politics of capital exploitation that these practices conceal. Research has shown that the production of user-generated content can be understood as a form of 'free labor,' a labor that is exploited by web 2.0 corporations to generate income and value (Jakobsson and Stiernstedt, 2010; Van Dijick and Nieborg, 2009; Bauwens, 2008; Andrejevic, 2003, 2009; Jarrett, 2008; Terranova, 2000, 2013; Huws, 2003; Fuchs, 2007, 2013; Scholz, 2013).

This chapter explores the different ways in which the Italian and Spanish activists, who had been greatly affected by precarious working conditions and unemployment, were critically reflecting on the issue of digital labor. It will argue that despite being critically aware of the corporate exploitation and surveillance to which they were exposed, activists were willing to share information on web 2.0 platforms and negotiate with digital capitalism. Bringing together my own empirical findings with critical Marxist approaches in anthropology (Graeber, 2002; Turner, 2006), the chapter argues that in order to understand activists' processes of negotiation we need to re-frame theories of digital labor, by looking at the concept of *value* in anthropological terms and appreciating that the production of human value goes well beyond rationalist/reductive economist paradigms. In doing so, the chapter will demonstrate that the production of value online cannot be perceived merely as the production of data to be turned into a commodity. It is only by looking at the human value that activists actively produce on corporate web 2.0 platforms that we can start to appreciate the meaning these technologies have for political participation and to look at the many margins of freedom from online corporate surveillance that activists actively construct.

The focus on the problems of corporate surveillance or digital labor can be crucial in exploring the political economy of the web. Yet another problem, which is still under-investigated, is the problem of temporality of the internet (Hassan, 2003, 2007, 2009; Leong et al., 2009), which I will explore in *Chapter Five*. The chapter will argue that mobile media and web 2.0 technologies are creating a temporal context that is based on the notion of 'immediacy' (Hassan, 2007; Tomlinson, 2007; Virilio, 1995). Combining the literature on capitalism and hegemonic time consciousness (Thompson, 1967; Thrift, 1990) with the one of the anthropology of time (Gell, 1992; Munn, 1993), the chapter will explore how the hegemonic temporal consciousness of immediacy is impacting political and democratic processes. The aim is to show that although it is true that web developments have accelerated the possibility to share information and mobilize action in fast and effective ways, the temporality of web technologies is affecting processes of political reflection, discussion, and elaboration in negative ways. This is not only because online communication tends to simplify radical reflections and discourses but also because the pace of information exchange reduces political discussions and creates insurgent networks (Castells, 2009) of action, which rely on weak affinities and strong emotions but not on shared political projects. These transformations are having a strong impact on the lived experience of political activism, and people are looking for ways to cope with the logic of immediacy. Drawing on activists' testimonies, I will argue that – alongside the issue of surveillance and control – the notion of the temporal context promoted by web 2.0 platforms is one of the darkest effects of web developments and really challenges the democratic potential of these technologies and the political processes that they make possible.

Chapter Six will critically explore how the anxieties and frustrations that activists experience in their everyday encounter with digital capitalism on web platforms are radically transforming their relationship with printed media. Drawing on the anthropological literature on material culture and exchange (Appadurai, 1986; Miller, 1997), this chapter will reflect on the continued importance of activist magazines in the context of CSC and *Ecologistas en Acción*. The chapter speaks both to the changing nature of oppositional groups and the ways that technological developments are embedded in the wider processes of human comprehension, interaction, and negotiation. It argues that looking at why people – and especially grassroots political organizations – remain attached to material forms of communication, while at the same time developing online ones, can raise critical questions on the connection between subjectivity, political association, and new technologies.

After exploring the different ethnographic tensions experienced by activists in their everyday web uses, and reflecting on the way in which these tensions are impacting activists' relationship with printed media, the concluding chapter of the book will, therefore, explore the current transformations in web developments. In particular, I will focus on the issue of big data. I will draw from the main arguments of the book and present some empirical evidence on the ways that activists are understanding and negotiating with what is being understood as the next big 'technological revolution.' The chapter is influenced by the latest critical internet research (boyd and Crawford, 2012; Gitelman, 2013; Couldry and Powell, 2014) and will argue that it is of pivotal importance to critically deconstruct the current 'technological hype' around big data and reflect once again on the complex relationship between technological transformations, digital capitalism, and the unpredictability and creativity of human practices.

NOTES

1. Democracia Real Ya was a web platform and political reality created by different political groups active in Spain, such as Anonymous, ADESORG, Estado del Malestar, No le Votes, Ponte en Pié, and Juventud en Acción, which sparked the mass mobilizations of the 15 of May (15M) and the rise of the 15M/Indignados movement.
2. According to the two scholars, the forces of indignation that have fueled criticism to capitalism have more or less remained unchanged and can be divided into four sorts: a) capitalism seen as a source of disenchantment and inauthenticity; b) capitalism seen as a source of oppression; c) capitalism seen as a source of poverty and profound social inequalities; d) capitalism seen as a source of opportunism and egoism (2007:37).
3. Resonance is intended here as a non-linear and unpredictable dynamic by which meaning constructed in a particular context becomes significant in another with both predictable and unexpected effects. Rather than diffusion – which signifies migration – resonance signifies movement, mutation, and active translation (Khasnabish, 2008:8).
4. Anthropologists' interest in media technologies dates back to the early twentieth century, and this is especially true if we consider the many different contributions in the field of 'visual anthropology.' However, although anthropologists were interested in the different and complex dimensions of the visual, it was only in the 1990s that they started to research and theorize about people's engagement with mass media or internet technologies (Marcus, 1996; Herzfeld, 2000; Peterson, 2003).

1 The Ethnography of Digital Activism

INTRODUCTION

The use of media by social movement actors is certainly not new and has long preceded the development of internet technologies. Anderson (1991) and Tarrow (1998) suggested that the rise of small press publications was partly responsible for the development of different social movements during the eighteenth century. In the United States, Downing (1995) traced the roots of dissident publications back to the revolutionary pamphleteers of the American War of Independence and showed that media activism has been a central form of political action from the nineteenth-century women's press and the suffragette movement to the civil rights movements of the 1960s (1995:180–191).

In the last two decades, the media produced by social and political minorities have become a growing area of interest in media and communication research. 'Radical media' (Downing, 2000), 'citizens' media' (Rodriguez, 2000), 'alternative media' (Atton, 2002), 'community media' (Howley, 2005), 'activist media' (Waltz, 2005), 'autonomous media' (Langlois and Dubois, 2005), 'tactical media' (Garcia and Lovink in Hall, 2008:128), 'our media' (McChesney and Nichols, 2002), and 'critical media' (Sandoval and Fuchs, 2010) have all been used to provide insights into the multiple varieties of the media produced at the grassroots level. Within these works a picture emerged that described these media as complex communication systems defined by participatory practices and content that is more or less in explicit opposition to the one of mainstream media[1] (Downing, 2000; Atton, 2002; Curran and Couldry, 2003; Coyer et al., 2007; Waltz, 2005).

In the last decade, scholarly research in the field has grown exponentially, especially due to the developments in internet technologies and the extension of 'digital activism.'[2] In fact we have seen a rapid proliferation of studies that have looked at how internet technologies and digital media have affected activists' practices (McCaughey and Ayers, 2003; Juris, 2008; Castells, 2009; Hands, 2010; Rodriguez et al., 2009; Joyce, 2010; Earl and Kimport, 2011; Gerbaudo, 2012) or transformed alternative and activist media (Meikle, 2003; Atton, 2004; Lievrouw, 2011). All these works demonstrated that digital activism has widened the scope and reach of media activism, enabling the proliferation of new media forms and strengthening activists' ability to mobilize and organize collective actions and mass protests in cheap, fast, and effective ways (Earl and Kimport, 2011).

Although we have seen a growing number of important analyses on activists' digital media practices and on the opportunities and challenges of digital activism (e.g. Joyce, 2010; Earl and Kimport, 2011; McCurdy, 2011; Gerbaudo, 2012; Mattoni, 2012; Treré, 2012; Cammaerts et al., 2013; Wolfson, 2014), current research in the field – with the exception of some works in social anthropology (Juris, 2008, 2012; Postill, 2014; Juris and Khasnabish, 2013) – is constrained by a fundamental problem. This is the problem of 'ethnographic refusal' (Ortner, 1995). In fact even when scholars of digital activism claim to have used the ethnographic method (e.g. Gerbaudo, 2012), they often rely on a combination of participant observation and qualitative interviews. In doing so they distance themselves from the notion of 'ethnography' as developed by anthropologists who believe that the richness of the ethnographic method is based on a quest for thickness and holism[3] (Marcus, 1998).

The chapter argues that lack of a 'thick' ethnographic engagement in the field of digital activism can have a serious repercussion on the type of data and knowledge that we have available about social movements and internet technologies. Drawing from Ortner (1995), I contend that ethnographic refusal leads to the production of a type of data that does not take into account the social life and internal politics of political groups, providing us with a 'thin' appreciation of the political cultures in which they are embedded. In contrast to these approaches, the chapter will argue that it is only through an in-depth understanding of activists' political cultures that we can fully appreciate the way in which they organize their media practices.

Therefore, the first part of the chapter will describe the historical development and political cultures of the three organization studied. The chapter will argue that in order to understand the complexity of activist cultures we need to look at the relationship between political *imagination* and practice and we must appreciate how activists' everyday political practices are shaped by specific political projects (Castoriadis, 1998; Taylor, 2003). This understanding, it will be shown, is essential also to the analysis of activists' media practices. In fact, by introducing the concept of *media imaginary*, the chapter will argue that the relationship between political project and practice is at the very heart of activists' media uses.

ACTIVIST CULTURES AND DIGITAL ACTIVISM: AN ETHNOGRAPHIC APPROACH

Digital Activism and the Problem of 'Ethnographic Thinness'

In the mid-nineties anthropologist Sherry Ortner (1995) argued that studies of resistance in the social sciences lacked an ethnographic perspective and that the failure to properly engage with the ethnographic method directly impacted the type of data that we had available on social movements. In the first place, according to Ortner (1995), the lack of engagement with the ethnographic method led to a 'sanitization of the internal politics' of resistant groups or, in other words, to the failure on the part of scholars to take into account the power relationships and hierarchies that defined the everyday realities of social movement actors (1995:176–180). In the second place, studies of resistance failed to appropriately contextualize social movements within broader cultural environments and did not appreciate issues of cultural complexity and variation. Consequently, according to Ortner (1995), they contributed to the 'thinning of culture' (1995:180–183). In the third place, the failure to use the ethnographic method in the study of social movements has produced a type of data that describes actors in broad terms as 'resistant subjects' but with little exploration of their biographical narratives (1995:183–187).

Almost 20 years after Ortner's seminal contribution, it is striking that the study of digital activism today seems to be encountering the same problems that she described at the time. Not only do we have little knowledge of the internal politics of resistant groups and of how the biographical narratives of activists are intertwined with technological developments, but also we are often co-participants with the process of 'thinning of cultures.' Key examples of these problems can be found in works of those scholars who have chosen to study digital activism mainly by focusing on web platforms (e.g. Earl and Kimport, 2011; Hands, 2010; Stein, 2011) or in the works of those – like Gerbaudo (2012) or Castells (2012) – who despite maintaining a sociological stance do not consider the social complexities of activist cultures. Both authors, in fact, focus on the example of different movements, from Tunisia to Iceland, Egypt, Europe, and the United States, neither providing us with a thick analysis of the different cultures in which these movements are embedded nor offering us an insight into the complexity of their political cultures.

In contrast to these approaches, anthropologists have shown how important the ethnographic method is for the study of digital activism (Juris, 2008, 2012; Khasnabish, 2008; Postill, 2014; Juris and Khasnabish, 2013). In these works, ethnography is understood not simply as a set of qualitative methodologies, including participant observation and interviews, but also as a mode of analysis and writing (Juris and Khasnabish, 2013:3). Their approach is of central importance because it enables us to understand that activist political cultures, although inspired by specific waves of protest movements, are in fact the product of open-ended and complex processes of social construction, which change from context to context, from group to group. The research presented in this book was inspired by these approaches and was based on the understanding that what we are missing from current research on digital activism is an ethnographically thick understanding of activist cultures and of their everyday processes of negotiation with web technologies.

Understanding the Social Complexity of Activist Cultures

The project presented in this book was born out of a will to highlight the social complexities that define the relationship between activist cultures and digital technologies. In order to do so, I have chosen to work with three different organizations, in three different countries, and belonging to three different movements. The idea of the project was to shed light on the social tensions that emerge in activists' web uses, by looking at the history of the three different organizations and considering the biographical narratives of the activists involved. Methodologically the research project was designed following the 'old,' 'new,' and 'newest' distinction in social movement studies.

During the 1980s, 'new social movements' scholars argued that the late 1960s and 1970s had seen a profound transformation in the political repertoires of social movements and that old social movements based on class struggles were being replaced by movements based on identity politics and single-issue campaigns (Touraine, 1985; Laclau and Mouffe, 2001; Melucci, 1996; Castells, 1983). In the late nineties, following the Zapatista uprising and the establishment of the 'movements for global justice,' newest social movements' scholars highlighted another fundamental cultural shift in the political repertoires of collective action. They argued that the 'politics of demand' of the 'new social movements' had gradually been replaced by an understanding that the emancipations of political identities are constantly instrumentalized by power forces (Holloway, 2002; Day, 2005; Hands, 2010). The newest movements, according to the scholars, did not believe in the importance of identity politics and challenged the very idea of representative democracy in favor of a politics based on the notion of political autonomy.

The theoretical distinction between 'old,' 'new,' and 'newest' social movements has influenced the methodological choices of the research presented in this book. In fact, I have chosen to work with an organization that was embedded in the 'old' political culture of the Labor Movement and two organizations that were instead embedded in 'new' and 'newest' social movements, like the environmental and autonomous movements in Spain and Italy. Although the project was inspired by the debates in social movements studies, and by the classical distinction between 'old,' 'new,' and 'newest,' when I approached fieldwork I realized that such distinction does not capture the social complexities of activist cultures. Calhoun (1995) has rightly argued that the new social movement scholars of the late eighties, in order to mount the challenges to 'old social movements,' have exaggerated the extent to which labor politics was based on a Marxist meta-narrative of class unity, overlooking the importance of identity politics (1995:178–184). According to him, the main problem in the literature is that scholars keep focusing on transition rather than on the interplay between different political repertoires in the shaping of activist cultures. This same problem emerges also within the work on the 'newest' social movements (Holloway, 2002; Day, 2005) and in the research on digital activism (Earl and Kimport, 2011; Joyce, 2010; Hands, 2011; Gerbaudo, 2012; Castells, 2012). Scholars often emphasize the linearity and novelty of repertoires of political and media action without considering the complex interplay between old and new political cultures and without taking into account social movements' internal ability to renew themselves.

It is important to understand that an approach that focuses on 'transition' rather than renewal and that does not consider the complex dialectics between change and continuity is flawed. Such an approach does not take into account the fact that different repertoires of political and media action coexist in a tension. Looking at this tension is of central importance to social analysis. This is because it sheds some light on social movements' internal, innovative, and creative struggle to find new possibilities to bring about social change. In the next parts of the chapter I will explore the historical development and changing political repertoires of the three organizations studied. I will try to provide an analysis of the social movements in which they are embedded and will map the political projects and beliefs that define their political cultures.

THE CUBA SOLIDARITY CAMPAIGN AND THE LABOR MOVEMENT IN BRITAIN

The Labor Movement, a Century of Struggle and the Creation of Solidarity Campaigns

Crossing Oxford Street on a Saturday morning in June 2007, I felt surprised to find it completely deserted. The early morning and its emptiness imposed a surreal atmosphere upon one of London's busiest streets. It was early June and, before I realized it, I found myself once again in front of Trade Union Congress House. The Trade Union Congress (TUC) is the national federation of trade unions in Britain, comprised of 54 national unions affiliated with a total of about 6.2 million members. The Trade Union Congress House is located on Great Russell Street in Central London. It was constructed in 1958 as a memorial to the sacrifices made by trade unionists in the two World Wars, and since then has been the headquarters of the TUC. With its 1960s' architecture and the sculpture by Jacob Epstein in the courtyard, Congress House has been one of the overlapping spaces of my multi-sited ethnographic research (Marcus, 1998). As often occurs in familiar spaces, that morning I knew where to go. I walked down the metal staircase, looked at the TV screens – which were announcing the SERTUC (Southern and Eastern TUC) Conference on Global Solidarity – and found my way to the plenary hall.

The TUC was founded in 1860 after more than a century of repression and criminalization of organized labor in Britain. In 1889, the TUC founded the Labor Representation Committee in the endeavor to stand for Parliament, and this led to the creation of the Labor Party in the early years of the twentieth century (Webb and Webb, 1919:570; Cole, 2001:182). The Labor Movement in Britain was a key contributor in the progressive and democratic transformations in Britain in the twentieth century. In the years following the First World War and leading to the Great Depression, trade unions largely increased in membership size and in political influence gaining many different successes in the development of workers' rights. During the Second World War, trade unionism played a fundamental role in strengthening the domestic economy of war (Wrigley, 1997) and supporting the European anti-fascist movement (Buchanan, 1991). In 1945, the Labor Party won the national election and proceeded to introduce a free National Health Service (NHS), a free education system, and a state welfare system meant to protect each British citizen from the "cradle to the grave" (Hollowell, 2008:486).

The political and economic influence of the British Labor Movement kept on increasing in the postwar period until the late 1970s.[4] The winter of 1978–1979, famously known as the 'Winter of Discontent' for a series of major strikes against the Labor Government, marked a fundamental setback for the Labor Movement and the beginning of a sharp decline in the political and economic influence of the unions. This was due to the fact that the inability of the Labor Government to deal with the trade unions was one of the causes for the victory of Margaret Thatcher and the Conservative Party in 1979, which quickly proceeded to create a series of laws and policies that were all directed at weakening the power of the trade unions (Dorey, 2006:155).

During the 1980s, under the government of Margaret Thatcher, trade unions lost much of their political and economic influence. In a decade of struggle and defeats two events have become particularly emblematic. One is the failure of the yearlong Miners Strike (1984–1985), which was perceived as a success for Thatcher's government. The second one was the abolishment in 1986 of the Greater London Council, which was led by Ken Livingstone and other Labor councilors and clashed with Thatcher's government. Thatcher's policies largely impacted the movement's political and economic influence.

In addition, during the 1980s and 1990s under John Major's government, unions had to come to terms with the re-structuring of capitalism, globalization, and the casualization of labor (Mayo, 2005). In this framework it is not surprising that between 1979 and 2000 trade union membership largely declined. To get an idea of this decline it is important to look at the numbers presented by the TUC website. In 1979, for instance, the membership of the Transport and General Workers' Union (TGWU) was 2,086,000 (making it easily the largest union then); by 2000 it had fallen to 858,000. Over the same period, the 253,000 members of the National Union of Mineworkers (NUM) had shrunk to 5,000.[5]

During the years of decline in membership numbers, the Labor Movement witnessed the emergence and strengthening of different single-issue political organizations created by trade unionists. Among these was a sharp rise in international solidarity campaigns. One fascinating aspect of these solidarity groups was the fact that a great majority of international solidarity campaigns in Britain – that are linked to the trade unions – are showing their 'solidarity' to Latin American countries. This is not surprising. Indeed, as Tariq Ali (2008) suggested, many within left-wing organizations in the UK believe that these countries stand as examples of 'alternatives' to the global neo-liberal system and give hope to people who fight for socialist ideals, workers' rights, and state welfare (Ali, 2008). In this framework, showing solidarity to these countries, creating trade union networks, and defending their representations in the British national media are all considered important political acts by the people involved.

International solidarity organizations are a particularly interesting site of research for the study of digital activism. This is because practices of transnational action had always existed, especially if one considered the history of workers' solidarity (Thorn, 2006); however, digital activism has facilitated and transformed these forms of transnational activism. Indeed, as some scholars have shown – although in the past international trade unionism was anchored to notions of working-class unity and traditional left-wing discourses – in the last decades the notion of international solidarity has been transformed by the advent of new technologies and the creation of global networked movements (Alvarez et al., 1998; Castells, 1996; Dagnino, 1997; Hardt and Negri, 2000; Waterman and Wills, 2001). When I approached fieldwork at the end of 2006, I believed that the context of international solidarity organizations in Britain was a very interesting field of research, where one could properly investigate the techno-historical transformations of the last 15 years by looking at people's personal histories and testimonies, and considering how practices of international solidarity had changed.

The Cuba Solidarity Campaign

Although the different international solidarity campaigns are in fact interconnected and members and organizers often overlap, I decided to focus my research merely on the *Cuba Solidarity Campaign* (CSC), which was the oldest international solidarity organization within the Trade Union Movement. The organization, previously known as British Cuba Resource Centre (BCRC), was born in 1978 out of a group of trade union members and individuals who aimed at gathering and sharing information on Cuba's socialist achievements and on its economic blockade. At the time – in the middle of the Cold War in Britain – information on the socialist country was scarce and, most of the time, biased; traveling to Cuba was quite rare, and personal relationships with Cubans were infrequent.[6] The information available in Britain was based mostly on firsthand individual experience or on the cuttings from *Granma Newspaper.*[7] Just before the 'Winter of Discontent' and at the very beginning of the Thatcher years, BCRC organizers gathered in a room of the Casa Latina in North London to discuss Cuba's achievements in terms of public health and education and compare these with the political and economic situation in Britain. At the time, the group produced a newsletter of information on Cuba. This newsletter, which later became the *CubaSí* magazine, was the very heart of the organization.

The fall of the Soviet bloc in 1989/1990 had a profound impact on the BCRC; all the members of the executive committee almost disappeared, and the resources for producing the magazine were no longer available. Although some would suggest that people withdrew from the organization because after the collapse of USSR, no one believed that socialism in Cuba was going to survive; other details seem to imply that the crisis was triggered by the fact that socialism and the socialist states were being questioned at the time by the people who saw themselves as socialists. Despite struggling, the organization managed to survive, and in 1992 it was transformed from a resource center into the *Cuba Solidarity Campaign*. By binding effective political and economic networks with the major trade unions in Britain, it largely increased its membership size and political influence. Consisting of 4,000 individual members, 450 trade union branch affiliates, 28 local groups on national territory, and two sister organizations in Northern Ireland and Scotland, CSC has become today the leading political organization in Britain with a focus on Cuba and Latin America.

CSC and Its Political Project

When I first entered CSC and was introduced to office workers, members, and volunteers, I started to acquire the certainty that I had been thrown into a profoundly British, white, male-dominated, middle-aged, middle-class reality. Despite some members coming from different Latin American backgrounds, overall people within CSC are usually British nationals, who identify strongly with Cuba. By showing their solidarity to Cuba, the principal aim of the campaign is to show that there is an alternative to the neo-liberal system. The political project of the campaign is directed towards defending Cuba's right to national sovereignty, independence, and self-determination, without outside interference. After 50 years of blockade, the *Cuba Solidarity Campaign* calls for the end of the blockade and for the normalization of diplomatic, economic, and cultural relations with the island. It is for this reason, as argued elsewhere (Barassi, 2012), that their campaigning strategies are all directed towards the construction of a positive image of Cuba though a complex and fascinating *game of mirrors*. The *game of mirrors* between Cuba and Britain is sustained by the shared idea among members and organizers that Cuba represents an example, an alternative reality, which helps to highlight the contradictions of the political system in Britain, and possibly transform it.

By placing the policies of the Cuban and the British governments in antithesis, the aim of the campaign is to argue for the importance of putting social welfare first. Their intention is not to propose that Britain should undergo a socialist revolution, but to argue that state intervention – and a limitation to corporate power – can lead to important civic transformations. One fascinating aspect of the *game of mirrors* between Cuba and Britain is that it is often played on notions of class conflict, where Cuban achievements are compared to the achievements of the working classes in Britain. In this respect, I found it extremely interesting that at a South London CSC meeting a volunteer and organizer in her fifties compared the Cuban health achievements to the working classes' battle for the NHS in the UK just after the Second World War. For many within CSC, the Cuban Government had done for its citizens and workers what they believed the Labor Government should have done for them. Indeed, as I have been told once by a volunteer for CSC: "The example of Cuba shows to all of us the lost promises of the Labor government, in terms of public health, and free education."

We cannot fully understand the social context of CSC without acknowledging the fact that this is a context where progressive policies, activism, workers' rights, collectivism, and state welfare constitute the means for the construction of shared meanings. Within this context particularly important is the notion of *international solidarity*. The notion of international solidarity has been essential to the development of the Labor Movement, which has been influenced by the socialist values of the Third International (Borkenau, 2013). Within the movement, solidarity means solidarity among workers at the global level,[8] but it also means solidarity with socialist governments and states. The creation of international solidarity organizations, along with the continuous political and economic support that trade unions provide for these organizations, is an indicator of the importance of international solidarity for the Labor Movement.

The way in which CSC builds international solidarity has changed enormously during the years. At the beginning, solidarity was largely expressed through the collection and the shipping of aid material to Cuba or the construction of international trade union networks. In the late 1990s, the situation radically changed. Today, the campaign's involvement with material aid has decreased to the point that it is limited to the shipping of musical instruments or ballet shoes through the *Music Fund for Cuba*.[9] In contrast to the past, solidarity is expressed through symbolic action, which is aimed at defending the 'image' of Cuba in Britain. This transformation can only be understood if we consider a shift in the political project of The Cuban Institute of Friendship with the People (ICAP, Instituto Cubano de Amistad con los Pueblos). The organization, which is funded and run by the Cuban Government, is in charge of coordinating the global solidarity movement with Cuba. In 2003, ICAP explicitly asked CSC to stop sending material aid and to focus instead on producing information on Cuba and on countering the negative representations of its government in Britain.

The overall idea is that, in an internet-connected world where information flows freely from one country to another and the message of political movements reaches a global scale, paradoxically the 'wall of silence' between Cuba and the rest of the world seems to be stronger than ever. In the majority of cases Cuba is not a matter of focus for global broadcasting companies and newspapers. It is not news; it is an old, outdated issue. When issues on Cuba are covered, these merely focus on negative representations of the socialist government. In this context, therefore, media action has been charged with a new and fundamental importance and has come to dominate the agenda of the *Cuba Solidarity Campaign* in Britain. Therefore, counteracting negative representations of Cuba has become for CSC members a matter of great importance, one that shapes their understanding of international solidarity and defines 'what they do.'

The importance of challenging the misrepresentation of Cuba emerged very well in an interview with Kate.[10] During the interview, she explained the importance of deconstructing the misrepresentations of Cuba and building a network of political support for the island.

V: How do you define political solidarity?

K: How do I define political solidarity? What, specifically about the political solidarity that CSC does?

V: yes ...

K: Well ... It is about giving a voice to Cuba in Britain, although it isn't the voice of Cuba, because we are not the Cuban Embassy and we don't say what the Cuban Embassy says. But we put Cuba in context in Britain to try to explain what is good about Cuba, what its achievements are. [...] When Cuba gets mentioned in the media it is always misrepresented, and our aim is to counter that misrepresentation of Cuba. But also, we aim to be a kind of center for gathering support. Departing from individual members who have networks and inform people but also at a much higher level within parliament and attempting to influence the British government policy over the blockade [...]. [We also] put pressure on the American government ... that has a real outcome for Cuba. So political solidarity for me is not only to say 'I am with Cuba' but it's actually achieving something, achieving some change for Cuba, and influence the British Government. That's how I see political solidarity.

As Kate explained, political solidarity is expressed in a variety of ways by the campaign, and the definition of the meaning of political solidarity keeps changing. In the understanding of activist political cultures, therefore, it is important to highlight the fact that these are not 'systems' that can be studied and analyzed as such but they are complex social processes of human construction and negotiation, which are always evolving. It is for this reason that it is crucial to consider the notion of political culture by exploring the socio-historical context in which they are embedded.

Fieldwork within CSC was carried out between the end of 2006 and the beginning of 2008, at a time of great social and political transformation for the Labor Movement. At the time trade unions and solidarity organizations were swept by a profound sense of disillusionment in the New Labor Government. This emerged effectively from an interview with Tasha. Tasha was employed as a campaigns manager in 2003, but after four years commuting from London to Brighton, and sleeping at the homes of friends and relatives, she decided to accept a job in Brighton for an academic institution. During the time she was not working for CSC, she helped out at events and kept saying how much she missed working there. Only five months later she returned to work for the campaign as communication officer. During her interview, she explained the profound disillusionment she felt towards the politics of Tony Blair and the New Labor.

T: When Labor came to power I had really, really high expectations because it was brilliant, it was a party, and there was a real sense of hope. I thought: what's going to happen? It's going to be fantastic! I was looking forward to major transformations. But then everything turned into a fucking nightmare. And now you have to really re-consider whether you vote for them again.

V: But what did you think it would do? What are according to you those 'major transformations' that didn't occur?

T: It's not so much about the major transformation that didn't occur. Because, you know, when it comes down to it, there are still major parts in the capitalist system, which are not going to change despite the government. It's the bad things that they did. That you didn't expect them to do, like start dismantling the NHS or carrying on supporting arms trade, and the wars. Before the election I always identified really clearly as a Labor voter, since the election, possibly since working at CSC as well, but now I don't know.

Discontent, disillusionment, and skepticism in the Labor Party and in governmental politics in general were pervasive elements among trade unions and other networked organizations at the time of fieldwork. In this context people's identifications with Cuba and Latin American politics acquire a great social significance, which should be contextualized by looking at Laclau's concept of *dislocation*. For Laclau (1996) all identities are dislocated. This is because identities are discursive constructs that clash with the reality/structure of things. According to him, the feeling of dislocation, although traumatic, is also a condition of possibility, of social and political creation and re-articulation. For Laclau, dislocation makes alternative politics possible, because people become politically involved and construct their identities as a response to this feeling of dislocation (1996:60–65). His argument, I find, fits very well with the standpoint of this research. Cuba and Latin America, for the British Labor Movement, are important spaces of imagination in order to resist a feeling of dislocation. It is in the imagination of Cuba as an 'alternative' to neo-liberalism that individual understandings and experiences become shared images in the definition of their political culture.

ECOLOGISTAS EN ACCIÓN AND THE ENVIRONMENTAL MOVEMENT IN SPAIN

Spanish Environmental Activism between Conservationism and Radical Politics

It was a sunny day in Madrid, fresh but not chilly, on 19 November 2010 when I walked through the neighborhood of Malasaña – known for its creative and countercultural scene – and down Marqués de Leganés, a small street just off Gran Vía, where the offices of *Ecologistas en Acción* are located. After three months of online ethnography and email exchanges, that day I was finally going to meet the people involved with the organization. I found myself in front of a small door on the ground floor of an old residential building, and few minutes later I was sitting in front of Barcia. Barcia greeted me with cordiality and showed me around the office. With yellow walls and 14 individual office spaces, the office seemed to be structured in a very horizontal way. Office staff looked friendly and very busy with more or less an equal number of men and women whose ages spanned from the late twenties to mid-fifties. I sat down with Barcia in one of the meeting rooms; we talked about my research and he started introducing me to the history of the environmental movement in Spain. In the following months I interviewed a variety of people in that room; I carried out research on the old issues of the magazines and participated in book launches and debates. In those months of research I slowly added testimonies and insights to what Barcia had told me that first day, and pieced together the different parts of the history of the organization and its political project.

The Spanish environmental movement – in contrast to other environmental movements in Western Europe – developed only during the 1970s when, after 36 years of dictatorship, Spain started to take the first tentative steps towards a democratic society. Historically the first environmental organizations emerged towards the end of Franco's regime, with the creation of the organization ADENA (1968), founded by people close to Franco, and later the foundation of AEORMA (1970), which was the first organization in Spain to begin the debate around nuclear energy (Sánchez, 2005; Colon Diaz, 1987). However, at the time 'political association' was still discouraged by the regime and the environmental movement struggled to take hold. It is only since the end of the dictatorship and the beginning of a period of political transition in the late 1970s that Spain has seen a rapid proliferation of a variety of different environmental organizations (Recio, 1992; Sánchez, 2005; Colon Diaz, 1987). During the years that followed the end of the dictatorship, the environmental movement arose thanks to the influence of different political cultures and tensions. In the first place environmental activism was triggered by local needs and influenced by ideas of regional autonomy that were linked to the national question (Recio, 1992:81–83). In the second place environmentalism in Spain was influenced by other new social movements, especially by feminist and pacifist social movements (Sánchez, 2005) as well as by anarchist discourses (Recio, 1992).

In October 1976, a group of environmental activists belonging to different organizations, including environmentalists who worked within ADENA or AEORMA, created an organization called AEPDEN (*Asociación de Estudios y Protección de la Naturaleza*), which promoted the first assembly of the *Federación del Movimiento Ecologista* (Federation of the Environmental Movement). The third and last assembly of the federation was organized in 1978 in Daimiel (Royal City) and it was during that assembly that a document was written indicating the manifesto of Spanish environmentalism, which emphasized the anti-capitalist and libertarian spirit of the movement (Varillas cited in Sánchez, 2005:62).

During that year, the movement was defined by the emergence of a conflict between two different ideologies (La Calle Dominguez et al., 2001:405). On the one hand, there were the *conservacionistas* (conservationists), who were grouped under the 'umbrella' organization CODA[11] (*Coordinadora para la Defensa del Ambiente*, Coordinator for the Defense of the Environment), which believed in a political culture of environmental activism based on the philosophy of conservationism and environmental protection. On the other hand, there were the *radicales* (radicals) who were represented by more radical organizations, such as *Amigos de la Tierra* (Friends of the Earth, Spain) and *Greenpeace*, who believed that environmental activism needed to be radical and political.

The decade of the 1980s was a period of political transformation in Spain but also of disillusionment for the environmental movement. In 1982, the socialist party PSOE won the election, giving rise to a series of expectations for environmental activists. However, the filo-European and neo-liberal policies of the new government, which emphasized 'economic growth' and 'modernization,' soon revealed that the government was not going to implement a real change in environmental politics. The decade was also defined by an increased fragmentation of the environmental movement. During the 1980s and the beginning of the 1990s, within the *conservationists* and the *radicals* internal conflicts started to emerge creating further contrast, division, and fragmentation. In 1985, for instance, in Madrid – which is the focus of my research – the former AEPDEN was affected by internal tension between environmental activists who sought to promote a more radical politics by joining forces with other social movements and others who did not agree with the focus on direct action and radical politics. In this context a new organization was created and called ADENAT (*Asociación Ecologista de Defensa de la Naturaleza*). Founded in Madrid, ADENAT extended on national territory and grouped different environmental organizations that shared a radical political culture.

The history of the 1980s and beginning of the 1990s confirms the fact that, as Rootes (2003) has argued, the environmental movement in Spain, in contrast to other movements in Western Europe, has been extremely fragmented. However, the decade of the 1990s was a very interesting decade for the environmental movement in Spain when important steps against its intrinsic fragmentation were taken, and the opposition between conservationists and radicals decreased.

The decade of the 1990s transformed significantly the political culture of the movement as organizations such as ADENAT became involved in the global justice movements. Two key dates mark this involvement. In autumn 1994, Madrid had been chosen as a site to celebrate the fiftieth anniversary of the creation of the International Monetary Fund (IMF), the World Bank (WB), and the General Agreement on Tariffs and Trade (GATT).[12] During the days of the summit – from 26 September to 3 October 1994 – social movements across Spain organized the *'Foro Alternativo'* (Alternative Summit), titled *'Cinquenta Años Bastan'* (Fifty Years Are Enough). The forum consisted of days of social and political unrest, conferences, demonstrations, and meetings to oppose the World Organizations. It was during these days that the Spanish social movements, including environmental organizations, started to become involved with what later became the movements for global justice. Another important date in this regard was the organization of the second world meeting in solidarity with the Zapatistas, which was organized in July 1997 and was titled the *Segundo Encuentro Intercontinetal contra el Neoliberalismo y para la Humanidad* (The Second Intercontinental Meeting against Neoliberalism and for Humanity).

Ecologistas en Acción

The creation of *Ecologistas en Acción* (Environmentalists in Action), in 1998, was the direct expression of the transformation that affected different areas of the movement, which saw different organizations seeking to establish a more radical stance. During the 1990s, the above mentioned umbrella organization CODA – which at the beginning of the 1990s brought together more than 500 local groups – started to reconsider its political culture and to include more radical groups. In 1996, CODA organizers together with the organizers of other umbrella organizations, such as ADENAT, C.E.P.A.[13] and other environmental organizations in different regions, started to discuss the idea of creating a unique organization, with a unique name, and a shared political manifesto. Reflecting on the process, one of the founders said, "It was a very complex process where groups were asked to reject their names and their identity as organizations. Few groups resisted and did not join, but the great majority joined."

Today *Ecologistas en Acción* is composed of 300 small[14] autonomous local groups organized in 19 different territorial confederations and 12 working groups at the national level, which deal with various environmental themes (climate change, water, transport, urban development, etc.). In contrast to CSC where the national office plays a fundamental part in the coordination of action, *Ecologistas en Acción* relies on a complex organizational structure based on participatory democracy. Local groups have the ultimate power to make their own decisions and manage their members and their campaigns. All the groups meet at the annual general assembly (AGM). Representatives of territorial confederations and of thematic confederations meet on a quarterly basis. In between meetings, it is the national office of the confederation based in Madrid that deals with the day-to-day choices and requirements of the organization. The very structure of the organization, which is based on a total autonomy of groups, makes it impossible to have an exact figure of the number of members. However, according to office staff, the organization counts around 20,000 members, 5,000 of which are militant activists.

The Political Culture of *Ecologistas en Acción*

The very history and structure of the organization suggest that the political culture of *Ecologistas en Acción* is based on ideas of autonomy and participatory democracy and is defined by a plurality of biographical experiences and beliefs. This emerged vividly during my research. From interviews and informal conversations it became evident that the organization brings together different ways of understanding and experiencing environmental action. Despite the plurality of beliefs, personal experiences, and areas of engagements, the organization is based on the ideology of the *ecologismo social* (social environmentalism), which brings together radical left and anti-capitalist beliefs with a concern for environmental justice. This political philosophy is based on the understanding that the current environmental crisis is the result of the capitalist economic system and its model of unlimited growth. Consequently, the people involved with *Ecologistas en Acción* believe that it is impossible to engage in environmental activism without dealing with issues of social justice and a political critique of capitalism.

This latter point becomes clear if one reads a document written following the general assembly of 2005, which brings together the ideological principles of the organization. The document begins by explaining the fact that, according to *Ecologistas en Acción*, the destinies of human societies and natural ecosystems are inseparable, and environmental activists need to tackle the global economic crisis by considering simultaneously environmental damage and human inequality. It is for this reason that the 12 ideological principles listed in the document, which are the basis of the political culture of the organization, bring together environmental issues such as pollution, nuclear energy, and animal rights with social issues such as the right to labor, the gender gap, the unfair divide between Global North and Global South, and the importance of localism and participatory democracy.

The ideology of the *ecologismo social* presupposes a commitment to the ideology of *decrecimiento* (de-growth). The concept of de-growth was originally introduced by the Romanian-born economist Nicolas Georgescu-Roegen ([1971] 2011), but historically ideas of de-growth have been part of different liberal-left movements and theoretical approaches. Key examples of this can be found in the Arts and Crafts movements in the UK during the Victorian age, which emphasized the importance of man over the machine, and in the writings of Gunther Anders or Hannah Arendt. In recent years, the concept has been popularized by Latouche (2009).

Within *Ecologistas en Acción,* the notion of *de-growth* is based on the assumption that the current modes of production and consumption are unsustainable and that individuals and governments need to find ways in which to downscale the process of capitalist production, accumulation, and consumption. According to the concept of de-growth, the downscaling of capitalist growth improves human conditions and the quality of life, reinforces local economies, and promotes human equality and environmental sustainability. In fact, the overall idea is that societies should live according to their own means and should democratically decide how to distribute their resources.

From the perspective of the *ecologismo social* the concept of de-growth is of central importance as it enables activists to critically reflect on and politically engage with a variety of different themes. In fact the concept is used to criticize ideas of 'sustainable development' in the Global South, to challenge the techno-optimism of the Western model of progress and technological advancement, and to propose different alternatives for social, political, and economic organization. Fieldwork among the *Ecologistas en Acción* revealed that – despite their internal differences and the variety of political and personal backgrounds – the notion of de-growth was at the very heart of their actions and their experience and involvement in environmental activism. As this book will show, the notion of de-growth was also at the very heart of activists' everyday critique of web technologies.

Research was conducted between July 2010 and July 2011, at a time of economic and social crisis in Spain, when the politics of Zapatero's Socialist government was coming into question and mass mobilizations of 15M movements gave rise to a long period of social unrest and critique in the squares of Madrid, Barcelona, and many other Spanish cities. The financial crisis and the peak in unemployment figures had created an opening for the environmental discourse to affect different levels of society. At the political level we witnessed the creation of the environmental party EQUO in June 2011, which became the ninth most supported party after the 2011 General Election, while at the grassroots level the anti-capitalist critique gave rise to different environmentally informed political initiatives.

THE *CORSARI* AND THE AUTONOMOUS
MOVEMENT IN ITALY

The Social Centre Movement and the Struggle for Political Autonomy

The first time I attended a meeting of the *Corsari*, it was a cold November evening in 2010. We were sitting in the garden of the ARCI Bellezza, a center for social and cultural events managed and run by the left-wing association ARCI with a low-budget bar and a restaurant. That evening the bar and restaurant were closed, but the head of the co-operative in charge of the center had given us access to the garden area. We were sitting in the dark, on bitterly cold white plastic chairs positioned in a circle, and the activists started to talk, to discuss various issues that had happened, and strategize future actions. It was cold, and there was the shared understanding that the meeting needed to end at a reasonable time in order to avoid the risk of clashes with neo-Nazi groups that could be waiting outside of the ARCI. I had been introduced and been given access to the meeting by an old friend, who was one of the key members of the group and vouched for me. For months I had been reading their blog on a daily basis, but online ethnography was limited by the fact that I had to gain access to their autonomous mailing lists where much of the exchanges took place. That evening I was there to negotiate my access to the group; I spoke briefly about the research and answered some questions, I observed and listened to the various issues that arose within the meeting, and I thought about the role of the *Corsari* in the Italian Autonomous Movement and all the things I knew and was going to learn about a very complex and ever-changing social movement.

The Italian Autonomous Movement finds its roots in the movements of the late 1960s and established itself during the 1970s, when different political realities started to organize moved by a quest for political autonomy. On the one hand, there were the autonomous worker groups such as *Autonomia Operaia* (AO) that sought to assert their grassroots independence from both the management of factories and the unions, which were linked to the Italian Communist Party (PCI). On the other hand, the movement owes its legacy to the feminist, student, and youth collectives that during those years were seeking to establish their autonomy from the Italian political and social context, which was defined by a system largely influenced not only by capitalist exploitation but also by blatant patriarchal costumes, and the legacy of fascism.

During the 1970s and beginning of the 1980s, a time that is usually known as 'Years of Lead,'[15] groups of youths, feminists, and activists became involved in a movement of reclaiming the city, by engaging in the occupation[16] of private and public spaces (Moroni, 1994; Ruggiero, 2000; Montagna, 2006). These spaces became known as *centri sociali* (social centers) and became proper landmarks of many Italian cities as they hosted different political and subcultural activities. Each city had a variety of social centers, which were organized by autonomous collectives of activists through practices of participatory democracy and *autogestione* (self-management). During the 1980s, some of these centers became particularly famous such as the *Leoncavallo* in Milan, the *Pedro* in Padoa, and *Corto Circuito* in Rome.

From the very beginning the social center movement defined itself by its 'autonomous' ideology. In fact the movement was based on a cross-regional organizational model, which recalled one of the 'net' constituted by nodes, independent and autonomous from one another but connected by similar political ideologies and struggles (Maroni, 1994; Ruggiero, 2000; Montagna, 2006). In Milan, which is the focus of my research, social centers such as the *Leoncavallo, Pergola, Conchetta, Torkiera, Bulk, Panetteria Okkupata,* and *Orso,* just to mention a few, have defined the history of the militant left from the 1980s throughout the 1990s and the early 2000s.

In 1994, the Mayor of Milan Marco Formentini[17] ordered the eviction of the historic *Leoncavallo* social center, and in the autumn of the same year he made a public statement claiming that from that day onwards the militant movement in Milan had been defeated and that what remained of it were only 'specters.' As a response to his claim, on 10 September 1994, during the demonstrations that followed the eviction of the center, activists took to the streets dressed in white overalls to recall the 'specters.' The demonstrations were organized with the support of other social centers on national territory – especially the ones of Padoa and the Northeastern region, as well as the *Corto-Circuito* in Rome – and the network between the different social centers gave rise to the famous '*Tute Bianche*' movement (*White Overalls*).

As some scholars have pointed out, the *White Overalls* became a strong political symbol within the movements of the 1990s well beyond the Italian context (Juris, 2008; Jordan, 2004; Starr, 2005). The political philosophy behind the *White Overalls* was new in essence. In the first place the *White Overalls* movement was seen as a way to challenge the very notion of identity and represented the enactment of multiple singularities becoming a mass, so to a certain degree these were the first forms of political actualization that inspired the Negrian 'multitude' model (Hardt and Negri, 2000). Furthermore, the *White Overalls* became known for challenging the dichotomy of violence versus non-violence, and for the fact that – in contrast to the blue overalls – they were meant to represent the changing regimes of labor, from Fordism to post-Fordism.

From the mid-1990s to July 2001, therefore, the Milanese autonomous scene was defined not only by the activities around the *Leoncavallo* and the *White Overalls* but also around a variety of different social centers. In 1997, an autonomous political collective of secondary school students was created under the name of RASC. This political collective occupied and created the famous Milanese social center named *Deposito Bulk*, which hosted one of the first Hacklabs in Italy, and played a pivotal role in the organization of the 2001 G8 protests in Genoa.

The 2001 G8 demonstrations in Genoa marked the end of the *White Overalls* and the beginning of a period of decline for the social center movement. The police brutality, with a protester killed, and the infamous School Diaz[18] episode signaled the beginning of a period of repression by the newly elected right-wing government lead by Silvio Berlusconi. After Genoa, the social center movement in Northern Italy was defined by the internal conflicts between the *Disobbedienti* (Disobedients) on the one hand – who were based in the North-East and particularly Padoa and who were grounded on the political philosophy of Tony Negri – and the activists of the North-West region on the other, whose key node was Turin and who have become key actors in the NO TAV movements against the High Speed Trains (Della Porta and Piazza, 2008).

In a context of tension between the North-East and North-West areas of the movement, the Milanese autonomous scene largely suffered. Particularly problematic for the movement in Milan was the politics of repression supported and enacted by the Vice-Mayor of Milan, Riccardo De Corato, a former representative of the Fascist Party MSI (*Movimento Sociale Italiano*), who was a representative of Berlusconi's center-right PDL (*Partito della Libertá*). While repressing left-wing social centers and the radical left militant movement in Milan, the city administration tacitly supported the strengthening of extreme right groups. In 2003, Milanese activists had to come to terms with the strengthening of far-right groups and the killing of Dax, a militant of the social center *Orso*. In 2005, they had to come to terms with the eviction of the famous social center *Bulk*, which was followed by the eviction of many other centers across town. In March 2006, around 300 activists from within the social center movement rioted in the streets around Corso Buenos Aires, near the center of Milan, and 40 of them were arrested. For many within the movement the episode represented a major defeat and the evidence of a lack of internal unity. By 2008, with the overwhelming victory of Berlusconi's coalition at the general elections, many radical left political parties had been excluded from Parliament. In a context of political disillusionment and repression where many people believed that the movement had died in Milan, in the summer of 2008 the *Corsari* collective was created.

The *Corsari* Collective

The *Corsari* collective was created in July 2008 and brought together the activists who belonged to different Milanese social centers (especially *Bulk, Orso, Panetteria Okkupata,* etc.) that had been closed down by the right-wing Milanese city administration with student groups (*collettivi studenteschi*) – which were involved in the 2008 student movement known as *Onda Anomala* (Anomalous Wave). At the beginning of 2008, Maria Stella Gelmini, the Education Minister of the Berlusconi Government, put forward a controversial decree aimed at cutting state funds for the education sector (Caruso et al., 2010; Treré, 2012). By October 2008, at national level a large student movement emerged that was not only defined by the participation of students (high school and university students), but also by the participation of young activists and precarious workers (Caruso et al., 2010; Mattoni, 2012).

At the time of fieldwork (2010–2011) the *Corsari* was a relatively small group, counting around 100 militants who gathered on a weekly basis in various spaces to organize direct actions and discuss a shared political strategy. In November 2010, the *Corsari* decided to organize a three-day-long occupation and to test the number of followers and supporters that they had. The occupation of a disused building near the center of Milan, which was called by the activists ZAM Racaille 2.0, was organized on social media and resulted in three days of concerts, political debates, and activities. After the successful three-day occupation, in January 2011, the *Corsari* occupied an abandoned building in Barona, a working-class area in the suburbs of Milan and they created the social center ZAM (Autonomous Zone Milan), which was evicted in May 2013. A few weeks later they occupied an old abandoned school in the center of Milan, which was evicted in July 2014.

Today the *Corsari* collective is no longer known as such, the members and organizers of the collective having given rise to a much larger political project called *MilanoinMovimento* (Milan in Movement). *MilanoinMovimento* brings together different autonomous collectives and political realities, including the social centers (ZAM and Lambretta), student networks, Ambrosia (a radical feminist collective), MaCAO (a radical cultural and artistic center), and many other political collectives. All these groups are self-managed and autonomous; they are based on horizontal structures, participatory democracy, and voluntary contributions. Given the organizational structure of *MilanoinMovimento*, which is based on the rejection of the notion of 'member,' as well as given the fact that these groups constantly change and merge, it impossible to have an exact figure of the number of participants involved. Interviews revealed that an approximate figure is around 5,000.

The *Corsari*, ZAM, and Their Political Project

When in 2008 the *Corsari* collective was created as a direct action group, it focused on a variety of different yet interconnected themes. The first theme was the issue of *public space*. Interviews revealed that, following the years of repression and neo-liberal expansion in Milan, it had become clear that the main political goal of the city administration was to control human experience by making sure that sociality happened only within the confined spaces of bars, restaurants, and pubs, thereby ensuring that individuals were turned into consumers. Therefore, one of the key political projects of the *Corsari* was to reclaim the space through direct action and practices of occupation and thus resist the neo-liberal enforcements and ideologies that had come to dominate much of public life in Milan in those years.

With the creation of ZAM, their goal was to establish an 'autonomous zone' for the construction of social realities, which escaped the neo-liberal logic. The building was owned by a private landlord and had been abandoned for a period between eight and ten years. When the *Corsari* together with other collectives occupied ZAM in January 2011, the building was full of weeds and rats. The two years of 'occupation' had radically transformed the space. The people of ZAM had invested all their resources in building a concert hall, one bar, one exhibition center, and a gym. All the different spaces and cultural activities were organized through the practice of *auto-gestione* (self-management), which is based on a radical criticism of representative democracy, the rejection of any kind of bureaucratic hierarchy, and the adoption of horizontal and participative forms of decision-making processes (Andretta, 2004).

The political project of the *Corsari* was not only defined by the issue of space but also encompassed a variety of other different yet interconnected themes. One of these was the issue of *labor* and *precarious work*. As Mattoni (2012) has shown, the movement against the casualization of work life has been particularly strong in Italy. Within the ethnographic context of the *Corsari,* fieldwork and interviews revealed that the majority of the people involved in the *Corsari* were either unemployed or on fixed-term contracts, and those who were still studying had no real prospects for the future. The economic and financial crisis had exacerbated an already problematic situation in Italy with figures of youth unemployment rocketing from 25.30% in June 2009 to 39.10% in June 2013.[19] As argued before, many activists involved with the *Corsari* came from the social center *Bulk*, which was part of the 2001 May Day struggle and which gave rise to a project called *Chain Workers* (see Mattoni, 2012), which later became *Intelligenza Precaria* (Precarious Intelligence). Influenced by the works of the Autonomous Marxists as well as from other currents within the movement, the activists involved with the *Corsari* not only participated to different demonstrations alongside the more radical trade unions such as FIOM but also argued for the importance of challenging the casualization of labor and life.

At the time of fieldwork there were two other themes that defined the political culture of the *Corsari*: anti-fascism and anti-racism struggle on the one hand, and equal rights and female emancipation on the other. The anti-fascist struggle was brought ahead in a variety of ways, either by creating strong networks of support with old associations of partisans who had managed to defeat fascism during the Second World War or through everyday resistance against extreme right groups in Milan. The struggle for female emancipation and equal rights was instead brought ahead by an autonomous group that was created by key female members of the *Corsari* and was originally called *Gruppo G* and later *Ambrosia*. All these themes were an important terrain of struggle during Berlusconi's second mandate, which saw the establishment of an authoritarian neo-liberalism based on the rein-forcement of neo-fascist ideologies and a blatant sexism.

As it can be seen, there were many different and interconnected themes that defined the political culture of the *Corsari*, yet these themes were always evolving in a continuous process of collective self-reflection and elabora-tion. In fact as Canny, who at the time of fieldwork was 29 years old and employed on a fixed-term contract at an insurance company while trying to read for a degree in Sociology, explained to me:

C: Our group mechanism is based not so much on a shared ideological coherence of thought but on the constant re-definition. We are all very different people; we come from different backgrounds, and are of differ-ent ages. We may have some common themes but we are very different from what might have been other political groups in the past – when activists acted on a shared political analysis and reflection. We are dif-ferent [...] our mechanism is not based on an ideological structure but rather on defining common desires and needs.

The process of political reflection, redefinition, and renewal was a key aspect of the ethnographic contexts of the *Corsari* and ZAM, and it is for this reason that since the beginning of fieldwork in 2010 this context has radi-cally transformed itself, making it a fascinating site of research for explor-ing activists' use of web technologies. Fieldwork was carried out between 2010 and 2011. These years of great transformation for Italian politics saw the defeat of Silvio Berlusconi's political monopoly. In Milan, in May 2011, Giuliano Pisapia – the left-wing mayor of Milan – was elected after 18 years of ruling by the center-right coalition. At the time of Pisapia's election a large part of the autonomous movement supported his election and actively campaigned for him. During his two years of administration, however, Pisa-pia instead of supporting the growth of cultural and social spaces within the city was involved in a politics of repression against the social centers. As it happened, in the context of CSC and *Ecologistas en Acción,* the context of the *Corsari* was pretty much defined by a great sense of disillusionment in institutional politics.

ACTIVIST CULTURES, POLITICAL IMAGINARIES, AND INFORMATION ECOLOGIES

Understanding Political Cultures and the Importance of Imagination

The above description of the historical development and political cultures of the three organizations reveals that, as Castoriadis (1998) has noticed, activists' everyday lives are defined by the *imagination* of a different type of society, which is based on a profound critique against capitalism and the neo-liberal agenda of governments. For the *Cuba Solidarity Campaign* it is a society that it is based on the defense of public welfare and a greater intervention on the part of the state in order to limit corporate exploitation. For the *Corsari* it is a society that respects the self-management and determination of groups and integrates individual differences without suppressing them. It is also a society that reclaims the importance of public spaces, collective congregations, and the expression of collective creativity. For *Ecologistas en Acción* it is a society that is sustainable; that relies on local networks and promotes collective organization in respect of the environment and of social equality.

The concept of *imagination,* therefore, is central to the understanding of activists' cultures and of the way in which they organize their everyday practices in order to bring about social change. In *The Imaginary Institution of Society,* Castoriadis (1998) argues that imagination is a defining element of humanity. Grounding his understanding in Aristotle's claim that 'The soul never thinks without phantasms (images)' he recognized that imagination, intentionality and action were inseparable (1998:194). As a critical Marxist, Castoriadis brought together Marx and Freud and argued that dream, desire, wish, pleasure, and fantasy are all at the core of our social processes, and they are also at the core of political institutions and resistant groups. Castoriadis's work is of central importance in the understanding of activist cultures because he establishes a link between imagination and resistance, and by doing so – as Elliot suggested (2003) – his theory of imagination moves beyond a focus on the human subject and opens possibilities of research that enable us to understand it as a social process (Elliott, 2003:85).

Drawing from Castoriadis (1998) and bringing his theory together with contemporary anthropological theory, I understand imagination as detached from an idea of fantasy, which carries with it a connotation of unrealistic thought divorced from projects and actions (Appadurai, 1996:7; Graeber, 2007). On the contrary, in Castoriadis's terms, I see imagination as a social *activity,* something that *we do* (Ingold, 2000:416), which carries forward internationality, project, and action of a kind. As Ingold suggested, metaphorically imagination can be understood as something a chess player does when, sitting apparently immobile and without touching the pieces of the board, he or she proceeds to work out a strategy (Ingold, 2000:416). Drawing from the work of these scholars, I came to the conclusion that 'imagination' can be seen as a personal as well as a collective process that enables people to organize their actions/practices according to specific images. The understanding of imagination as a collective process is central if we want to explore the construction of activists' political cultures and the fact that these political cultures bring forward specific political projects.

Particularly insightful in the understanding of imagination as a social process is the concept of imaginary, as developed by Taylor (2003). According to him, a social imaginary is not a set of ideas but is "that common understanding that makes possible common practices and a widely shared sense of legitimacy" (2003:24). Taylor's (2003) argument is strong and important, precisely because it unravels the relationship between collective imaginations and shared practices.

Now in the last few years the concept of 'imaginary' has come into scrutiny by anthropologists (Sneath et al., 2009). There are three main problems with the concept. In the first place, as Sneath et al. have noticed, the concept can be seen as sharing many lines of similarities with earlier concepts of culture or ideology (2009:8–10). In the second place the concept has often been used in an instrumental and functionalist way, where the notion of 'imaginary' was seen as indicating the way in which humans make sense of the world they live in (2009:9). In the third place scholars have ascribed a 'positive' and 'romantic' purpose to the process of imagination. According to Sneath et al., therefore, one way to move beyond these problems is to focus on the "technologies of the imagination" and the way in which "imaginary effects may come about" (2009:19). If we do so, the scholars believe, we may develop an approach that does not presuppose that imaginaries are a kind of 'holistic' backdrop that conditions human activities (2009:19).

Similarly to Sneath et al. (2009), I personally believe that it is pivotal to move beyond the notion of imaginary as some kind of holistic backdrop that structures human activities. However, although the scholars wish to move away from the anthropological literature on imagination to focus on the effects of imaginaries, I wish to draw on this literature to explore *imaginaries* as social processes. In fact I personally believe that one important aspect of the notion of 'imaginary' is the understanding that, as Crapanzano (2004:12–15) has shown, this notion – although constructed on ethnographic realities and understandings – extends itself from the reality of the here and now. Sneath et al. (2009) agree with this understanding (despite criticizing Crapanzano for his romanticism) and, influenced by the philosophy of Kant, they argue that imagination is defined by the human ability to bring to mind that which is not entirely present to the senses (2009:11–12).

During fieldwork, the concept of 'imaginary' enabled me to study and understand the different political cultures of the activist groups and also appreciate the fact that there is a bound relationship between activists' political projects and the organization of their everyday practices. Furthermore, and most importantly, the concept of 'imaginary' has also enabled me to explore activists' relationship with media technologies and understand the different 'information ecologies' (Nardi and Day, 1999; Treré, 2012) that they build.

Media Imaginaries and the Construction of Activists' Information Ecologies

At the end of the 1990s, as communication scholars were eager to explore the impacts of internet technologies on different levels of social experience, Nardi and Day (1999) argued that rather than focusing on specific media technologies, scholars had much to gain if they looked at the *'information ecology'* of a particular local environment and, thus, considered the interconnection between "people, practices, values and technologies" (1999:para1). According to the authors, the ecological metaphor enables us to appreciate the complexity of how technology is used in local settings and is shaped by human relations. In addition to this, it enables us to highlight the fact that information ecologies are constantly changing, because the "different parts of the ecology *coevolve,* changing together according to the relationships in the system" (Nardi and Day, 1999). Treré (2012) has applied the concept of information ecology to the investigation of the relationship between social movements and media technologies and has rightly highlighted the fact that activists develop complex information ecologies, which bring together old and new media technologies, as well as specific understandings of technological use.

The understanding that there is a bound relationship between human values and technological use and that this relationship is defined by local settings is at the very heart of the *media as practice* approach (Couldry, 2004; Brauchler and Postill, 2010). Couldry (2004) has argued that in order to fully understand people's media practices scholars must focus on the principles and beliefs whereby these practices are ordered. This is particularly true when we think about the context of social movements because, as scholars have shown, activists and activist groups develop self-reflexive perceptions of the "things" they do with and expect from the media at large (Atton, 2002; Downing, 2000; Mattoni, 2012).

My research was largely inspired by these works. However, during fieldwork among the three different organizations, I realized that within the communication or media anthropological literature, scholars had paid very little attention to the concept of imagination as defined above and to the fact that people often *imagine* "what they do" with media technologies according to specific political cultures and projects. Now as the anthropological literature on 'social imaginaries' has shown, it is impossible to divorce these projects/ideals from everyday practices and to overlook how everyday practices are often organized following specific political projects.

During fieldwork, therefore, I used the concept of *media imaginary* as a methodological and analytical tool to highlight the fact that the three different collectives often develop 'different understandings' of what they wanted to achieve from media technologies, which was largely inspired by their political projects and which determined the way that their media practices were organized. Therefore, and as we shall see in more detail in the following chapters of the book, the concept of *media imaginary* enabled me to shed light on the relationship between activists' political projects and their media practices. In fact, it became clear that activists used the technologies available to them according to their different needs and goals. These needs and goals were defined on the basis of their different political cultures and led to the creation of very different *information ecologies.* The understanding that there is a strong relationship between political projects and media practices is of great importance for the study of digital activism, because it enables us to appreciate the fact that if we want to study activists' information ecologies we have to have in-depth knowledge of their political cultures.

CULTURAL DIFFERENCES IN MEDIA IMAGINARIES AND INFORMATION ECOLOGIES

The Complexity of Information Ecologies

The information ecologies of the three organizations studied for this book were complex multi-dimensional systems created by the interaction of different old and new media outlets, a hybridity of media networks, media values, and human relationships. In addition, these information ecologies have been evolving since the beginning of fieldwork and are continuously changing. Acknowledging the fact that it is impossible to provide an overview of such a complexity, here I simply want to a) sketch the different media outlets of the organizations, b) map some of the important media networks, and c) identify some of the most common understandings that shaped the different ecologies. The following parts will therefore highlight the difference in the information ecologies and will argue that is only through an in-depth understanding of activists' political cultures and media imaginaries that we can fully appreciate the 'information ecologies' that they build (Nardi and Day, 1999; Treré, 2012), and hence their relationship to web technologies.

The Information Ecology of CSC

Media Outlets   At the time of fieldwork, the *Cuba Solidarity Campaign* relied on a variety of different media outlets. These included a non-interactive HTML website (www.cuba-solidarity.org), an email newsletter, which was sent out on a weekly basis to CSC members and 4,000 other subscribers in the Labor Movement, a non-interactive YouTube channel, a Facebook group (at the time it counted around 1000 likes, against the 3,643 likes on 15 November 2014) and a Twitter account (at the time it counted 400 followers, against the 3,124 followers on 15 November 2014). Despite the many online media platforms, the *Cuba Solidarity Campaign* still invested its few economic resources, often at a loss, to publish a glossy magazine on a quarterly basis, the *CubaSí*. At the time of fieldwork, the organization printed 5,000 to 6,000 copies, which were then distributed freely to all members and affiliated organizations, as well as to key figures in the trade unions. The magazine was also sold for £2.00 to the general public at conferences and events or for £0.75 to all local groups that wished to sell it at their own meetings.

Media Networks   The information ecology of the organization was defined by a plurality of media networks, especially with the media produced by other international campaigning organizations, trade unions, and Cuban media outlets such as *Granma International*. Among all the media networks, members and organizers showed a particular attachment to the *Morning Star* daily. The *Morning Star* was launched in the 1930s as the organ of the Communist Party of Great Britain and was known as the *Daily Worker*. In 1966 it was re-launched as *Morning Star*, and since then it has been produced by a co-operative of people. Today the newspaper is an integral coordinator of the trade union movement. The *Cuba Solidarity Campaign* constantly publishes news and information on Cuba in the *Morning Star* and a representative of the newspaper sits on CSC's executive committee.

Media Imaginaries   All the media practices of the campaign were built on the political project of counteracting the negative representation of Cuba in the UK and constructing a specific image of Cuba, one that focuses on 'revolutionary and progressive achievements' of the socialist government. A shared understanding among campaign members and organizers was that there are so many negative messages about the socialist island that 'every column inch spent on lamenting an aspect is one less spent on more important issues' (*CubaSí*, Winter 1999:12). All the media outlets are therefore used as important space for the construction of positive news on Cuba and also for the promotion of the events of the campaign. One important aspect of all the different media practices of the campaign is that they are all directed towards the production of a 'unique coherent message' that reaches the public through a complex dynamism of intertextuality.

The Information Ecology of Ecologistas en Acción

Media Outlets   Similarly to CSC, *Ecologistas en Acción* also relies on a variety of online media, including an HTML website (www.ecologista-senaccion.org), and different social media accounts. However, the organization relies on a much wider range of social media platforms than CSC. In fact, alongside a Facebook group (with 12,000 likes at the time of fieldwork and 165,636 on 15 November 2014), a Twitter account (with 4,000 followers at the time of fieldwork and 76,200 followers on 15 November 2014), and a YouTube TV channel, *Ecologistas en Acción* also relies on other social media that are particularly popular in Spain such as Tuenti. com and Eskup. In addition, *Ecologistas en Acción* publishes a printed magazine titled *Ecologista*. At the time of fieldwork, the organization printed around 10,000 copies of the *Ecologista* quarterly. Magazines are sent to members and organizers free of charge, distributed to local groups that sell them at local events, and also are sold for €2 by a few newsagents in Madrid.

Media Networks   The information ecology of *Ecologistas en Acción* was extraordinarily complex and relied on a variety of media networks. It is difficult to trace the different media networks of the organization, because these are constructed by all the autonomous groups and extend on national territory. In Madrid, different activists expressed a real appreciation for the newspaper *Diagonal*, a bi-weekly alternative media newspaper, which was founded in 2003 to support the production of independent news among progressive social movements in Spain. Their information ecology was also shaped by the creation of different 'autonomous' projects that acted within the organization but that focused specifically on media-related issues. One of these projects was *ConsumeHastaMorir* (Consume until you die), a counter-advertising project that was created in 2002 and meant to offer a critical reflection on our relationship to advertising and consumerism. Another project is *Libros en Acción*, which is a publishing house run by the organization that publishes books about social environmentalism.

Media Imaginaries   The media practices of *Ecologistas en Acción* were organized on a very different political project than the one of CSC. The production of news and content – although it was certainly directed towards the promotion of the events and activities of the organization – was not guided by the shared belief that it was essential to build a unique and coherent message but rather it was based on the understanding of the plurality of voices and beliefs that shaped *Ecologistas en Acción*. This latter point is particularly evident if we consider the production of content in the magazine. In fact the magazine was used to produce in-depth journalistic reportages, which were based on empirical and scientific evidence and that addressed a variety of environmental and social issues affecting the different areas of the confederation. In addition, the different online platforms were used in very strategic ways in order to facilitate the co-ordination of the organization as a whole while respecting and reinforcing the autonomy of the local groups and their multiple messages.

The Information Ecology of the *Corsari*

Media Outlets   The information ecology of the *Corsari* was very different from the one of CSC and *Ecologistas en Acción*. The main difference was defined by the fact that the group relied on the autonomous internet infrastructure network known as Autistici/Inventati, which was founded in March 2001. Autistici/Inventati (A/I) is an autonomous service provider that at the time of fieldwork hosted more than 5,000 email addresses, around 500 websites/blogs, and over 700 mailing lists. A/I is managed by a voluntary tech collective, whose objective is to create an autonomous internet network among different activists' organizations in Italy in order to facilitate social movements' anonymity and privacy.

A/I provides political activists with an email address and blog without requesting the input of personal data and, thus, enables them to enjoy a certain degree of autonomy from the commercial and governmental tracing of digital identities. At the time of fieldwork, in order to organize and mobilize action, therefore, the *Corsari* relied mostly on different A/I mailing lists (see Barassi and Treré, 2012). They also posted their information on two different A/I Noblogs.org, one titled CORSARI MILANO and one ZAM. Despite relying on the autonomous infrastructure network of A/I, the group also relied on corporate social media platforms. When I started fieldwork, the group had just created different collective pages on Facebook: one for the CORSARI MILANO (with 1,839 likes shortly after the end of fieldwork in 2012 and 1,673 on 15 November 2014) and one for ZAM (5,179 likes shortly after the end of fieldwork in 2012 and 12,662 on 15 November 2014). Particularly central to the information ecology of the time was the YouTube platform because it enabled activists to post and share the videos of the different direct actions they had done. Although YouTube was particularly important for activists, at the time of fieldwork they were very skeptical about the usefulness of Twitter, as they believed that it was a platform aimed at 'professionals.' In fact, they had opened a Twitter account, which despite the fact that it has more than 400 followers, it had only five tweets.

Today, the media outlets that define the information ecology of the activists who were involved with the *Corsari* have radically changed, and this is because the group has merged into a much broader umbrella organization called *MilanoinMovimento* (Milan in Movement) which relies on an interactive website, a Facebook page (with 7,489 likes on 15 November 2014), a Twitter account (with 3,319 followers on 15 November 2014), and a YouTube channel (with 298 subscribers and 242,112 views on 15 November 2014).

Media Networks   The media networks of the *Corsari* extended at the national level and were defined by the constant exchange between individual activists and different social centers, student collectives, autonomous collectives, non-profit organizations, trade unions, and left-wing parties. It is impossible to map the plurality of these exchanges. However, on the website of *MilanoinMovimento* there is a list of 'independent media partners,' which is indicative of some of the media networks that were established at the time. Particularly important for the activists is the network with *Global Project,* the information hub of the social centers and radical collectives across the North-East region, or the link to the live stream of *Radio Onda d'Urto,* a radical radio based in Brescia that played a key role in the movements of the 1990s and during the 2001 G8 summit in Genoa.

Media Imaginaries   The media practices of the *Corsari* were organized according to very different political projects than the ones of CSC and *Ecologistas en Acción.* In fact, they were shaped by the shared belief that the primary role of their different media outlets was to coordinate and organize real-life meetings, direct actions, and events on the ground. Blog and social media posts (of both the *Corsari* and ZAM), as well as most of their email discussions, were aimed at organizing and coordinating actions. Only occasionally these sites were used as spaces for political discussion and elaboration. With the development of the umbrella organization *MilanoinMovimento,* the media imaginaries of the activists I met had changed, and this is because their political project had changed. *MilanoinMovimento* aimed at bringing together different autonomous collectives operating within the city. The role of the website and the other media platforms was thus to create a sense of shared unity by linking different networks together and respecting groups' individual autonomy. Their online media outlets (and in particular their website) became not only a hub of information for the movement in Milan but also a space for political elaboration and reflection.

CONCLUSION

This chapter has looked at the historical development and political cultures of the organizations studied. It has argued that activists' political cultures are shaped by specific political projects and practices of imagination and that these projects directly influence the organization of activists' media practices. The study of digital activism has been constrained by a lack of a 'thick' ethnographic engagement with activist cultures. This has led to the production of a type of data that provides us with a 'thin' appreciation of the political cultures in which activists are embedded. By introducing the concept of 'media imaginary' and highlighting the bound relationship between political projects and everyday media practices, the chapter has argued that it is only through an in-depth understanding of activists' political cultures that we can fully appreciate the 'information ecologies' that they build (Nardi and Day, 1999; Treré, 2012).

As the chapter has shown, the information ecologies of political groups are complex systems that are defined by the interaction of different old and new media outlets, a hybridity of media networks, media imaginaries, and human relationships. In addition, these information ecologies are in continuous transformation, and it is impossible for scholars to fully grasp their social complexity. What we can do is focus on specific aspects. In this book, I have decided to focus on a social tension that emerges in activists' everyday use of web technologies: the tension created by the encounter between activist cultures and digital capitalism. In the next chapter I will endeavor to develop a theoretical standpoint that will enable us to fully understand this tension.

NOTES

1. In this book I refer to 'mainstream media' to identify large media corporations that are essentially business groups, concentrated and globally interconnected, highly diversified and geared primarily by profit-related concerns (Castells, 1997, 2009).

2. In this chapter I use the umbrella term 'digital activism' to describe activists' media practices that involve the use of internet technologies as well as the digitalization of images and texts.

3. Of course, the tension between the different ways in which communication scholars and anthropologists approach the ethnographic method is not new. In the 1990s, Nugent (1993) argued that when talking about 'ethnography' cultural studies scholars and anthropologists referred to completely different concepts. In this chapter I do not wish to dwell on the polemic between anthropologists and communication scholars, but I simply want to argue that, within the study of digital activism, the lack of engagement with ethnographic thickness has had an enormous impact on the type of data that we have available about the relationship between activist cultures and digital technologies.

4. This is despite the fact there were internal tensions and conflicts especially due to the conflict between communist and non-communist union members who felt the pressure of the Cold War.

5. To face this situation, in the last two decades different unions have been forced to merge, and this merging activity has defined much of my fieldwork with CSC. Union mergers in the public services were dominated by the creation in 1993 of UNISON (which has remained the largest union since) and the eventual emergence in 1998 of one very large civil service union, the Public and Commercial Services Union (PCS), covering all but the top and specialist grades. After that, most large unions continued to absorb smaller ones in the private sector (Trade Union Congress website http://www.unionhistory.info/timeline/1960_2000_5.php, date accessed 03/05/09).

6. Information gathered during fieldwork, as I was talking with my informants.

7. *Granma Newspaper* is the official newspaper of the Central Committee of the Cuban Communist Party; it was founded in 1965, and is available in weekly international editions in English, Spanish, French, Portuguese, German, and Italian.

8. Here it is important to appreciate that the notion of solidarity is a conflicting terrain of meaning and practice among trade unions. The TUC International department, for instance, is constantly trying to establish a hegemonic idea of international solidarity, whereby the interests of British companies (and hence British workers abroad) are not challenged or undermined. This understanding of international solidarity is not supported by more radical organizations within the movement, which try to criticize and go against the wrongdoings of British corporations in developing countries.

9. The *Music Fund for Cuba* was first established in memory of the singer Kirsty MacColl who before dying in Mexico had been involved with the CSC. The *Music Fund for Cuba* was set up as a charity with the political intention of reaching those people who would want to get culturally engaged, but not politically engaged, with Cuba.

10. Fictional name to protect the interviewee's choice of anonymity.

11. The organization was originally called *Coordinadora para la Defensa del las Aves* (Coordinator for the Defence of Birds), indicating the conservationist character of its origins.

12. The World Trade Organization replaced the GATT in 1994/1995.

13. An Andalusian organization, *Confederacion Ecologista Pacifista Andalusa* (Ecologist, Pacifist, Andalusian Confederation).

14. At times only three individuals may compose groups.
15. In the last years of the 1970s the Italian government approved a law allowing the police to open fire on protesters. Repression reached its peak; different sections of the autonomous movement organized in guerrilla-terrorist groups, which led to the armed struggle. In 1978, one of these groups, the Red Brigades, kidnapped and killed former Christian Democrat Prime Minister Aldo Moro. The 1970s and the early years of the 1980s were years of violence, repression, armed robberies, kidnappings, and exile. They were bloody years for Italian politics, and have been known as the years of lead.
16. Within this book I have decided to use the term 'occupation' rather than 'squatting' because this is the term used by the people involved in the movement, and also because the Italian 'social centers' cannot be really considered 'squats' as people do not usually live or sleep in them.
17. Formentini was a representative of the far right, independentist party Lega Lombarda (Lombard League, which later became known as Lega Nord, the Northern League). The party, which is based on populist and xenophobic ideologies, remained an important political player, as it was a key ally of Berlusconi's government.
18. On the third night of the G8 summit, after three days of brutality in the streets, the police raided the School Diaz, where 93 protesters were sleeping and injured 86 activists before arresting them and taking them to the Bolzaneto prison.
19. (http://ycharts.com/indicators/italy_youth_unemployment_rate_lfs).

2 Web 2.0 and the Agency of Technologies

INTRODUCTION

After exploring the different political cultures and information ecologies of the three organisations studied, in this chapter I plan to develop a theoretical approach for the understanding of the tension between activist cultures and digital capitalism. In the last decade, the rapid growth in usage of web 2.0 technologies has triggered the rise of different and contrasting approaches in communication research. As mentioned in the introduction to this book, some scholars have seen new web technologies as tools of democratic empowerment (Shirky, 2008; Castells, 2009; Stiegler, 2009; Ellison et al., 2009). Others have argued that far from being democratic, new web 2.0 platforms have become the material support of new forms of corporate control (Bauwens, 2008; Fuchs, 2007; Terranova, 2000) and state repression (Morozov, 2011). To a certain extent these debates on the web 2.0 appear to be a more up-to-date and technologically aware version of earlier discussions on the internet, when scholars were divided between those who believed that online technologies were tools of collective empowerment (Rheingold, 1993; Negroponte, 1996; Rash, 1997; Toffler, 1995; Castells, 1997) and those who highlighted that they were becoming the material support for the development of digital capitalism (e.g. Schiller, 2000; Kellner, 2002).

This chapter will argue that at the very heart of these recurring debates between techno-optimists and techno-pessimists lies the question of 'technological agency' and the very utopian (and dystopian) Western assumption of the socially transformative (and almost 'magical') qualities of new technologies (Mosco, 2004; Morley, 2006). This chapter will contend that one way to critically consider the question of technological agency, and move beyond the binarism that defines much research, is to develop a theoretical standpoint that enables us to understand the complex relationship between technological discourse and practice. This theoretical standpoint is of central importance if we want to comprehend the encounter between activist cultures and digital capitalism.

There are three fundamental steps that we need to take in order to develop this theoretical standpoint. In the first place we need to reconsider the 'power of discourse' in the making of technological agents. In fact, the first part of the chapter will reflect on the agency of technologies by highlighting some of the problems with Latour's (2005) actor-network-theory and exploring the relationship between technological discourse and processes of technological fetishism (Harvey, 2003). It will argue that one of the first steps to be taken in the understanding of the impacts of web technologies, in the study of political activism, is to start appreciating the power of discourses associated with them (Morley, 2006; Mosco, 2004; Hindman, 2008) and to consider how techno-utopian discourses have impacted the everyday practices of activists.

Once we understand the power of discourses associated with technologies and we appreciate their impact on activists' practices, we can take a step further and highlight the fact that digital discourses have become *contested spaces of meaning* and the basis of some of contemporary hegemonic struggles. An example of this is certainly the concept of *network*. As it will be shown, not only the concept of network has become an ideological construction within the context of social movements (Graeber, 2002; Gerbaudo, 2012) but also political activists need to come to terms with the way in which the network is used as an ideological discourse by businesses and governments. The chapter will thus argue that the concept of 'network' (like any other digital discourse: e.g. participation, interactivity) needs to be considered as 'empty signifier' (Laclau, 1996), which defines the basis of contemporary hegemonic struggles.

The understanding that web technologies are contested terrains of imagination and practice (Kelty, 2012) enables us to take a third step in the development of our theoretical standpoint. It fact, it enables us to look at the difference between the imaginaries and practices of 'the weak' and the ones of power. As it will be shown, the imaginaries and practices of power have a spatial dimension (De Certeau, 1980), in the sense that they shape the social environments that we live in. This understanding, as we shall see, applies very well to the analysis of the web 2.0. There is no doubt that the web needs to be understood as a complex socio-technical environment defined by the interactions of different cultures, human relationships, and social processes. Nevertheless, as argued in the introduction to this book, within this socio-technical environment, like elsewhere in society, the capitalist logic is hegemonic and thus capitalist discourses and strategies have largely shaped this environment. The chapter will, therefore, argue that it is by looking at the tension between the 'strategies' of power and the 'tactics' of the weak – as De Certeau (1980) has beautifully theorized it – that we can start to understand the complex relationship between activist cultures and digital capitalism.

THE IMPACTS OF DIGITAL DISCOURSES ON EVERYDAY POLITICAL PRACTICE

Constructing Technological Actors, Techno-Fetishism, and Techno-Utopianism

The understanding of the 'agency' of technologies, as Hands (2010) has shown, is a complex topic of academic debate, shaped by a variety of different theoretical and philosophical traditions. Here I want to focus on Latour's (2005) actor-network-theory (ANT), because it has largely influenced the standpoint of the research presented in this book. According to Latour (2005), the social should be understood as a networked movement, which is defined by the multiple interconnections of human and non-human actors. Objects are active actors in the construction of the social, because action is not limited to the intentional activities of humans; anything that modifies the state of affairs is an actor (2005:71). Latour's contribution has been important to media and communication research because it challenges techno-deterministic and functionalist understandings of the social impacts of media (Couldry, 2008:6). In fact ANT has shown that technologies are shaped by, and shape, human relations through an open-ended process constructed by everyday practice.

Despite being central to the general approach of this research, there is, as Couldry (2008) has argued, a problem[1] with ANT's understanding of technological agency. In fact the spatial virtue of ANT is connected with the relative neglect of time and thus ANT is not well equipped to understand the consequences of the *representations* that technologies embed and the effects of these representations on everyday life (2008:163–165). My understanding is that one way to enrich the application of ANT is to appreciate the fact that often technologies become 'agents' because they are embedded with specific digital discourses (Mosco, 2004; Morley, 2006; Hindman, 2008) that have an impact on the organization of human practices. In fact, my belief is that new technologies always bring about social transformations. This is because technologies transform the way in which people communicate, organize their daily routines, and redefine their practices and choices. Yet often it is not the technology itself that brings about social transformations, but the human discourses 'naturalized' within the technology itself (e.g. web technologies = openness/freedom; social networking sites = participation/empowerment), that have a profound effect on the everyday layers of social experience (e.g. understandings of political opposition; communication strategies, etc.).

In order to understand this process, it is important to look at the notion of *technological fetishism* (Harvey, 2003). In social theory, one cannot start to analyze processes of technological fetishism without taking into account Marx's ([1867] 1990) discussion on 'commodity fetishism.' According to Marx, within the capitalist mode of production, humans are alienated from the objects they produce. These objects are turned into commodities, which acquire a mystical and supernatural power. Harvey (2003) was obviously highly influenced by Marx, and he argued that technological fetishism is the process whereby humans invest technological objects with specific forms of powers and believe that these objects are able to move and shape the world (2003:3).

In the understanding of technological fetishism, I believe, it is important to combine Marxist approaches with the anthropological literature on fetishism and thus take a step further. Anthropologists have argued that fetishism is a human process that can be found in a variety of cultures well beyond capitalism (Hornborg 1992, 2001; Graeber 2007). However, they have also highlighted the fact that 'technological fetishism' is often at the very heart of Westernized notions of modernity and progress (Hornborg, 1992; Pfaffenberger, 1988), and this is a particular point that needs to be understood if we want to fully appreciate our very Western obsession with investing technologies with 'magical' qualities (Mosco, 2004; Morley, 2006).

It is by looking at technological fetishism that we can fully understand the way that we construct the agency of technologies through human discourses. One interesting aspect of this process of technological fetishism is represented by the fact that it cannot be fully understood without looking at the peculiarly Western attitude towards *techno-utopianism* or, in other words, the belief that technologies can become important tools of social and political liberation. This belief lies at the very heart of Western thought. As Segal (1985) has argued, techno-utopianism can be found in a variety of works of social theory from Tommaso Campanella to the nineteenth-century thinkers like Saint-Simon, Comte, Owen, Fourier, and of course Marx and Engels (Segal, 1985:2). All these works share the understanding that technologies, and in particular new technologies, can enable us as humans to construct a more just and democratic society.[2] As the next part of the chapter will show, the history of the internet has been largely shaped by these techno-utopian discourses, which have had a profound impact on everyday life, including the everyday life of political activists.

The Historical Development of the Internet and the Power of Digital Discourses

The relationship between techno-utopianism and technological fetishism has defined the historical development of the internet. During the mid-1990s, different scholars were quick to come to conclusions on the so-called revolutionary and transformative impacts of the internet. Rheingold (1993) highlighted the fact that new technologies were facilitating the emergence of a new form of social life: the virtual community, which was self-governed and horizontal in essence. Toffler and Toffler (1995) argued that internet technologies were creating a 'third way,' a new civilization, which distanced itself from older forms of political organization. Negroponte (1996) believed that the internet had created a new shift for political organization, enabling societies to move away from the centralized politics of the nation state. All these works not only constructed internet technologies as 'agents' (*techno-logical fetishism*) able to transform the world but they also argued that, as agents, internet technologies were going to bring about important political and democratic transformations (*techno-utopianism*).

The 'hype' over the so-called revolutionary qualities of the internet slightly decreased with the burst of the dot.com bubble (Mosco, 2004:3–5). However, as Mosco argued, technological hypes are cyclical (Mosco, 2004:3–5). This is particularly true if consider the fact that with the development of web 2.0 technologies the ideological discourse on the 'new,' 'democratic,' and 'revolutionary' qualities of the internet re-established itself with a sur-prising force. In 2005 Tim O'Reilly announced the creation of a new type of web based on a new 'architecture of participation' ([2005] 2009). The dominant discourse was that the new technology was going to reinforce human cooperation with positive impacts on democratic processes and social change. Again, as it happened during the 1990s, scholars were quick to jump to conclusions on the revolutionary qualities of new the web. This is particularly true if we consider the work of those scholars who argued that web 2.0 platforms, for their interactive character, were radically transform-ing political freedom and facilitating the emergence of grassroots organizing (Tapscott and Williams, 2006; Benkler, 2007; Shirky, 2008; Castells, 2012).

As it can be seen from the above paragraphs, technological fetishism and techno-utopianism have defined the early developments of the internet and the creation of the web 2.0. Therefore, it is of fundamental importance that communication scholars engage in a critical deconstruction of the Western-centric and techno-utopian understandings of web technologies. We can do this in a variety of ways. We can choose to explore the processes of con-struction of the 'digital sublime' (Mosco, 2004), we can focus on challeng-ing the 'myths of digital democracy' (Hindman, 2009), or we can critically consider how web discourses legitimize new forms of capitalist exploitation (Fisher, 2010). All these approaches are valid and important. Here, however, rather than focusing on the deconstruction of digital discourses, my aim is to empirically explore their impact on everyday political practice. This latter point is particularly important in the study of digital activism and emerged well from the ethnographic context of the organizations that I studied. As the next part of the chapter will show, in the context of political activism digital discourses have had a profound impact, as they redefined groups' political practices and priorities.

The Everyday Construction of Technological Fetishes among Activists

One afternoon in early 2011, I sat down for an interview with Elena,[3] one of the full-time staff of *Ecologistas en Acción*. In the hour-long interview, Elena discussed her personal and political development; she talked about her ten-year involvement with the organization and reflected on how internet technologies had transformed her everyday political practice. The transfor-mation, according to her, was not abrupt or rapid but was rather the product of a slow process of change and renewal. During the interview, she recounted that at the end of the 1990s and beginning of 2000s – when she first started to work for *Ecologistas en Acción* – the organization only had one computer that was connected to the internet and all members of staff shared a unique email address. She laughed, looked away, and said: "It's almost impossible to imagine how it was. Isn't it?" I agreed. I started to imagine how their everyday working lives had to be structured at the time; I tried to picture the collective tensions that would arise from sharing a unique email address and to envisage how the office space must have been organized, but I failed. More than ten years later, with the extension of wireless technologies, the proliferation of email accounts, and social media, it was difficult for me to relate back to her first experience and imagine the office of *Ecologistas en Acción* then.

Elena was not the first activist I encountered during fieldwork who asked me to 'imagine' everyday life before the extension of internet technologies. I remembered talking with Mary,[4] an old-time member of CSC and trade union activist, and listening to her account of the trade union general strikes of the 1980s. She talked about the labor-intensive and time-consuming process of producing information. She explained that when she wanted to produce information on a specific event or demonstration, she would have to take photographs with an old camera, wait a couple of days to get the photos developed, write a bulletin, and then send everything via post to networked organizations, mainstream media, and friends. By the time the information was ready to circulate almost a week had already passed. I remembered also talking to Marco,[5] who has long been involved in the autonomous movement in Italy, and who described activists' struggles during the 1990s as they tried to communicate with different areas of the movement located in different cities and regions. During the interview, he remembered in particular one night in 1996, when together with other activists from the *Deposito Bulk,* he spent hours trying to fax a document to the Roman social center *Corto Circuito*, while the fax machine kept on breaking and stalling.

Throughout my research activists asked me to imagine how life was before the internet because it was difficult for them to describe the challenges they faced at the time when they tried to exchange information, build networks of support and solidarity, or 'get their message across.' Their different life narratives did not only reveal a collective memory of past challenges and difficulties but also a collective recognition that the internet had radically (and positively) changed their everyday practices, opening new possibilities for political organization and imagination.

Many of the activists that I had the pleasure to meet during fieldwork and to interview could remember when the internet became a pervasive tool of political action and the transformations it brought. In an interview with Luis, for instance, he provided a comprehensive reflection of how the internet had transformed political action within the organization. At the time of the interview Luis was 36 years old and one of the key coordinators of *Ecologistas en Acción*. He had first become involved with environmental activism during the 1990s' global justice movements. He remembered the uprising in Chiapas and the construction of the Global Action Network. He also remembered the way in which internet technologies started to become widely used by social movement actors:

L: Velocity and quantity were the main transformations of the internet, and this has affected the way in which we relate to one another. Today, much of our communication is being mediated all the time. For us as a group it has enabled our internal democratic processes. Local groups can participate in the coordination of the organization. The internet has also provided us with a greater autonomy, in the sense that we do not have to rely on dominant media and their politics to transmit our messages.

Similarly to the story of Luis, activists' life stories, across the three organizations, were more or less defined by a linear narrative of technological development, with the older activists remembering and recounting the advent of internet technologies and the younger ones talking about the advent of web 2.0 technologies. In all instances activists would talk about a 'revolution' of sorts that completely transformed their everyday practices.

When activists discussed the radical transformation brought about by internet technologies, they often focused on two different yet interconnected themes. On the one hand, they highlighted the fact that internet technologies provided them with a greater degree of communicative autonomy from mainstream media. On the other hand, they emphasized the fact that internet technologies had strengthened their networking practices and enabled them to organize and co-ordinate political action in fast and effective ways.

Here we can trace lines of similarities between activists' experiences and the works of scholars like Castells (1997) or Juris (2008) who argued that the internet had radically transformed political participation because it extended activists' ability to build networks of communication and action. These works reflect to a certain degree the reality on the ground. My research convinced me that it is undeniable that the extension of communication networks reinforced the very human process of social networking (Juris, 2008, 2012), providing activists with a greater communicative autonomy from mainstream media and dominant powers (Castells, 2009, 2012).

In his interview Luis talked about a radical and largely positive change to the way in which the people involved with the organization communicated and organized, but he also talked about the fact that activists' attitude towards internet technologies in the last decade became increasingly more critical. At first, he argued, internet technologies appeared to be tools of social and political liberation, which enabled activists to circumvent the power of mainstream media and expand the reach of their messages and political networks. Yet at the beginning of the 2000s, it started to become evident that far from challenging the existing powers of society, internet technologies often reinforced them, and this was particularly true if we considered financial and corporate power.

A similar situation of 'disillusionment' emerged also in the context of CSC. When in 1996/1997 CSC launched its website, the emphasis on the political possibilities brought about by internet technologies was an influential discourse within the organization. In the autumn 1996 *CubaSí* issue, which followed the launch of CSC's first website, 'immediacy,' 'efficiency,' and 'world-wide direct online action' were key words used in the articles to highlight the advantages the internet would bring to their cause. In the same issue, the national office of the campaign expressed its enthusiasm about the fact that they finally could get their message across to the high centers of global power. Such enthusiasm faded shortly after. One year later, in the winter 1997 issue of the magazine, a reader who defined himself as a 'net-enthusiast,' reports on his own failed attempt to pressure a governmental institution through online action. When he wrote to the White House an email full of anger and discontent about U.S. policy on Cuba, the White House responded via snail mail:

> Thank you for your message. I've been touched by the many expressions of support and encouragement I have received from people everywhere who care deeply about my Administration and about the future of the United States and the world. I am doing all I can to help us meet the crucial challenges that face all of us. Sincerely, Bill Clinton (*CubaSí* Magazine, Autumn 1997–1998, p. 28)

The early enthusiasm for the internet was thus replaced by a certain degree of skepticism as activists started to realize that, although the new technologies were enabling them to organize and mobilize action in fast and effective ways, internet networks did not necessarily challenge existing powers; in fact they often reinforced them.

However, as mentioned above, technological hypes often function in cycles (Mosco, 2004), and this is certainly true if we consider the history of the organizations I had the pleasure to work with. Towards the end of 2007 – as the *Cuba Solidarity Campaign* started to take the first steps in the world of social media by creating a YouTube account, opening a Facebook group, and setting up a profile on Twitter – internet practices within the office were largely shaped by the understanding that it was of fundamental importance to 'secure a presence' on social networking sites. The dominant discourse was that the organization had to draw on the new possibilities of social media technologies and spread the message of the campaign.

In order to comply with this discourse, the organization started to invest its few economic resources in developing social media platforms and in redefining its political practices in order to give a particular importance to social media action. This move was not seen favorably by everyone. Different activists within the organization started to question the importance of redefining their political and communication strategies in order to focus on 'social media action.' This latter point is expressed well in the following conversation between two members of CSC Matt and Claire,[6] who at the time of fieldwork were in their mid-twenties and active participants of the Labor Movement.

C: I think it's noticeable in the last years, among the different campaigns and the Trade Unions, things have changed. Today people think that having a Facebook group is a level of political activity, and they concentrate on online media action a lot. But then things are deteriorating. Members start to think that merely joining a Facebook group shows that you are committed. But actually it doesn't mean anything, it doesn't change things. There is too much information around, to be effective.

M: You are right, but I think it's also useful.

C: I mean it's useful in terms of advertising and promoting what we do. But you also want lobbying, you want demonstrations, you want protests. Facebook and other online spaces are useful in terms of promoting these activities but cannot be perceived as a substitute. But that's what's happening now.

Claire and Matt's conversation was not unique. Within the three different groups, activists felt that the belief in the possibilities of online communication often determined the fact that internet practices were given 'too much importance' to the detriment of other forms of political organization and participation. Therefore, activists were constantly engaged in defining the boundary between online action and other forms of action and in critically appraising how much they 'valued' their online communications. One fascinating aspect that emerged from this process of negotiation was represented by the fact that activists expressed their worry about the fact that they were being co-participants in processes of *technological fetishism* and were transforming web technologies into agents, able to redefine their political practices and transform their everyday life.

One day, for instance, I was interviewing Emma[7] who worked for *Ecologistas en Acción*. In the interview Emma highlighted the fact that activists were transforming online technologies into a "way of life."

E: Everything has changed [since the advent of the internet]. The way in which we manage space, time, resources, labor, we have gained agility in communicating, organizing, and creating actions. We reduced space and we can co-ordinate activities with local groups more easily, we can create texts simultaneously. Everything is much, much easier. But then there are the downsides to this; like the information overload that we are subjected to and also the fact that I think we rely on the internet too much and we tend to forget that it is just a technology, a tool, not a way of life. For us the net has come to be just that. It is our life; it shapes our everyday capacities of dealing with resources, our understandings of work and time.

A few months after my chat with Emma, I was sipping an espresso in Italy with one of the first founders of the *Corsari*, Nik, and I was surprised to notice that he shared the exact same understanding as Emma. At the age of 34, Nik had dedicated much of his life to political activism and was well known within the autonomous movement in Milan. I asked Nik how new technologies had changed the practice of political activism and to talk about his own experience:

N: Everything changed. It is inevitable that it did. Perhaps ten years ago I would have replied differently, because when new technologies became a new 'trend' for political activism … as it always happens … these situations trigger certain types of collective enthusiasm, which are at times out of proportion. Now the situation is different, these technologies have become part of our everyday life, they are part of normality, and they are mostly used instrumentally as 'tools.' The problem is when people forget that these are 'tools.' Technologies should never lose their instrumental nature.

Nik's and Emma's interviews validated my belief that as humans we are co-participants in the construction of technological agency, through our enthusiasms, ideologies, and political imaginations. We enable digital discourses to reshape our everyday practices. Both Nik and Emma seemed to have a clear understanding of this when they suggested that we tend to 'forget that technologies are tools.'

It seems to me that in the context of digital activism, therefore, scholars would miss important keys of analysis if they investigated technological agency without exploring the connectedness between the construction of digital discourses and their impacts on activists' everyday political practices. Once we understand the power of digital discourses on political activism, we can take a step further and explore a) the way in which digital discourses have become contested spaces of meaning in our Western societies and b) the tension between the digital discourses of capitalism on the one hand and activist cultures on the other.

ACTIVIST CULTURES AND DIGITAL CAPITALISM: SOCIAL TENSIONS BETWEEN DIGITAL DISCOURSES

Digital Discourses as Contested Spaces of Meaning and the Network as Empty Signifier

In the previous part of this chapter I have argued that it is important to look at the impact of techno-utopian discourses on everyday activist practices. Here, however, we need to appreciate the fact that it is equally important to critically reflect on the fact that digital discourses have become *contested spaces of meaning*. A good example of a digital discourse that has become a contested terrain of meaning is the concept of 'network.'

The study of digital activism in the last decade has largely focused on the analysis of the 'power of networks,' where the 'network' became the epitome of much of contemporary techno-utopian discourses. According to Castells (1996, 1997, 2009, 2012), for instance, the network has completely redefined political and social organization with important consequences for democratic processes. For Hardt and Negri (2000) the network has made possible the creation of the 'multitude,' a new form of political struggle, which does not rely on discipline but on creativity, communication, and self-organized cooperation (2000:83). Within these works, the network has been constructed as a 'political agent' – capable of transforming politics by fostering new and horizontal forms of political organization – and defined by the conjunction between a self-organizing collective intelligence and internet technologies.

In contrast to these approaches, Gerbaudo (2012) has argued that the 'network' is not a political agent but a 'political ideology.' Looking at the movements of 2011, he argued that far from being 'horizontal' and 'leaderless' contemporary social movements often have their leaders and reference points and use digital discourses, and especially the notion of network, to enable the creation of a 'soft' type of leadership (Gerbaudo, 2012). Gerbaudo is right to argue that the notion of 'network' is intrinsically connected to the ideologies of contemporary social movements, and his work is important because it highlights the fact that digital discourses are entwined with the political cultures of movements. However, what is missing from his account is an appreciation of the fact that the 'network,' as any digital discourse, has become a contested terrain of meaning, which is imagined and constructed in different ways by different political cultures.

The concept of 'empty signifier,' as developed by Laclau (1996), enables us to clarify this point. Laclau powerfully suggested that our societies depend largely upon 'empty signifiers' and that 'empty signifiers' define the basis of hegemonic struggles. In order to prove his argument he takes as example the concept of 'democracy,' which is an empty signifier because it is a concept that is essentially ambiguous. Empty signifiers are ambiguous and represent the power of the absence, because instead of reflecting reality, they are absent from it (1996:38–46). Despite not reflecting reality, empty signifiers still have a fundamental meaning for human beings; their absence has an immense power. Laclau's insight lies in the fact that he understands hegemony as the processes through which 'different forces attempt to fix meanings to these empty signifiers' (1996:38–46). The concept of 'network,' as Stalder (2006:169) has argued in his critique to Castells, can be perceived as an empty signifier. In fact, in the last decades, different social movements and power forces have tried to fix it with a meaning.

The fact that the concept of 'network' can be perceived as 'empty signifier' emerges particularly well in the ethnographic work of Green et al. (2005). The scholars undertook research on three different European Union–funded projects for the development of the information and communication infrastructure in Manchester. The projects largely reflected European policies, which were based on the 'imperative to connect' and on the idea that information and communication networks were a solution to technical, economic, and political problems in the making of Europe (Green et al., 2005:806). One of the most fascinating aspects of their work lies in the fact that they show that, although European policy makers had an 'imagination' of the network that reflected their political project, this imagination clashed with different understandings of networks that were advanced by local actors, who in the development of ICT sought to empower the local communities.

Equally, in the everyday lives of social movements, activists need to come to terms with the tension between their digital discourses on the meaning of networks and the digital discourses constructed by others. This latter point is particularly evident if we consider the fact that not only the political imaginations of the network vary from movement to movement (e.g. the autonomous network of the *Corsari* is very different from the notion of transnational network of solidarity as developed by CSC) but also that these imaginations clash with the ideologies promoted by corporate interest and web developers. Within business models, in fact, the 'network' has become the material expression of participatory consumer engagement and new flexible forms of capitalist production, consumption, and exploitation (Castells, 1996; Boltanski and Chiapello, 2007; O'Reilly, [2005] 2009; Fisher, 2010).

The concept of network, therefore, enables us to clarify the fact that all digital discourses[8] are contested spaces of meaning; they are empty signifiers that constitute the basis for some of contemporary hegemonic struggles. In order to understand these hegemonic struggles we need to refer back to the idea of *imaginary*[9] and explore the relationship between imagination and practice. This is because *imagination* is central to processes of discursive construction. As Kelty (2012) has shown, in the study of web technologies, the concept of imaginary is pivotal because it shows us that web technologies are imagined by different cultures in different ways and these imaginations define everyday web practices. It is for this reason that we need to understand the web as a '*contested* terrain of imagination and practice.' Once we do so, however, as the next part of the chapter will argue, we need to look at the difference between the imaginaries and practices of 'the weak' and the imaginaries and practices of 'power.'

IMAGINARIES AND SOCIAL PRACTICES: UNDERSTANDING THE DIFFERENCE BETWEEN POWER AND COUNTER-POWER

Strategies, Tactics, and the Everyday Experience of the Web

In recent years, as argued in the introduction to this book, different scholars interested in the analysis of the relationship between social movements and internet technologies have adopted the 'practice' approach to challenge much of the techno-determinism and techno-utopianism that can be found in current communication research (Mattoni, 2012, 2013; Treré, 2012; McCurdy, 2011; Cammaerts et al., 2013). One of the key influences in the development of the media practice approach in the study of social movements is a seminal essay written by Couldry (2004). Couldry (2004) argued that media scholars needed to move beyond a focus on media as texts or technologies and embrace the study of *media as practice.*[10] To develop his paradigm, Couldry (2004) brought together the contributions of key social theorists – such as Bourdieu, Latour, and Foucault – with sociological research on media practices and argued that it is important to consider the principles and beliefs whereby media practices are ordered. Despite being extremely interesting, one current dimension is missing from the media practice approach in media and communication research, namely the understanding that – as argued elsewhere (Barassi and Treré, 2012) – the 'practices of power' are very different from the 'practices of the weak'. This is because they have a spatial dimension and ultimately define the social environments that we live in.

This latter point emerges very well in the seminal work of De Certeau (1980). In his study on the understanding of everyday social practices, De Certeau (1980, 1984) argues that institutions and power structures usually have a spatial dimension in which they operate and, therefore, their practices can be understood as *strategies* that shape specific social environments (e.g. business and the internet). De Certeau believes that the practices of power (*strategies*) need to be differentiated from the practices of the 'weak,' which instead need to be understood as *tactics. Tactics,* in contrast to *strategies,* reflect the relationship between 'negotiation, practice and experimentation, they have a temporal dimension and they are connected to the idea of cultural adaptation' (1980:7). According to De Certeau (1984:11), the weak must continuously turn to their own ends forces that are alien to them.

As a social environment the web is a fundamental example of this. As I have argued in the introduction to the book, drawing on Curran (2012), I understand the web in very simple terms, namely as the construction and establishment of a user interface that provides a method of organizing and accessing distributed data across internet networks (2012:35). As mentioned elsewhere, there is no doubt that the web needs to be understood as a complex socio-technical environment defined by the interactions of different cultures, human relationships, and social processes. However, as different scholars have shown (Curran, 2012; McChesney, 2013), this user interface in the last decades has been largely shaped by the imagination and practices of corporate power. This is not only because web developments are constantly shaped by business rhetoric and practice, but also because giant corporations such as Facebook and Google are designing web platforms in such a way that they can exploit the user-generated data to turn it into profit. These practices need to be understood as *strategies* in De Certeau's terms (1980), because they are able to shape the web as social environment.

This understanding was shared among the activists I met during fieldwork. Informal conversations and interviews revealed that activists perceived the web as a 'public space' that was controlled and shaped by corporate interest. One day, for instance, I had the pleasure to interview Javier, who was in charge of the web development strategies of *Ecologistas en Acción*. In his forties, Javier had dedicated much of his life and work to finding tactical ways to strengthen digital activism. During the interview, he discussed the increased corporatization of the web, but also explained why it was important that activists accessed corporate web platforms.

J: From my own perspective digital spaces are public spaces that at present are owned by private corporations. We [activists] cannot afford not to enter and use these public spaces; we need to go where the people are. If the people are in a coffee shop we need to go there. If they are in a shopping center we need to go there. But we also need to convince them to go in the squares, in the streets and in all those places that are not owned by private corporations. The same thing happens on the internet, we need to use social media but at the same time we need to create our own spaces. [...].

As we shall see in the upcoming chapters, not only activists like Javier are critically aware of the fact that web platforms are largely shaped by the digital discourses and strategies of corporate power but their everyday internet uses of the web are defined by the process of negotiation with digital capitalism.

As argued in the introduction to this book, this process of negotiation is giving rise to a series of different 'ethnographic tensions' or, in other words, a series of collective experiences that are defined by the tension between activists' democratic needs on one side and digital capitalism on the other. The next chapters will explore three different ethnographic tensions faced by activists when using internet technologies as tools of political action and critique: *networked individualism, digital labor, and immediacy.*

CONCLUSION

This chapter has argued that if we want to understand the relationship between activist cultures and digital capitalism we need to develop a theoretical standpoint that approaches the question of 'technological agency' by looking at the relationship between digital discourses and digital practices. The development of this theoretical standpoint requires that we take three main conceptual steps. In the first place, we need to consider the fact that often technological agency is bestowed upon the technology through discourse and through the process of fetishism, which constructs the technology as an autonomous and magical agent (Harvey, 2003). This understanding enables us to appreciate the power of digital discourses and their impact on everyday practice. It has been shown, in fact, that techno-utopian discourses on the so-called revolutionary qualities of new technologies have not only defined the history of the internet and the development of the web 2.0, but also they have largely impacted activists' everyday practices by redefining political priorities and transforming understandings of political participation.

Once we are aware of the 'power' of digital discourse and of its impact on everyday practice we can take the next conceptual step. This involves the understanding that digital discourses have come to define some of our contemporary hegemonic struggles and that web technologies have become a contested terrain of imagination and practice (Kelty, 2006). If we need to understand that the web is a contested space of imagination and practice, we also need to appreciate the fact that there is a fundamental difference between the imaginaries and practices of the weak and the ones of power. In fact as it has been shown, the practices of power have a spatial dimension (De Certeau, 1980) and ultimately define the social environments that we live in. This is evident if we consider the web, which is largely shaped according to the imaginations and interests of corporate power.

As the next chapters will show, activists find themselves negotiating with the corporate structures of the web, and this process of negotiation is giving rise to a series of different 'ethnographic tensions.' Appreciating these tensions has become a key priority in the study of social movements. In fact as Silvia, of the *Corsari*, nicely put it:

s: [Web] Technologies have made an irruption into our lives, and now is the time for balance and negotiation.

NOTES

1. From an anthropological point of view there is a further problem with ANT, which I do not have the space or time here to explore. As Edwards et al. (2008:6) suggested, when ANT was established as a theoretical approach in the 1980s, its claims shared many lines of similarity with anthropological theories, and this is specifically true if we consider the work of Appadurai (1986) on the social life of things or if we look at Gell's (1998) anthropology of art and his analysis of things as social agents. Yet, there was a difference between the work of the science, technology, and society scholars (STS) and that of anthropologists. This is because, as Edwards et al. (2008) suggested, STS scholars were interested in showing how networks of human and non-human agents created social discourses, and they were especially concerned with the construction of science and scientific facts. Anthropologists, on the contrary, were interested in the human relations that made networks and connections possible, and they sought to uncover the meaning of these relations (2007:5–7). In this framework, as Knox et al. (2006) contended, the problem with much of the work of STS scholars is that it maintains a distance from the lives of the people it is focused on, in such a way that people become abstractions in the description of a scientific process (Knox et al., 2006:127).
2. The other side of this belief is techno-dystopianism, which fetishizes technologies as agents that construct unjust and unfair societies.
3. Fictional name to respect the informant's choice of anonymity.
4. Fictional name to respect the informant's choice of anonymity.
5. Fictional name to respect the informant's choice of anonymity.

6. Fictional name given the informant's will to remain anonymous.
7. Fictional name given the informant's will to remain anonymous.
8. A similar argument can be made also if we look at many other different digital discourses such as 'participation,' 'interactivity,' 'co-operation,' etc. All these concepts have come to signify different things in different social contexts.
9. As explained in the previous chapter, the concept of imagination needs to be detached from the idea of fantasy, which carries with it a connotation of thought divorced from projects and actions (Appadurai, 1990:7, Graeber, 2007), and should instead be regarded as a social *activity*, something that *we do* (Ingold, 2000:416), which carries forward intentionality, project, and action of a kind. Imagination is understood here as a social project, as referring to those social processes that enable people to construct total images of themselves and society and organize their everyday practices to fit these images. The concept of 'imaginary,' therefore, enables us to explore precisely this bound relation between imagination and practice (Taylor, 2003:24).
10. Prior to Couldry (2004), the concept of practice has often been central to the anthropology of media (Ginsburg, 1994; Ginsburg et al., 2002; Peterson, 2003; Askew and Wilk, 2002; Turner, 2002). However, as Brauchler and Postill (2010) have noticed, one problematic aspect of the media anthropology literature is represented by the fact that the concept of practice has not been properly defined or problematized. The authors therefore collected in the last years important contributions from media anthropologists and others, which thoroughly engage with practice theory and propose a more nuanced and thorough understanding of *media as practice* (Bräuchler and Postill, 2010).

3 Social Media Activism
and the Critique of Mass
Self-Communication

INTRODUCTION

The emphasis on the power of discourse associated with technologies, as argued in the previous chapter, enables us to better appreciate the fact that web technologies are contested terrains of imagination and practice and, thus, explains the tensions between activists' tactics and the strategies of digital capitalism. This chapter will consider one of the first ethnographic tensions that I have explored during fieldwork, which arises from the encounter between the self-centered architecture of social media and activist collective cultures. Research on social media has shown that the very architecture of these platforms supports and develops a form of communication that is individualized and egocentric (boyd and Heer, 2006; Hodkinson, 2007; Castells, 2009). In contrast to those who argue that the rise of 'mass self-communication' has been positive for political participation (Castells, 2009, 2012; Ellison et al., 2009; Stiegler, 2009), this chapter will show that the self-centered logic of social media is presenting a variety of challenges for political activists. This is not only because it is fomenting a type of political participation that does not necessarily translate in participation on the ground (Christensen, 2011; Morozov, 2011) but also because the increased visibility of the individual over the collective is challenging collective processes of meaning construction and impacting the internal politics of political groups (Fenton and Barassi, 2011). The chapter will therefore argue that, in the understanding of the individually centered networks of social media, we need to consider the strong connection between online self-communication, individualism, and the capitalist discourse. If we do so, we would realize that activists' everyday experience of social media is defined by the tension between the 'neoliberal individualistic autonomy' (Castoriadis, 1991) of digital capitalism and their understanding of 'political autonomy.' Therefore, the chapter will argue that the relationship between social media and political activism is defined by activists' negotiation with the 'self-centered' logic of these web 2.0 technologies.

This process of negotiation, it will be shown, varies from context to context. This is because activists need to shape their social media practices with reference to their own imaginaries. The chapter will, thus, focus on the contexts of CSC and the *Corsari*, which have completely different understandings of the meaning of 'collective identity' and political autonomy, and will argue that we need to understand social media activism by considering the cultural variation in *media imaginaries* and by appreciating the fact that this cultural variation leads to different social media practices.

WEB 2.0 TECHNOLOGIES, DIGITAL CAPITALISM, AND NETWORKED INDIVIDUALISM

The Self-Centered Structure of Social Media

The understanding that the architecture of social media supports the development of individualized and egocentric forms of communication can be found in the very early stages of social media research. Boyd and Heer (2006), following an online ethnographic research on *Friendster* and *MySpace*, argued that social networking sites, through the practice of 'friending,' created imagined egocentric communities. According to boyd and Heer (2006:para 50), in contrast to earlier virtual communities where interests or activities defined a group (Usenet, mailing list, chatroom, etc.), one of the key characteristics of social networking sites is that within these online platforms the context is created by the individual and his or her connections. A similar understanding is also shared by Hodkinson (2007), whose research on the Goth online community investigated the transition from online chat forums to individual blogs. He argued that individual blogs, although being interactive and socially oriented, are particularly consistent with the notion of individualistic rather than group-centered patterns of sociability (2007:648–650).

The earlier analyses of the self-centered structure of social media recall the work of Castells (2001). Castells was one of the first to point out the fact that online technologies, and especially new interactive web platforms, enable a form of communication and sociality that is self-centered. This type of sociality, according to him, had little to do with the idea of 'virtual community' that permeated earlier understandings of social interaction in the online world (Rheingold, 1993). Drawing from Wellman (2001), Castells contended that the new sociality promoted by the internet is one in which the individual becomes the central actor; it is the sociality of *'networked-individualism'* (2001:131). According to Castells, networked individualism is a social pattern, not a collection of isolated individuals. Rather individuals build their networks online and offline on the basis of their interests, values, and affinities. In this way networked individualism organizes around communities of choice that are flexible, fluid, and ever changing.

In 2001, Castells argued that, with the extension of internet technologies, networked individualism was becoming the dominant form of sociality, and at the time he concluded that the costs of this sociological transformation were still unclear (2001:133). In a more recent work on *Communication Power* (2009), he reconsidered the role of networked individualism in the global context by looking at the way it coexisted with other cultural patterns. In fact he argued that global culture is affected by a tension between globalization and identification, between individualism and communalism (Castells, 2009:116–117). According to him, these cultural trends intersect with one another, creating the coexistence of four cultural patterns: consumerism (signified by brands), networked individualism (signified by the internet), cosmopolitanism (be it ideological, political, or religious), and multiculturalism (2009:119). Therefore, although Castells argued that networked individualism today coexists with other forms of sociality, he also argued that networked individualism is a model of sociality that is promoted primarily by online technologies. By considering the development of web 2.0 technologies, he came to the conclusion that in the contemporary global context we are witnessing a transformation of information and communication means, where the 'mass communication of the self' has increasingly become an established phenomenon. This form of communication is defined by the fact that the self-generated messages created by individuals have the possibility of reaching global audiences and, hence, are a form of mass communication (2007, 2009:58–71).

The understanding that, on social media, individuals have the power to rely on personal networks to create their own context and display their identity has often been seen as a radical and positive transformation, which democratizes media production and empowers individual agents to bring about social change. This point is vividly expressed by Castells (2009), who contends that web 2.0 platforms empower individuals to re-program networks and re-channel messages from the grassroots level, leading to important social changes and political transformations (2009:412–415). Furthermore, he refers to Eco's idea of the 'creative audience' and argues that self-expression through social media platforms empowers individuals providing them with a new type of 'creative autonomy' (2009:127).

A similar line of reasoning is shared also by Ellison et al. (2009:9) who contend that social media platforms have positively influenced the organization of social movements and other political processes because they allow people to connect, communicate, and take action at the grassroots level through individual networks. A different perspective, yet still concerned with the positive consequences of individualized communication, can be found in the work of Stiegler (2009). Stiegler contended that social media – in contrast to mass media – are empowering tools because they enable people to develop new techniques of the soul and challenge the contemporary political economy through the self.

As argued elsewhere (Fenton and Barassi, 2011), one fundamental problem of the accounts of scholars like Castells (2009), Stiegler (2009), and Ellison et al. (2009) is that they focus on a discourse of empowerment and fail to consider the relationship between digital capitalism and mass self-communication. The creative autonomy of individuals enabled by new communication technologies that Castells (2009) heralds as liberatory can be interpreted, drawing on Castoriadis (1991), as 'individualistic autonomy' conducive to neo-liberal practice. In fact, it is the individual that is asked to communicate, share interests, and construct a profile on social media networks. Although this can lead to many positive and empowering situations at the individual level, in the context of social movements, the problem of positive understandings of networked individualism and creative autonomy is precisely that they prioritize individual agency over the political and ideological context.

Individualism, Web 2.0 Technologies, and Capitalism

In this book, rather than sharing the techno-optimism of the above scholars, my understanding is that it is impossible to explore the bound relationship between online communication and networked individualism without exploring the relationship between capitalism and individualism. In the social sciences, different scholars have shown that capitalism, more than any other economic system, is based on an individualist 'supporting philosophy' (Callero, 2013:24–25). This 'supporting philosophy,' as Callero (2013) would call it, finds its roots in the earlier development of capitalism in 'merchant' Europe (Goody, 2013) and was largely influenced by the Protestant ethic and by the development – after the French Revolution – of a form of political thought, which brought together the ideology of the market and liberalism with an almost sanctified understanding of individual rights and private property (Macpherson, [1962] 2011; Dumont, 1992; Goody, 2013). Therefore, it is important to understand that the relationship between Western capitalism and individualism has affected different layers of social experience, and as Goody (2013) has argued, it has multiple facets whether we consider political-legal issues, economic issues, family values, or religion.

My understanding is that with the development of web 2.0 technologies this relationship has acquired a new facet, and social media have become the spaces where individualistic practices are reinforced for corporate interest. Within social media platforms, rather than being empowered, the individual has a limited margin of freedom. This is clear if we consider the fact that the fixity of profiles often diminishes users' agency (Marwick, 2005). Furthermore, this is even more evident if we appreciate the fact that the self-disclosure that is fostered and encouraged by web 2.0 platforms is aimed at creating large datasets of user data that can be exploited for corporate purposes (Jakobsson and Stiernstedt, 2010; Van Dijck and Nieborg, 2009; Bauwens, 2008; Andrejevic, 2003, 2009; Jarrett, 2008; Terranova, 2000, 2013; Huws, 2003; Scholz, 2013).

Consequently, in the understanding of networked individualism as a form of communication and social organization promoted by web 2.0 technologies, we cannot fail to consider the bound relationship between capitalism and internet technologies, and we must appreciate the fact that, as Fuchs (2009) argued:

> The empowerment discourse issue is individualistic because it focuses research primarily on how individuals use SNS for making connections, maintaining or receiving friendships, falling in love, creating autonomous spaces etc. It does not focus on how technology and technology use are framed by political issues and issues that concern the development of society, such as capitalist crises, profit interest, global war, the globalization of capitalism, or the rise of a surveillance society.
>
> (Fuchs, 2009:18)

The recognition that there is a complex connection between digital technologies and a type of networked individualism, which is rooted within the history of Western capitalism, is of central importance in the understanding of the communication processes enabled by social media and how they are impacting digital activism. As the next parts of the chapter will show, self-centered communication processes are affecting the internal politics of political groups and clashing with the collective nature of political activism.

SOCIAL MEDIA ACTIVISM AND THE CRITIQUE OF MASS SELF-CENTERED COMMUNICATION

Individualism and Slactivism? Changing Cultures of Political Participation

When I first approached fieldwork with CSC in 2007, social media technologies were becoming new tools for political communication, organization, and action. At the time, as we have seen in the previous chapter, within the Labor Movement members and activists believed that it was of central importance to 'tap into the possibilities of social media' and to transform their own communication strategies and political practices. These beliefs were influenced by the assumption that social media were going to attract younger generations, and this was an important strategy for trade unions. At the time of fieldwork most of the trade union members and organizers that I interviewed believed that their politics no longer appealed to younger generations and showed a great deal of distress with the idea that 'their world was dying.' When confronted with the question of why they thought that the Trade Union Movement was no longer appealing to younger generations, most of the people I talked to would simplify the problem by stating that 'young people just didn't care.' Others would look confused and claim that they didn't know. Occasionally, however, I have been confronted with thorough reflections on the issue, reflections that took into consideration the economic and historical transformations brought by Thatcher, the new culture of individualism promoted by neo-liberalism, and the self-centered nature of web 2.0 communication.

This latter point emerged vividly in a joint interview, which I mentioned in the previous chapter, with Matt and Claire[1] who were both in their early twenties. According to Claire, trade union organizations were focusing too much on online action to the detriment of older forms of political engagement. She argued that such a strategy could prove right to attract younger generations, but she also stressed the fact that online participation often creates an 'illusion' of political activity, because online communication is not enough to promote real change at collective and societal levels. Matt found himself agreeing with her and added:

M: People no longer believe in collective action, and I do think that this is partly due to what is going on around the internet. It is all so individualized. You know, all people want is to focus on blogs and they say that it is good to focus on blogs, but that is so individualistic, and in terms of collectively changing society it doesn't bring anything.

Interviews revealed that, like Matt, many who were involved in the British Trade Union Movement believed that web technologies are embedded in a broader political culture that emphasizes individualism versus collective action and belonging. At Trade Union conferences and events I found myself involved in a variety of different conversations, where people complained about the 'too individualistic logic' of web 2.0 technologies and argued that these technologies are promoting a political culture based on individual distance and laziness.

The understanding that social media technologies are fomenting a new type of individualism that challenges processes of political participation and aggregation was a shared belief also among the Spanish and Italian activists. Within *Ecologistas en Acción*, Barcia, whom I mentioned in the introduction to this book, for instance, argued that social media technologies 'allow people to relate at a distance' while making people simultaneously more detached from collective experiences and collective political processes. Also Juan,[2] another full-time staff member of *Ecologistas en Acción,* shared Barcia's understanding. In his interview he explained that part of the problem was the 'multimodality' of web technologies, which is giving individuals the 'illusion' that they are constantly connected to the collective experience.

J: During a single day we may be on Skype, on social media accounts, writing emails, or uploading information on a website but all these are individual actions, which encourage a form of individualistic experience of collective action with consequences for collective forms of political participation.

During my research, I found a similar belief also within the social context of the *Corsari*. Piero,[3] who at the time of fieldwork was 24 years old, argued that social media isolated individuals, giving them the illusion of being part of a collective. In a variety of interviews and informal conversations, different activists asked me to understand that individual participation on social media could not really be perceived as politically important or meaningful for collective action. The only time such participation was perceived as meaningful was when it was aimed at producing and sharing content about the group's political beliefs, activities, or events. Yet they also argued that the production and sharing of oppositional content alone could not be the only form of an individual's political engagement, as it was a form of lazy politics.

All the evidence collected within the different organizations, therefore, relates well to some contemporary theoretical critiques against 'slactivism' (Christensen, 2011; Morozov, 2011), which have shown that online individual participation alone cannot lead to political emancipation. However, an analysis of the different ethnographic contexts also brings this critique forward because it highlights the fact that individualized forms of communication are rendering the individual more visible over the collective and this is having an impact on the internal politics of political groups.

The Networked Self, the Visible Individual, and the Challenge to the Collective Life of Political Groups

One of the greatest challenges faced by activists when dealing with the networked self was represented by the problem of 'visibility' of the individual over the collective. What emerged from my research is that many activists believed that in an era of selfies and social media, individual messages are often given the same importance as the messages that have arisen out of the tensions and negotiations of a collective of people. Therefore, they believed that the 'collective messages and voices' of oppositional groups become suffocated by the information overload of the online space and by the sheer abundance of individual messages. This shared understanding among the activists across the three organizations was making them question the very idea that web 2.0 technologies create a space in which their voice can be heard. The overall debate was that social media technologies were making the individual more visible over the collective, and in doing so they were challenging collective processes of meaning production.

One day in spring 2007, for instance, I was talking to Rob, the director of the *Cuba Solidarity Campaign*. In his early forties, Rob had been involved with the Trade Union Movement and international trade unionism since the mid-1980s, at a time of great political and economic change for British politics. During fieldwork we often went for lunch together with the other members of the office of CSC, and we would have long and informal chats about the campaign, trade union politics, the difficulty of managing resources, and of course about the impacts of internet technologies. That day over lunch, Rob was discussing the self-centered nature of social media communication and was highlighting the fact that the sheer abundance of individual messages produced on social media was threating the visibility of their collective message. He discussed the difficulty of getting the campaign's 'message across' to mainstream media and public opinion. He then added: 'We try our best. But what should we do when the message of a single eleven year old can achieve a greater importance than our own?'

A few years later, while the tents of the 15M movement were occupying Puerta del Sol in Madrid, I sat down for an interview with David[4] who had long been involved with the organization. In the interview David discussed the issue of self-centered communication on the internet in the same way as Rob had done years before, and talked about the fact that the messages of the collective are often suppressed by the abundance of individual messages.

D: I think the internet is a dangerous tool for political action. It creates isolated social relationships, which are based on individualism. Furthermore the internet fosters alienation. Even if one can find some interesting content, there is also a great amount of content that is produced by individuals and distracts people and detaches them from serious issues, in this way it alienates them. Everybody says that there is no censorship on the internet, or at least only in part. But that is not true. Online censorship is applied through the excess of banal content that distracts people from serious or collective issues.

According to David, the quantity of individual messages online creates a form of social noise, which distracts people from more serious, collective concerns. David, like Rob, was critical about web 2.0 technologies because, according to him, the online visibility of the individual was impacting activists' ability to transmit their collective messages. Both activists considered the problem of the 'visible individual,' therefore, by reflecting on the difficulty their organizations faced in getting their messages across.

Yet it is important to understand that the problem of the 'visible individual' can have also another impact on political activism: It can affect the internal politics of political groups and create internal tensions. Illustrative in this regard is an interview with Franz, one of the founding members of the *Corsari*. Franz's personal biography is deeply embedded in the militant movement in Milan. He started his political activity at the beginning of the 1990s, when he participated in the creation of the *Tute Bianche*. Towards the end of the 1990s Franz was one of the founders of the social center *Deposito Bulk*, which was a key player in the Italian global justice movements. His life narrative is deeply interlinked with the collective narrative of the movement, and it was a pleasure for me, after almost a year of research on the *Corsari*, to sit down for a long interview with him. During the interview, I asked Franz to discuss his biographical narrative and also elaborate and reflect on the findings that I had collected within the group. In one part of the interview he discussed the relationship between web technologies and individualism and explained the fact that the problem of the 'visible individual' was impacting the internal politics of the group.

F: I don't want to be the nostalgic type who says that now children stay at home in front of their playstations and computers whilst before they used to play together in the streets. It's true. But that's ok, the world changes; it evolves itself. What we have to do is to negotiate with change not resist to it. However, it is clear that the use of technologies facilitates processes of individual isolation, especially if you think about it in terms of society. It is clear that we live in a society where there is a tendency to use new technologies in an individualistic way.

V: And what do you think about the impact of these forms of individual communication on collective action?

F: I am not entirely sure there is a link between the expansion and growing pervasiveness of individualist technologies with a growth of individualistic forms of political action. I think that the fact is that there is a growing tendency in society as a whole to promote individualism and that this is affecting our relationship to technologies as well as our relationship to political action [...]. If you think about our own group, the situation is the following. Many of us use social media technologies to 'amplify' and disseminate information on our collective actions, and this is very positive. [...]. However, all these technologies facilitate the public dimension of the single individual and this is problematic. Here I am making an example that may be seen as a bit of an extreme. Let's imagine that you were a supporter of LSD drug use. In the past, you would share this information only with the people you wanted to share it with, but now if you have a Facebook account and you are not very careful on how you are managing your information, then this information can become public. Now let's imagine that you belong to a political group that, alongside other things, campaigns against drug use. Then the public juxtaposition of your personal belief and the collective one becomes problematic. Without reaching such extremes, I think that new technologies facilitate a new visibility of the individual (and the individual political actor) and now activists have to judge whether their individual choices and interests can have an effect on the life of the collective [...]. You see, ideally I think that everyone should have a coherence between one's own private and public life but if you are not coherent and don't take care of your individuality you end up weakening the collective.

As it can be seen from the above section, individualistic forms of communication can represent a real challenge for collective processes of political participation and meaning construction and for the internal politics of collective groups. As argued elsewhere (Fenton and Barassi, 2011), contemporary communication research does not recognize this challenge. An example of this is, of course, Castells's (2009) theory of 'creative autonomy.' As mentioned above, Castells refers to Eco's idea of the 'creative audience' (2009:127) to argue that web 2.0 platforms have provided individuals with a greater communicative autonomy. His argument is based on the belief that the construction of communicative autonomy is directly related to the development of social and political autonomy (2009:414). Now, as the following part of this chapter will argue, this is not necessarily true, and we need to take into consideration the fact that the communicative autonomy of the consumer, which is promoted by digital capitalism, clashes with the political autonomy heralded by activist cultures.

DIGITAL CAPITALISM AND ACTIVIST CULTURES: THE NETWORKED SELF AND THE QUESTION OF POLITICAL AUTONOMY

Activist Cultures, Political Autonomy, and the Construction of the Self

In the last two decades, activist cultures – especially in Europe and the United States – have been largely influenced by the notion of 'political autonomy' as developed by the global justice movements.[5] During the nineties, the movements for global justice started to show that there were new political possibilities available in the construction of political belonging and opposition. One of these political possibilities was represented by 'autonomy' and the idea that social struggle can happen beyond the state. Influenced by the Zapatista teachings and understandings that the state is a form of relationship (Deleuze and Guattari, 1987), the movements for global justice acted on the logic of autonomy. In a similar line to the classical anarchists of the nineteenth century, such as Kropotkin and Laundauer, these movements argued that state relationships 'capture' and 'control' minorities (Day, 2005). Hence, their aim was to enact forms of communitarianism and non-hierarchical relationships through direct action and participatory democracy. The way in which they organized themselves collectively and non-hierarchically, therefore, became not only a practice but also as Graeber (2002) suggested a form of ideology, an ideology that is based on anarchism and autonomism.

The autonomous discourses of the movements for global justice have created the basis for a new reformulation of political identity. During the eighties, scholars such as Laclau and Mouffe (2001) suggested that there was no longer a whole vision of society but only multiple and conflicting political identities (2001:34–39), and others – like Touraine – contended that society was not a system but a field of action, and that conflicts occurred over the control of the cultural, social, and political means of self-production (2001:750–754). Identity was therefore a key word in any debate that related to social and political struggle. In the late nineties, according to Day (2005), the 'politics of demand' fostered by new social movements had gradually been replaced by an understanding that the emancipations of political identities are constantly instrumentalized by power forces. Social movements were no longer interested in achieving recognition through the state for their marginal 'identities' because they no longer believed that the state could be perceived as a neutral arbiter. In other words, they no longer believed in representative democracy. On the contrary, these movements saw state relationships as the very reason behind social inequality. Among the movements for global justice, therefore, political identity was no longer a reason for struggle or the very ground for cohesion. It has been replaced by more hybrid and 'nomadic' understandings of engagement and participation, which focused on a politics of 'affinity' rather than a politics of 'identity.'

In order to better understand the characteristics of these new forms of belonging that are based on the notion of political autonomy, Agamben's (1993) definition of *coming community* is particularly interesting. According to Agamben, the coming communities are composed of different singularities; they have neither universal nor common subjects, and they do not work for the construction of collective belonging (1993:17–23). They are brought together spontaneously by relations of affinity. The coming communities, therefore, have many dividing lines but are interconnected and united by values and shared ethico-political commitments (1993:43–47). They rely on a politics of affinity, which is based on an understanding of 'groundless solidarity' (solidarity that is not based on identity) and 'infinite responsibility' (Day, 2005).

It is by looking at the concept of 'coming community' that we realize that, within social movements, the autonomous self is embedded in the collective; it is not an individualist agent. Therefore, the way in which activists have imagined the autonomous self in the last decades is very different from the individualistic notion of 'neo-liberal autonomous self' (Castoriadis, 1991), which is promoted by contemporary debates on social media as participatory technologies.

The understanding that there are different ways in which we can imagine the 'self' is key to classical anthropological theory on the 'category of person.' Anthropological approaches have largely been influenced by Mauss's famous understanding that there is a fundamental distinction between one's own sense of self (*moi*) and the social and cultural category of moral person (*personne*) (1985:3). Mauss argued that all human beings have a sense of self, which is different from the culturally constructed understanding of the moral/collective person (e.g. the good Christian, the good citizen, the good activist). Anthropologists have criticized Mauss's understanding that the sense of self (*moi*) should be understood as a universal category that survives in a Kantian way *a priori* (Collins, 1985), as the true side of individuals that is constantly masked by *personne* (the cultural category of the person). On the contrary, they have shown that within different cultures there are not only various conceptions of person but also different understandings of the 'self.' These understandings of the 'self' cannot be related to the construction of the individual in the West (Cohen, 1994; Morris, 1994).

The anthropological understanding that there are different culturally specific ways in which to analyze the construction of the self is pivotal if we want to appreciate the impacts of processes of 'mass self-communication' on political activism. This is because it enables us to appreciate the fact that activists' everyday experiences of social media are defined by the tension between the individualist autonomy of neo-liberalism (Castoriadis, 1991) and their notion of political autonomy, which is simultaneously personal and collective. This latter point emerged quite vividly in the interview with Franz:

F: I believe that political participation and the promotion of social change is inextricably connected to a collective process, it's not an individual process. It is obvious that, as an individual who partakes to a collective, you have to make sure that change happens not only outside of you but also within you, but political processes are first and foremost collective processes. This is why I believe that the concept of 'autonomy' linked to the idea of individuality can be extremely dangerous, political autonomy should be part of a collective process. I believe that new technologies tend to facilitate a form of individualistic autonomy. [...] But, if you want to be politically active you have to initiate or be part of collective processes [...]. Unfortunately new technologies favor – in a way that is absolutely superficial – an individualist autonomy, which is negative.

According to Franz, the 'individualistic autonomy' that is promoted by social media challenges the processes of 'political autonomy' where the self becomes simultaneously a subjective and collective subject. Unraveling the tension between networked individualism and the political autonomy of social movements is of central importance if we want to appreciate the impact of social media on collective action. However, this is just one step in our argument. The next step is to understand the fact that different political cultures negotiate differently with the networked self and that this cultural difference defines the very nature of activists' use of social media.

NEGOTIATING WITH THE NETWORKED SELF: ACTIVIST CULTURES AND MEDIA IMAGINARIES

Social Media Practices, Political Projects, and the Problem of the Networked Self

As argued above, social media activism cannot be fully understood without looking at activists' everyday negotiation with the individualist logic of social media. Here it is important to understand that the way that activists negotiate with the networked self will vary from context to context, from situation to situation. This is because processes of negotiation are defined by activists' need to shape their social media practices with reference to their own political cultures and projects.

In the previous chapters I have drawn on the work of different scholars (Appadurai, 1990; Castoriadis, 1998; Ingold, 2000; Taylor, 2003; Kelty, 2012) and argued that the concept of *media imaginary* can enable us to shed light on the fact that activists constantly 'imagine' what they do with media technologies with reference to specific political projects. Furthermore, I have argued that, as the anthropological literature has shown, it is impossible to divorce projects/ideals from everyday practices. The concept of *media imaginary* as developed in the previous chapters thus applies really well to the analysis of the ways that activists use social media and negotiate with the networked self. In fact their processes of negotiation are constructed around their political projects, and these political projects have an impact on the organization of their social media practices.

As argued elsewhere, CSC is a campaigning organization that by bringing forward the example of Cuba aims to show that there is an alternative to the neo-liberal system. The intention of the campaign is not to propose that Britain should undergo a socialist revolution but to highlight the fact that state intervention – and a limitation to corporate power – can lead to important civic transformations. Most importantly, by placing the policies of the Cuban and the British governments in antithesis, CSC is constantly trying to argue for the importance of defending the right to public health and education. Hence, the political project of CSC is that of building a strong message, a message that enables people to reflect on the contradictions and social injustices of the neo-liberal model.

Research within CSC revealed that the construction of a 'coherent and strong message' is not an easy task for the people involved in the campaign especially in a country where the dominant media attitude towards the issue of Cuba is largely critical. Therefore, in analyzing the way in which social media are understood within CSC, the researcher cannot overlook the ethnographic context of the campaign and the fact that social media practices are organized according to the specific political project of the organization.

During fieldwork, it emerged that within CSC people believed that one of the main problems of online self-centered communication is represented by the fact that the 'individual' would challenge and weaken the collective message of the campaign. Therefore, CSC organizers and members believed that one fundamental problem of social media activism was the problem of 'unmediated interactivity.' In fact, during fieldwork, many mentioned that in contrast to other forms of media production – such as the magazine or the website, which involves a process of collective negotiation and group production – social media platforms allowed individual members (and non-members) to post comments without negotiating with the collective. In this framework, transmitting a collective, coherent, and strong message on social media platforms is almost impossible because individual messages have the potential to challenge, deconstruct, and weaken the message of the campaign. This challenge can only be met through the constant and resource-intensive process of interactive discussion and deliberation that is simply too big an undertaking for a small organization such as CSC. Consequently, when the *Cuba Solidarity Campaign* opened its YouTube account, the national office chose not to allow others to post comments beneath their videos. The choice of not allowing people to post comments on their YouTube account was not motivated by a will to be undemocratic but by the fact that they didn't have the resources to monitor or reply to the posts. In the last years, especially with the development of the Facebook page and the Twitter account, CSC organizers and members had to embrace 'interactivity.' However, the resource-intensive task of interactive communication, for them, still represents a challenge.

For the *Corsari* the interactive element of social media was seen as positive. According to some of the activists that I interviewed, interactivity facilitated processes of individual participation. Thus, interactivity was important because it promoted practices of participatory democracy. Revealing in this regard is an interview with Giacomo, a veterinary student from Milan who at the time of fieldwork was 26 years old and had been with the *Corsari* since the beginning. When I asked him whether he believed that interactivity on social media would challenge the 'collective voice' of the group and whether activists should limit it, he replied:

G: I wouldn't limit comments on our blog or Facebook page, even the ones that are external to the group, because limitation and censorship do not belong to me. You know, everyone is free to criticize, and to have a personal opinion. If I were to give up my personal opinion, I would be giving up also my individual contribution to collective life and thus interrupt the political process itself. The new internet has enabled that sort of participation, which for us is very important, why would we censor it?

As it emerges from Giacomo's interview, the *Corsari*, in contrast to CSC, looked favorably at the issue of interactivity. However, it must be noted that the people involved with the group were finding the self-centered logic of the internet problematic for a different reason. Among the *Corsari*, many believed that the self-centered logic of social media was problematic because of the issue of privacy. As mentioned in the previous chapters, the group is very cautious about the information activists post on the web, to the point that they rely on an autonomous infrastructure network created by A/I. The main idea, as mentioned in the A/I manifesto, is:

A/I: In our glossy social networking age we tend to forget that technology is a tool, and as such we have to use it carefully and with the right amount of paranoia, so that it won't backfire on us all.

According to different activists involved in the *Corsari*, and especially those who had a long history of political activism, the main problem of self-centered communication is represented by the fact that individuals do not have the right degree of awareness when they post information on social media accounts. Within the group, at the time of fieldwork, there was the shared understanding that it was necessary to protect one's privacy on individual Facebook profiles in order to protect the privacy of the group. Consequently, activists were urged by the collective to 'untag' photos that might have identified them during an action and to limit the amount of data posted. These social media practices generated a great deal of tension within the group because individual activists misused their individual profiles and placed the privacy of the collective at risk.

We cannot understand these tensions or the logic behind their social media practices without looking at the political project of the *Corsari*. Within the *Corsari* 'direct action' was the key word. Their aim was to reclaim public spaces and oppose the neo-liberal laws, enforcements, and ideologies that had come to dominate much of public life in Milan. Furthermore, the political project of the *Corsari* was tightly interconnected to the promotion of 'self-management' and practices of participatory democracy. If we consider the political project of the *Corsari*, it is not surprising that social media uses were defined by a belief in the positive elements of interactivity and a fear of scrutiny and surveillance.

In conclusion to this part, it seems clear that the activists of both organizations negotiated with the self-centered nature of social media by referring to their political projects. Looking at how people imagine what they do with the media according to particular social and political projects is of central importance for our analysis of digital activism, because it sheds light on the multiple varieties of activists' use of web technologies.

CONCLUSION

In contrast to those scholars who emphasize the democratic possibilities brought about by the self-centered logic of social media and the 'mass-communication' of the self (Castells, 2009) this chapter has argued that in the study of digital activism, we need to critically consider the strong connection between online self-communication, individualism, and the capitalist discourse. If we do so, we would realize that activists' everyday experience of social media is defined by the tension between their understanding of political autonomy and the 'neo-liberal individualistic autonomy' (Castoriadis, 1991). In fact, as it has been shown, the individualistic autonomy of social media communication is having an impact not only on processes of political participation but also on collective processes of meaning construction and on the internal politics of groups. Therefore, the chapter has argued that the relationship between social media and political activism is defined by activists' negotiation with the 'self-centered' logic of these web 2.0 technologies.

As it has been shown, activists are not only critical about the self-centered logic of the internet, but also they are finding multiple ways that they can negotiate with this logic through their everyday media practices and beliefs. One fascinating aspect of this process of negotiation is represented by the fact that it varies from context to context, from situation to situation. While in negotiating with networked individualism CSC perceived interactivity as threat, the *Corsari* understood interactivity as a positive dimension of web 2.0 technologies. On the other hand, while for the *Corsari* the issue of 'privacy' was key in the negotiation with the networked self, for CSC the issue of privacy was only marginal. The chapter has thus argued that in order to understand this cultural variation in social media practices and beliefs it is important to turn to the concept of *media imaginary* and appreciate the fact that activists often *imagine* "what they do" with media technologies according to culturally and context-specific political projects.

NOTES

1. Fictional name to protect the informant's choice of anonymity
2. Fictional name to protect the informant's choice of anonymity.
3. Fictional name to protect the informant's choice of anonymity.
4. Fictional name to protect the informant's choice of anonymity.
5. The understanding that the notion of political autonomy as developed by the global justice movements had influenced activist cultures became particularly evident during fieldwork. In fact, during my research I came to the conclusion that the notion of political autonomy, as developed by the global justice movements, did not only influence the context of the *Corsari* or *Ecologistas en Acción*, whose political cultures were already largely shaped upon autonomous ideologies, but they influenced also the context of CSC. In fact, as I have argued elsewhere (Barassi, 2009), autonomous discourses have influenced a change in the way that political solidarity is perceived by CSC's members and organizers. The way that political solidarity as a rhetorical discourse is being understood within CSC is very different from the socialist logic of solidarity that was common in the 1980s. At the time of fieldwork, the notion of political solidarity had more to do with the type of networked logic of the global justice movements rather than with socialist ideology. When talking about political solidarity, the people involved with CSC often emphasized the importance of creating a 'common ground' and developing a broad campaign that included people from various political backgrounds. What I found particularly interesting during fieldwork is that in constructing a new understanding of political solidarity – which is based on an idea of joining forces for a common interest no matter if the people involved in the struggle come from conflicting backgrounds – many of the discursive practices of the campaign were directed towards a *systematic and conscious deconstruction of the concept of political identity*. Of course, although it is important to highlight how some of the discourses of 'groundless solidarity' that were central to the global justice movements have influenced the campaign, it is also important to be aware of the fact that despite reshaping their understanding of political identity in more flexible and networked ways, the people involved with CSC still strongly believe in the hegemonic project.

4 The Everyday Critique of
Digital Labor

INTRODUCTION

The previous chapter focused on one of the key ethnographic tensions triggered by the extensive use of web 2.0 technologies for political activism: the problem of networked individualism. As it has been shown, the everyday experience of social media activism is defined by the tension between the 'individualist autonomy' intrinsic to digital capitalism and the 'political autonomy' promoted by social movements. In this chapter I want to focus on a further ethnographic tension, which arises from the encounter between activist cultures and digital capitalism. In fact I will be focusing on the issue of *digital labor*, and I will discuss the issue by looking at the ethnographic contexts of the *Corsari* and *Ecologistas en Acción*.[1]

The first part of the chapter will engage with current debates on digital labor and will introduce the concept by looking in particular at its relationship to the ideas of 'immaterial labor' and 'free labor.' It will be argued that the concept of 'digital labor' is of central importance to communication research, because it enables us to uncover the way in which digital technologies are supporting a new type of capitalist domination, which is based on a politics of dispossession of personal data (Jakobsson and Stiernstedt, 2010; Van Dijck and Nieborg, 2009; Bauwens, 2008), on corporate surveillance (Andrejevic, 2003, 2009; Jarrett, 2008), and the exploitation of immaterial labor (Terranova, 2000, 2013; Huws, 2003; Fuchs, 2007, 2014; Scholz, 2013).

Although important for communication research, approaches on digital labor in communication studies seem to have been defined by a profound *economic determinism*, where scholars have focused on digital production as the production of data that can be turned into a commodity. This has led to the frequent (and sometimes unconvincing) pairing of 'free labor' online with the concept of exploitation (Hesmondhalgh, 2010) and to the emergence of critical questions in relation to the way in which people understand and negotiate with the exploitation of user data for corporate purposes (Andrejevic et al., 2014). Although it is clear that we need to critically reflect on emerging issues of exploitation in the digital economy, it is also clear that we need to consider the way in which digital production is intertwined with the production of social life.

These questions, I will argue, are of central importance in the study of digital activism. As it will be shown, activists' critique of digital capitalism is largely shaped by the understanding that there is a bound relationship between internet technologies and the emergence of new forms of labor that is exploited for corporate purposes. This understanding shapes activists political cultures as well as their uses of web technologies. However, the chapter will also show that, although activists are aware of the bound relationship between web technologies and new forms of capitalist exploitation, they also believe that it is important to use corporate digital platforms and negotiate with this exploitation.

In order to understand these processes of negotiation, it will be argued, we need to look at the concept of *value* in anthropological terms and appreciate that the production of human value goes well beyond rationalist/reductive economist paradigms (Graeber, 2002; Turner, 2006). In doing so, the chapter will demonstrate that in the understanding of the relationship between political activists and web 2.0 technologies scholars must bear in mind the different forms of value that they create through digital production and the many margins of freedom from online corporate surveillance that they actively construct.

WEB 2.0, THE QUESTION OF DIGITAL LABOR

Internet Research and the Importance of the Concept of 'Digital Labor'

In the last few years the concept of 'digital labor' has established itself within the field of communication studies as an important analytical tool, which has been used to critically reflect on the changing condition of labor in the digital economy. Internet researchers have used the concept to counteract the techno-optimism of scholars such as Benkler (2007), Tapscott and Williams (2006), and Shirky (2008) as well as many others who have argued that web 2.0 technologies were reinforcing a new, networked economy that was based on co-production and participation. On the contrary, by referring to the concept of digital labor, critical internet scholars claimed that the participatory culture promoted by web 2.0 technologies, rather than opening real possibilities for democratic empowerment, has strengthened an advanced form of capitalism based on the exploitation of users' digital production (Jakobsson and Stiernstedt, 2010; Van Dijck and Nieborg, 2009; Bauwens, 2008; Andrejevic, 2003, 2009; Jarrett, 2008; Terranova, 2000, 2013; Huws, 2003; Fuchs, 2008, 2013, 2014; Scholz, 2013). There is obviously a variety of different approaches to the understanding of digital labor in communication research, but as Scholz has argued, on whatever side of the argument we may fall, it is important to acknowledge the fact that scholars have referred to the concept of digital labor in the last years as a way to "dust off arguments about the perilous state of privacy, unequal wealth distribution, and the private exploitation of the public Internet" (Scholz, 2013:2).

In order to fully understand the concept of 'digital labor' we need to look at its relationship to the ideas of *'immaterial labor'* and *'free labor.'* The notion of immaterial labor has a long history and dates back to the nineteenth century (Khiabany, 2014); however, at the end of the 1990s, the concept was used mostly by the Autonomous Marxists (Lazzarato, 1996; Terranova, 2000; Hardt and Negri, 2000; Dyer-Whiteford, 1999, 2001) to shed light on the changing nature of labor and work in the digital and global era. The Autonomous Marxists argued that, with the emergence of post-Fordism, industrial modes of material production were being replaced by immaterial modes of production (Lazzarato, 1996; Hardt and Negri, 2000; Dyer-Whiteford, 1999, 2001). Therefore, they contended that scholars needed to consider those areas of labor that are involved in the production of "the informational and cultural content of the commodity" (Lazzarato, 2006:133). Furthermore, the Autonomous Marxists believed that the working class was increasingly involved in forms of immaterial labor, and that the exploitative relations of capitalism had pervaded areas that were relatively autonomous beforehand, creating the emergence of new possibilities for class struggle.

There are many flaws in the theory of immaterial labor as developed by the Autonomous Marxist tradition (Day, 2005; Gill and Pratt, 2008). We need to be critical about their notion of 'an extended working class' that is created by immaterial labor and is subjected to global capitalist exploitation. This is because the notion flattens a huge field of difference and does not take into account global inequalities (Day, 2005:145–146). In addition, we need to be skeptical about claims of 'immateriality' and about the overemphasis on the information economy that the concept of immaterial labor seems to take for granted (see Gill and Pratt, 2008).

Despite the flaws, at the end of the 1990s and at the beginning of the 2000s, the 'immaterial labor' argument was politically important because it drew attention to the new areas of labor that had emerged in the digital economy. The Autonomous Marxists largely influenced activists and political circles in Europe, who started to mobilize inspired by the understanding that the extension of internet technologies within the workplace – which was sustained by government's neo-liberal policies – was in fact strengthening a new 'political culture' of labor. This political culture was defined by the strengthening of 'flexible' forms of labor and the 'precarization'[2] of working life (Hardt and Negri, 2000; Virno, 2004; Lazzarato, 1996; Tari and Vanni, 2006). A beautiful study of the movements against precariety in Italy and their media practices can be found in the work of Mattoni (2012).

In social scientific terms, moreover, the concept of immaterial labor developed by the Autonomous Marxists played a fundamental role in the context of internet and communication studies because it enabled scholars to critically reflect on the relationship between internet technologies, capitalism, and changing modes of cultural production (Banks, 2010; Beck, 2005). As Terranova argued, what started to become clear to internet scholars was that new technologies "did not turn every user into an active producer and every worker into a creative subject" (2000:33). On the contrary – if one considered the creation of metadata – "co-creation on digital networks did not yield any power or control over the means of production" (2000:33), this power and control was concentrated in the hands of corporate power. Consequently, critical internet scholars argued that the 'new' participatory culture of the web 2.0 was creating a situation whereby the production of user data was systematically exploited by corporations to generate income and value (Andrejevic, 2003; Terranova, 2000; Fuchs, 2007, 2014; Bauwens, 2008; Jakobsson and Stiernstedt, 2010; Burston et al., 2010).

One particularly interesting aspect that emerges from these analyses of users' immaterial labor online is the understanding that this labor is *free*. Web users often produce value for web 2.0 corporations in their spare time making it difficult to differentiate between play and work, labor and non-labor (see Scholz, 2013). Within internet research, therefore, the concept of digital labor cannot be disentangled from the understanding of the role of 'free labor' within capitalism. In order to function capitalism has always relied on the exploitation of free labor, and this is particularly evident if we consider the role of women's reproductive or domestic labor within capitalist societies (Engels, [1884] 2010; Sayers et al., 1987; Trebilcock, 1997). However, the shared belief among digital labor scholars is that the increased pervasiveness of online technologies has brought a rapid increase in the exploitation of individuals' free labor. This is not only because individuals find themselves giving up part of their free time booking tickets, checking information, scanning supermarket items, etc. for the benefit of corporate interest, but also because on web 2.0 platforms processes of socialization and leisure are often exploited for corporate gain in unprecedented ways.

The concept of digital labor, therefore, enables us to uncover the bound relationship between internet use and a new political culture of capitalist exploitation in the digital economy. However, it is also important because it enables us to ask critical questions on the relationship between web 2.0 technologies and the emergence of new forms of corporate and political surveillance. Here the work of Andrejevic (2003, 2009) is particularly insightful, because he argued that through the extensive use of web 2.0 technologies individuals are not only constantly 'surveiled' for corporate or political reasons, but are also increasingly adopting practices of co-surveillance associated with marketing and law enforcement. According to Andrejevic (2003, 2009), therefore, web technologies can be seen as fostering the internalization of the strategies used by corporations and governments and their deployment in the private sphere. We can find a similar argument also in the work of Jarrett (2008). In contrast to Barry (2001) who differentiates interactivity from disciplining technologies – as defined by Foucault – Jarrett (2008) argues that interactivity can be seen as a disciplining technology and that this 'disciplining technology' is enforced within the digital spaces of web 2.0 platforms.

Therefore, the concept of digital labor has been particularly important for internet research because it has enabled scholars to deconstruct much of the techno-optimistic assumptions, which defined the earlier understandings of web 2.0 technologies, while highlighting the multiple complexities of the issue of labor in the digital economy. However, we need to be aware of the fact that there are some theoretical weaknesses in current internet research.

In the first place, as mentioned by Hesmondhalgh (2010), we have seen the development of a variety of approaches over-estimating the relationship between 'free labor' and 'capitalist exploitation' that are based on the understanding that digital production can only be seen as the production of data to be turned into commodity. In the second place, a weakness of contemporary research on digital labor can be found in the way in which exploitation is understood. In fact, as Andrejevic (2014) has argued, we need to seriously ask ourselves whether the exploitation of data can be really understood as the equivalent to other forms of exploitation of human labor that lead to human misery (in Andrejevic et al., 2014:1090). In the third place, a crucial problem with current internet research is that it tends to lump all users of social media into one (Khiabany, 2014) and does not take into account the empirical realities of users.

It seems to me, therefore, that as Fish (2014) has rightly argued, we have much to gain if – in the study of digital labor – we develop an "historically situated and ethnographically grounded approach complete with a degree of theoretical infidelity capable of appropriating both political economic and cultural studies approaches" (Fish in Andrejevic et al., 2014:1094). This approach, as the following parts will show, is particularly important in the study of digital activism and the effects of digital labor in their everyday contexts. This is not only because it enables us to highlight the fact that activists' political cultures are defined by a strong critique of digital labor, but also because it enables us to appreciate the fact that the everyday lives of activists are shaped by a complex process of negotiation with digital capitalism.

ACTIVISTS' CRITIQUE OF DIGITAL LABOR: BETWEEN LIVED EXPERIENCE AND POLITICAL IDEOLOGIES

In 2011, at the time of fieldwork, both the Italian and the Spanish contexts were defined by soaring unemployment figures coupled with a politics of austerity, tax inflation, and uncertainty. In Spain, the Spanish Socialist Workers' Party was being criticized for its inability to tackle the impacts of the economic crisis, and the country hit the highest rate of unemployment in Europe, with youth unemployment figures peaking at 49%.[3] In Italy, the government of Silvio Berlusconi was defined by multiple scandals as well as by the incapacity to deal with the country's economic decline. That year youth unemployment figures reached 30%, and zero-hour contracts and precarious working conditions became a social reality for millions of people, especially among younger generations. In this framework, it is not surprising that within both the ethnographic contexts of the *Corsari* and the *Ecologistas en Acción* the issue of labor was an important aspect of their political ideologies and activities.

I approached fieldwork in 2010 with a special interest in the issue of labor. Influenced by the work of the Autonomous Marxists and the critical internet scholars, I was particularly interested in exploring how activists understood the relationship between internet technologies and the changing politics of labor in the digital economy. As I followed them around at demonstrations and events, and I sat down for interviews and informal conversations, I realized that within both groups, activists were critically aware of the fact that the relationship between new media technologies and neoliberal governments had transformed the political culture of labor in Europe and had given rise to new forms of capital exploitation.

When critiquing these new forms of capitalist exploitation, however, the activists involved in the two different groups tended to focus on different aspects. Whereas environmental activists were more concerned with criticizing the expansion of free labor, the myth of dematerialization, and the issue of environmental exploitation, Italian activists often focused on the relationship between free labor, immaterial labor, and the precarization of labor and life. In the following parts of this chapter I will explore these different critiques.

The Expansion of Free Labor, Myth of Dematerialization, and Impacts on the Environment

At the very early stages of fieldwork in Madrid, I participated in a talk on the environmental impacts of capitalism on women's life in Latin America, where I expected to meet different members of *Ecologistas en Acción*. That evening in early spring, I walked down the narrow streets of Calle de La Fe, in the heart of Lavapies, one of Madrid's most multicultural neighborhoods. I headed to the headquarters of the *Diagonal*, which as mentioned in *Chapter One* is an alternative newspaper and an important media network for the activists involved with *Ecologistas en Acción*. The talk took place in the basement of the newspaper's headquarters and addressed different yet interconnected themes on women's free labor in Latin American countries. That evening I met Celia,[4] who had long been involved with *Ecologistas en Acción* and who spoke passionately about feminism and the problem of women's free labor under capitalism.

A few months later, I sat down for a coffee in a tapas bar just off Gran Via with her and had the pleasure to interview her for more than two hours. During the interview, Celia discussed her personal experience. She talked about the difficulties she encountered growing up under Franco's dictatorship and how she dedicated all her life to the cause of eco-feminism. In the interview, she revealed that she was seriously concerned about the changing forms of capital exploitation and the extension of free labor affecting society today. She argued that one of the reasons for such transformation had to be attributed to the developments in information and communication technologies.

C: I have always been interested in the fact that the majority of the hidden labor of capitalism is done by the woman. Corporate power needs to rely on free labor. But with the development of information technologies and the expansion of flexible labor arrangements, corporations are relying much more on the free labor and the financial resources of the laborer. One example is certainly the one of internet technologies, but we need to negotiate with a variety of different examples that affect everyday life, such as shopping centers, self-service machines etc. [...]. The service society and the online culture are certainly transforming things, all in the interest of corporations.

During fieldwork, within the organization, I met a variety of people who shared Celia's critical awareness about the changing politics of capital exploitation and its connection to the technological developments of the last decades. Interviews revealed that the Spanish environmental activists were not only concerned with the fact that the digital economy was enhancing new forms of capital exploitation but also that an economy based on computer and internet technologies was built upon the systematic exploitation of the environment.

It was by departing from the standpoint of the environment that activists often criticized me for using the term 'digital labor' when I referred to the production of content on the internet. On a number of occasions I was told that the problem with the term 'digital labor' is that it is often interconnected to the understanding that labor – within the digital economy – is 'immaterial.' In contrast to this belief, the environmental activists argued that within the digital economy – which is based on a satellite system that operates through the oil economy – everything is material. Each object, each site, and each technological application have a material history. In many regards, their argument resonated with the theoretical debates in contemporary communication research (Gill and Pratt, 2008; Hesmondhalgh, 2010; Khiabany, 2014), which critically question the 'immateriality' of digital technologies. Within the context of the Spanish *Ecologistas*, however, the argument was built on a harsh critique of the 'oil economy' (Fernandez Duran, 2008).

When I debated the notion of digital labor with them, the question at heart was one concerning the future. Rather than focusing on the present, most of the activists I interviewed critically reflected on the sustainability of a digital economy that was so dependent on oil. As mentioned by Luis, the co-coordinator of the organization, whom I introduced in the previous chapter:

L: The fact is that we really should ask ourselves for how long we'll rely on internet technologies, and a system that is entirely based on combustible fossils, you know we simply cannot afford them [...].

The ethnographic context of the environmental activists in Spain, therefore, demonstrated that activists engaged in an often complex and multidimensional political critique of the relationship between internet technologies and new forms of capitalist exploitation by considering the environmental impacts of this relationship.

This latter point shows us that the critique against digital labor was connected to the political cultures and ideologies of the organization. As the next part of this chapter will show, also within the context of the *Corsari*, activists were critically engaging with the question of digital labor. However, interviews revealed that rather than emphasizing the problem of free labor and criticizing the myth of dematerialization, Italian activists often focused on the relationship between immaterial labor and the precarization of work.

Immaterial Labor and the Precarization of Labor and Life

One day, close to the Easter holidays in 2011, I sat down with Alice for an interview. I had known Alice for more than a year and had often had the chance to spend time with her and discuss her personal experience as well as the motives that brought her to join the *Corsari*. Despite being only 20 years old, Alice had been involved in the social center movement in Milan for more than six years. During the interview, I asked Alice how she understood and perceived the relationship between labor and information technologies. Influenced by the debates intrinsic to the Italian left-wing social movements of the last decade, Alice answered the question by discussing the rapid proliferation of fixed-term contracts, internships, and flexible working arrangements, which were supported by the extension of digital technologies as well as by the Italian government's neo-liberal agenda. She used terms such as 'immaterial labor' and 'precariety,' which became important concepts within the autonomous movement in Italy thanks to the work of the Autonomous Marxists (Hardt and Negri, 2000; Virno, 2004; Lazzarato, 1996).

Alice was one of the many who, when asked to discuss how they perceived the relationship between labor and digital technologies, referred to such concepts. However, during fieldwork I realized that activists' understanding of the relationship between immaterial labor and precariety was rather different from the one of the Autonomous Marxists. According to the Autonomous Marxists, with the rise of immaterial labor, precariety had become the basis for the construction of new affinities and subjectivities of resistance, in other words, for the construction of a new class (in Neilson and Rossiter, 2008; Brophy, 2006). One of the problems with their work is that, as some have shown (Vosko, 2006; McDowell and Christopherson, 2009), the Marxist scholars did not analyze precariety with reference to insecurity. In contrast to their approaches, the Italian activists that I worked with perceived precariety as damaging for collective organization and resistance. In fact, resonating some of contemporary theoretical debates, they understood precariety with reference to insecurity, an insecurity that extends beyond the world of work to encompass other aspects of intersubjective life, including housing, debt, and the ability to build social relationships (Brophy, 2006; Tarli and Vanni, 2005; McDowell and Christoperson, 2009). In this framework, rather than the grounds for resistance, precariety was seen as a form of control, which is creating a great deal of anxiety and feelings of disempowerment. The interview with Alice highlighted this dimension of precariety.

V: Do you believe that precariety can become a terrain for collective mobilization and resistance?

A: Personally I cannot connect the world of precariety with resistance. Precariety destroys you. I used to work in a call center for a year and half, which is the key example of precarious working conditions. I studied during the day and in the evenings I worked for four hours in a call center, without a break. Every evening, I would find a new person sitting next to me and if I tried to sit next to a colleague who I knew, the managers would make me move to another location [...]. I think that precariety makes you lose the sense of human existence, you are abandoned to your own devices, you need to try to find ways of surviving. You are constantly dealing with uncertainty, questioning how you are going to pay the rent, whether you are going to have money tomorrow. It is profoundly alienating and separates people. I believe that collective action and resistance are grounded on completely different principles. I don't see how the focus on uncertainty and on basic needs would give you the space for revolution [...].

Many within the context of the *Corsari* shared Alice's skepticism and anxiety towards the question of precariety. Interviews and informal conversations often followed a similar narrative as the one of Alice, where activists not only immediately connected the critique of digital labor with the insights of the Autonomous Marxist tradition, but they went on to explore the relationship between immaterial labor and precariety as well. However, in contrast to the Autonomous Marxists, they argued that far from becoming a new terrain of struggle, precariety was having an impact on different dimensions of their everyday lives and threatening social cohesion. This latter point emerged very well in an interview with Edo, who had been involved with the social center movement since the mid-nineties. At the time of fieldwork he was in his late twenties and had just landed a permanent position working as a chef. During the interview, he mentioned Negri and some of the debates around precariety.

E: On the one hand he [Toni Negri] is right that precariety can trigger mass mobilizations. But this is simply because precariety creates social disintegration and this could create resistance. But personally, I see precariety as a social drama. I see most of my friends without a stable job,

I see myself being able to pay my pension only occasionally. In a month time, I am going to sign my first permanent contract, at the age of 28. This I feel it's like a miracle. [The problem] It's not only in terms of [work] contract; it is with reference to life as a whole, all my life is precariazed. I can afford rent simply because I share a flat with three other flat mates. [...] Precariety is a very individualistic experience; it means the fragmentation of the social fabric; it works against social cohesion.

Many others among the *Corsari* shared Edo's and Alice's belief that precariety is against social cohesion. Their understanding challenged the one of the Autonomous Marxists, who believed that immaterial labor and precariety were creating a new social class and a new terrain for resistance. Although disagreeing with the understanding that precariety is creating the grounds for resistance, the activists involved in the social world of the *Corsari* demonstrated a critical engagement with the question concerning the relationship between internet technologies and immaterial labor. They did so by focusing on a critique of the new working arrangements that this relationship – coupled with the neo-liberal policies of governments – had created.

In conclusion to this part, therefore, within both the context of the *Ecologistas en Acción* and the *Corsari*, questions on the social inequalities and environmental damages created by the very extension of digital technologies in the domains of labor and life were at the heart of their political critique against capitalism. What the preceding parts suggest is that not only were activists critically aware of issues of digital labor but they analyzed these issues through the lenses of their political cultures and ideologies as well. During fieldwork, therefore, I believed that it was important to question and investigate the way in which their critical awareness of issues of digital labor was having an impact on their internet uses.

WEB 2.0 USE AND THE EVERYDAY NEGOTIATION WITH DIGITAL LABOR

The Tactics of Political Activists against Digital Capitalism

When I approached fieldwork, I expected to find that activists' critical engagement with the issue of digital labor would directly impact and translate on their everyday internet uses and beliefs and would define the ways in which they related to web 2.0 platforms. Interviews and informal chats revealed that this was indeed the case. Activists showed a critical awareness of the fact that they were laboring for free for web 2.0 corporations and that the data they produced was being exploited for corporate purposes. This aspect emerged well in the interview with Javi, the web developer of *Ecologistas en Acción*, whom I introduced in the previous chapters.

J: The way I see it, is that we are playing a game that we need to play, but this game is risky as it is the game of those people who want to divide us and use us in the name of profit. If you subscribe to a web service, and it's free, then the commodity is you. We need to use social media but at the same time we need to create our own spaces. [...] That is our challenge. It would be a danger not to experiment in this regard and not to create spaces of freedom. It is impossible to live outside of capitalism but there are margins of freedom and it is a fact that we can produce contents and social relationships that are radically different.

Javi strongly believed that activists needed to find a way to use corporate web platform tactically, by escaping the logic of exploitation and using the technologies according their own goals. He also believed that it was essential to combine the use of corporate social media with the construction of autonomous digital spaces, and this belief largely shaped not only his personal web uses but also the way in which he tried to influence and develop the communication strategy of the organization. Others shared Javi's understanding within *Ecologistas en Acción*. Just after the 15M movement, I sat down for a long chat with Mariola. In her mid-twenties Mariola was committed to the cause of the *ecologismo social*, because as a teenager she had become involved in a local environmental struggle against the construction of a highway. During our interview, she was excited about the mass uprising of the 15M, and she described her involvement and participation in different activities connected to the movement. As we were talking about the role of social media in the organization and mobilization of political action, she recalled a meeting organized during the 15M movements in the neighborhood *La Latina*. She recounted the fact that at this meeting activists engaged in an extensive discussion of whether it was right for them to rely on corporate social media platforms or whether they should use autonomous networks. She concluded that the problem for activists is that:

M: You need to be there. The more I think about it, the less I like it. But you need to be there. These are closed, corporate and controlled spaces, but they are spaces where social movements can take important steps forward.

The understanding that activists need to use corporate social media platforms and combine their use with autonomous ones was a key aspect also of the *information ecology* of the *Corsari*. As we have seen in *Chapter One,* at the time of fieldwork the *Corsari* relied on the autonomous infrastructure network of A/I, which was built by a tech-collective of activists whose aim was to enable left-wing political groups in Italy to have an email address and blog without inputting personal data and, thus, to enjoy a certain degree of autonomy from the commercial and governmental tracing of digital identities.

Before 2005 the tech-collective relied on the internet provider Arruba. In 2005 Arruba allowed the Italian police to copy all its files without informing the A/I collective. When the issue emerged, the tech-collective realized that achieving a real internet autonomy was almost impossible, as they had to rely on often commercially driven and state-friendly internet providers. For this reason the group developed a new project of online resistance, which was named project R* (R = *rete*, "network" in Italian and R = *resistenza*, "resistance" in Italian). The R* plan for resistance communication was based on the principle that privacy needs to be established through the network and through individual initiatives of encryption. Furthermore, the project relied on a multiplicity of different servers based around the world. For the *Corsari*, the R* project was of fundamental importance because it protected the autonomy of political activism, and it enabled them to have an online space of resistance where they could discuss, share information, and coordinate action.

Although many activists within the *Corsari* understood A/I platforms as important tools in the mobilization and organization of collective action, they were also convinced that relying merely on this autonomous infrastructure could be detrimental, as it created processes of ghettization, and they argued – like Mariola and Javier had done – that activists need to be present on corporate social media and negotiate with the corporate structure of these technologies. This point emerged well in an interview with Carlotta of the *Corsari,* who explained the importance of combining the use of autonomous platforms with the use of corporate ones. At the time of the interview she was 24 years old and reading philosophy at university. As we sat down for lunch, Carlotta talked about her life and described what it meant to grow up as the niece of an important communist politician. She also talked about her political involvement with grassroots politics, and why as a political activist it was important for her to be on corporate social media platforms:

C: I know that there is a contradiction, I fight against the commercialization of certain aspects of my life (and in particular the spaces within the city) and not others. But I guess that the question is whether you want to be an outsider, or you want to act within society. I don't want to be an outsider, and although I know that Facebook and other social media are corporate enterprises I think that you can create spaces within them, which allow you to build yourself in creative ways. Independent platforms like A/I are great but they are closed systems, they speak to people that are looking for that information. Facebook is different, it gives you the possibility of reaching a wide variety of people, as many of your 'friends' may not be politically active at all.

A similar understanding was echoed also in the words of Canny, one of the founders of the *Corsari*, whom I introduced in *Chapter One*.

CA: Now we give up much information, which can be used for marketing processes. I am not very careful in protecting my privacy for corporate purposes. But, you see, it all comes down to compromise. If we want to use platforms that are *metafree* – so to speak that they are free on a condition – we need to compromise. It is a functional relationship, a bit like dealing with mainstream media. If you don't make these compromises you don't disseminate your actions. You know we rely on 'free' platforms such as A/I, and when we use these we don't have to compromise. Yet these are closed platforms; they are ghettizied. So it's all down to what you want really.

Both Carlotta's and Canny's interviews enable us to appreciate the fact that activists' internet uses were defined by the calculated use of corporate and autonomous platforms. The shared understanding among the *Corsari*, like it was highlighted by Javi and Mariola within *Ecologistas en Acción*, is that social media platforms are corporate spaces but that activists need to be on these platforms and negotiate with their corporate structure. Their understanding shares many similarities with the work of those scholars who have talked about the "Faustian Bargain of Web 2.0" (Zimmer, 2008) or the "Faustian Trade Off" (Langlois et al., 2009). Activists are aware of the fact that they are negotiating with the capitalist structure of web 2.0 platforms and, hence, to a certain degree 'dealing with the devil.' Yet they also believed that it is important to be on these platforms because there are ways to escape corporate control and use these technologies to subvert capitalist relationships, practices, and discourses.

This emerged vividly in an interview with Giacomo of the *Corsari*, whom I introduced in the previous chapter:

G: If you think about capital exploitation, that's everywhere. I drink coke. I buy objects. I put petrol in my car. But I think it's all a matter of negotiation. I know I can buy a coke, and use social media, but this does not mean that I can't use these technologies to change things. Everything is not static, it moves, it changes and I will always try to change things.

Therefore, in conclusion to this part, it is important to understand that activists' everyday lives are not only defined by a critical awareness of the relationship between new forms of capitalist exploitation and internet technologies but also by a process of negotiation with the corporate structure of web 2.0 platforms. The problem with current research on digital labor is that there is no acknowledgment of these processes of negotiation or of the many margins of resistance that people construct through their web uses. In fact, whereas scholars interested in the political economy of the web 2.0 argue that capitalism has a remarkable advantage over users whose creative content and free labor are systematically exploited (Jakobsson and Stiernstedt, 2010; Van Dijck and Nieborg, 2009, Bauwens, 2008; Jarrett, 2008;

Terranova, 2000, 2013; Huws, 2003; Fuchs, 2007, 2014), what I realized during fieldwork was that the activists involved with both organizations believed that they could use online production to produce a different type of *value* that escaped the logic of capital.

This understanding made me realize that we cannot approach the study of online production merely by looking at processes of data production that can be turned into commodity (Hesmondhalgh, 2010; Andrejevic et al., 2014). Although it is essential to be aware of the relationship between online production and new forms of capitalist exploitation and accumulation, it is also important that we realize that online production is intertwined with the production of a different type of value, which has much to say about how people construct their social worlds. In the next part of the chapter, therefore, I will argue that we need to reframe current debates on online production by looking at the connection between online production, human relationships, and the notion of *value*. In order to do so, we have much to gain if we look at the insights of Marxist anthropology and in particular at Turner's (2006) critical re-reading of Marx's *Labor Theory of Value*.

WEB USES, THE PRODUCTION OF SOCIAL RELATIONSHIPS, AND THE QUESTION OF VALUE

A Symbolic Re-Reading of Marx's Labor Theory of Value

The fiercest criticisms that have been made against Marx have been against his attachment to materialism and forms of material production (Morrison, 2006; Rockmore, 2002). However, as many anthropologists have shown, the stress on Marx's historical materialism fails to address some important aspects of Marxist theory. Indeed, as Bloch (2010) has argued, in *Capital* Marx himself protested against interpretations of historical materialism, which restricted the scope of his analysis. With his theory Marx seeks not only to reveal the internal structure of capitalism as a system of political economy but also to show how it generates forms of ideological construction and 'false consciousness' (Turner, 2006; Graeber, 2002). In this light, Marx was not only interested in materialism but also in the ways in which representations and meanings were constructed. Therefore, as Turner (2006) and Graeber (2002, 2013) pointed out, there is much to be gained from a symbolic reading of Marx's labor theory of value.

Marx developed his labor theory of value drawing from the work of Ricardo and Smith. Both scholars emphasized the connection between *labor* and *value* and believed that the former generated the latter. In this regard, particularly explicatory is Ricardo's formulation that value is created by labor, in the sense that is defined by the amounts of hours worked to produce a given object (Graeber, 2002; Turner, 2006; Morrison, 2006). In contrast to such understandings Marx developed a much more complex and over-embracing labor theory of value, which drew attention to the mechanisms of the capitalist mode of production as well as to processes of meaning construction. For Marx, value is not generated by labor but can be found in labor; that is, value resides in the *forces of production* or, in other words, in human *productive activity* (1976:163–178). However, value is also defined by the transformation of the productive activity into a category of meaning (e.g. commodity fetishism). According to Marx, therefore, value is defined by a dual dimension, which brings together both the forces of 'material production' and the forces of 'representation.' As Turner explains:

> Value is the theoretical category through which Marx connects function and structure, action and meaning, production and exchange, and the social organization of the division of labor with the semiotic representation of that activity through specialized symbolic media (in this case money).
>
> (Turner, 2006:8)

Turner was particularly interested in Marx's labor theory of value, because it highlighted the relationship between human productive activity, human value, and social representations. However, he was also interested in highlighting the fact that human productive activity is not only necessarily directed to the production of material goods but can also be directed to the *production of human relationships* (Turner, 2006:11). Therefore, inspired by a passage from *German Ideology* where Marx and Engels discuss the 'production of human relationships,' Turner (2006) applied Marx's labor theory of value to the analysis of the 'production of social relationships' within the ethnographic context of the Kayapo in Brazil. The result was the creation of a theoretical approach that demonstrated not only that social relationships are often 'produced' but also that they have a material and representative value.

Turner's (2006) understanding that relationships are constantly produced and that they come to have a material and symbolic value is a defining element also of theories of *social capital*. Within the social sciences, in the last 30 years the notion of social capital has enabled scholars to shed light on the fact that the construction and strengthening of social networks has a profound social value, which is simultaneously material and symbolic (Bourdieu, 1986; Coleman, 1988; Putman, 2001). Whereas Bourdieu (1986) referred to the notion of social capital to highlight the fact that the strengthening of social networks among social elites often enables them to retain social and economic power, Coleman (1988) argued that the construction of social networks is a very human process, which empowers elites and non-elites alike, and Putman (2001) believed that the human ability to construct and maintain social networks lies at the very heart of democratic processes and the making of communities.

In recent years, theories of social capital have been applied to internet research and especially to the analysis of the production of social value online

(Ellison et al., 2007; Valenzuela et al., 2009; Gauntlett, 2011; Steinfield et al., 2008; Chambers, 2013). Such approaches are important because they highlight the relationship between online productive activity and the production of human relationships. However, as it will be shown, current internet research that focuses on the construction of social capital online has been constrained by some fundamental weaknesses. These weaknesses, I believe, can be addressed by relying on the insights of Marxist anthropology.

Digital Labor, Production of Social Capital, and The Symbolic Value of Human Relationships

With the extension of social media and web 2.0 technologies, different scholars have turned to the concept of social capital to highlight the value of social relationships that are produced online (Ellison et al., 2007; Valenzuela et al., 2009; Gauntlett, 2011; Steinfield et al., 2008; Chambers, 2013). Among these works, Steinfield et al. (2008) argued that the processes of online disclosure of personal information, despite having clear implications in terms of threats to privacy, are important because they result mostly in bridging and bonding social capital with positive psychological consequences for individuals' self-esteem. Gauntlett (2011), instead, looked at processes of 'cultural production' and argued that web 2.0 technologies have facilitated the processes of 'making and connecting,' enabling people to build social capital in empowering ways.

Although this body literature can be considered interesting because it highlights the connection between online production, the construction of social relationships, and human value, there is a fundamental problem with these works. In fact, within this literature, scholars often refer to the concept of 'social capital' only as way to reach optimistic and techno-deterministic conclusions on how web 2.0 technologies enable the construction of 'social connections' (Ellison et al., 2007; Steinfield, 2008; Valenzuela et al., 2009; Gauntlett, 2011). These scholars understand social capital in very techno-deterministic ways: as a positive 'end product' that is determined by technologies.

In contrast to these works, Marxist anthropology enables us to focus on the online production of social relationships in a more critical way. In the first place, it reminds us that we cannot look at the relationship between online productive activity and human value as an 'end product' (e.g. social capital) but rather as a *complex social process*. In the second place it enables us to appreciate that online productive activity can enable users to build relationships, which are progressive or reactionary and can challenge or reinforce existing forms of power. Therefore, Marxist anthropology by focusing on the 'production of social relationships' as a *social process* detaches us from a positivist reading of the human value that is built online.

Throughout my research, the work of Turner (2006) enabled me to shed light on why activists believe that they can produce a type of 'value' online that challenges the corporate logic of web 2.0 platforms. During fieldwork, I realized that the social relationships that activists built online, as Turner (2006) has highlighted, have an enormous value for them, a value that is both material and representational. In fact, it is thanks to their social relationships that activists are able to spread their messages and mobilize and organize action in fast and effective ways. Yet at the same time these relationships are abstracted, and the number of 'friends' and 'followers' on their collective social media pages become the representation of their collective strength. This simple aspect explains why activists, despite being critically aware of the relationship between web 2.0 platforms and new forms of capital exploitation, are willing to negotiate with digital capitalism in order to produce a different type of value, a value that escapes the logic of capital and that enables them to build their social worlds.

CONCLUSION

This chapter explored how activists understand and negotiate with the issue of *digital labor*. In the last decade, the concept of digital labor has been of pivotal importance to highlight the bound relationship between internet technologies and the development of new forms of capitalist accumulation and exploitation. Although extremely important, this body of literature has encountered three main weaknesses. In the first place, digital labor scholars have often associated the notion of 'free labor' with the notion of 'capitalist exploitation' and have focused mostly on the production of data to be turned into a commodity (Hesmondhalgh, 2010). In the second place, digital labor scholars have under-theorized the notion of exploitation leaving us to question how people perceive 'exploitation' and whether the corporate use of personal data can be perceived as equivalent to other forms of exploitation that lead to human misery (Andrejevic et al., 2014). In the third place, digital labor scholars do not take into account the empirical realities of users (Khiabany, 2014).

In this chapter I tried to address some of these weaknesses by looking at activists' everyday lives and at the way in which they understand and negotiate with the issue of digital labor. I have argued that activist political cultures and ideologies are defined by a critical awareness of the issue. The chapter has shown, that whereas the Spanish activists believe that the development of information technologies has extended the capitalist exploitation of 'free labor' to different areas of social life with dramatic consequences for our environment, the Italian activists are concerned with the fact that the extension of internet technologies – coupled with the neo-liberal policies of governments – has given rise to the 'precarization' of labor and life. Despite their differences, activists' political critiques against digital labor shape and define their uses of web 2.0 technologies and how they negotiate with digital capitalism.

One interesting aspect of activists' negotiation with digital capitalism is represented by their understanding that there are many margins of freedom and resistance that they can build on corporate web platforms. Although scholars interested in the political economy of the web 2.0 argue that, within the online economy, capitalism has a remarkable advantage over users, the activists involved with both organizations believe that this advantage is not that evident. In order to understand these beliefs, I have argued, it is important to reframe the debate around digital labor by reconsidering the relationship between digital production and value and move away from the understanding that digital production can only be understood as the production of data that can be turned into a commodity.

A way in which we can do so is by learning from the insights of Marxist anthropology and by highlighting the connection between users' productive activity and the production of human relationships. As the work of different Marxist anthropologists has shown, humans constantly produce social relationships, and these social relationships have an immense value that is translated not only in material terms but also in representative terms. This chapter has argued that the understanding of the intrinsic value of human relationships, of their material and representative dimension, is key to an appreciation of the social importance of web 2.0 technologies (and especially social media) in the everyday lives of political activists.

NOTES

1. It is undeniable that the issue of digital labor/immaterial labor was important also for the Labor Movement in Britain. At the time of fieldwork I partook in a series of conversations with trade unionists about the changing economy and the rise of new areas of labor (e.g. service industries, digital corporations, etc.). During these conversations, many criticized the fact that the trade unions were reacting too slowly to these transformations. At the time of fieldwork, however, as a researcher I was not theoretically equipped to investigate how the activists involved with the Labor Movement in Britain were negotiating with the issue of digital labor. Hence, this chapter will focus on my later research in Italy and Spain where I investigated the question of digital labor at length.
2. In this chapter I decided to use the notion of 'precariety' or 'precarization' drawing on its Latin etymological definition, which denotes a different meaning from the English translation of 'casualization.'. In fact, as Appay (2010) has argued, in the concept of 'precarious' there is a note of danger, and of loss of control, which does not emerge from the English notion of 'casualization' (Appay, 2010:34–35).
3. http://epp.eurostat.ec.europa.eu/cache/ITY_PUBLIC/3-06012012-BP/EN/3-06012012-BP-EN.PDF
4. Fictional name to protect the activist's will to remain anonymous.

5   Digital Activism and the Problem of Immediacy

INTRODUCTION

In the previous chapters I discussed the multiple ways in which activists are negotiating with digital capitalism and focused on two different ethnographic tensions that they encounter in their everyday uses of web 2.0 technologies: the problem of networked individualism and the problem of digital labor. In this chapter I want to move a step further and argue that one of the most pressing questions in the analysis of the relationship between web technologies and democratic processes is the often neglected question of the temporality of the internet. The chapter argues that web 2.0 technologies and mobile media are creating a temporal context, which valorizes instantaneous communication, continuous connectivity, and technological dependency (Hassan, 2007; Leccardi, 2007; Tomlinson, 2007; Virilio, 1995; Lovink, 2007; Leong et al., 2009; Kaun and Stiernstedt, 2014) and which cannot be detached from a careful consideration of the changing cultures of capitalist accumulation, labor, and productivity (Lazzarato, 1996; Hardt and Negri, 2000; Gill and Pratt, 2008; Adkins, 2009, 2011; Hassan, 2007, 2009; Leccardi, 2007; Gregg, 2011; Fuchs, 2013).

The chapter will show that the relationship between new technologies, capitalism, and immediacy is creating a great deal of tension for political activists. Whereas the temporality of online communication exchanges can be beneficial for political and democratic processes, accelerating information sharing and mobilizing political participation, immediacy is affecting processes of political reflection, discussion, and elaboration in negative ways. This is not only because online communication tends to simplify complex reflections and discourses, but also because the pace of information exchange reduces political discussions and creates a type of 'political participation' that relies on weak affinities and strong emotions, but not on shared political projects and identities.

This chapter will, therefore, explore the negative effects of immediacy on political activism by looking at activists' everyday practices. In doing so, its aim is to challenge political economic approaches, which do not take into account how people negotiate with the temporality of web technologies. In contrast to these approaches, the chapter will draw on the 'anthropology of time' and the concept of 'temporalizing practice' (Bourdieu, 1964; Elias, 1993; Gell, 1992; Munn, 1992; Postill, 2002;

Adam, 1994) and will show how activists through their everyday practices simultaneously reproduce and resist the hegemonic temporality of capitalism.

UNDERSTANDING SOCIAL TIME, SPEED, AND FAST CAPITALISM

Capitalism, Social Time, and Everyday Practices

In order to understand the notion of the relationship between internet technologies and the social construction of time, we need to take a pretty large step back in history and look at the relationship between changing modes of production/consumption under capitalism, the development of technologies, and the construction of a collective time consciousness. The relationship between capitalism and the social construction of time has long been a topic of academic debate. In the *Manifesto of the Communist Party,* Marx and Engels identify 'speed' and the 'constant revolutionizing of production' as one of the defining aspects of the 'bourgeois epoch.' In *Capital* Marx discusses the notion of 'labor time' as one of the features defining the exchange value of the commodity (1990:302–314). What emerges well from Marx's analysis of the capitalist political economy, therefore, is the understanding of the intrinsic value of time under capitalism and of the need to maximize labor time in order to gain surplus value. This understanding, as Nyland (1990) has shown, has had serious repercussions on the organization of labor in much of industrialized societies, especially as work-time laws were introduced.

It is because 'time' is 'value' within the capitalist mode of production that, as Thompson has argued, between the fourteenth and nineteenth centuries in England, we have seen a gradual synchronization of human activities (Thompson, 1967:70–71). According to Thompson, in the Middle Ages in England there were only few places of exact timekeeping – such as monasteries or towns – and time was still organized around specific agricultural or social activities. However, from the fourteenth century onwards, with the Protestant ethics and the rise of earlier forms of capitalism, the 'time of the merchant' has gradually taken hold over other dimensions of time, with clocks entering households and taking over church bells in organizing the everyday lives of people (Thomson, 1967:82–86). In his analysis of the increased synchronization of time, Thompson draws to a certain degree on Weber's (1978) work and considers the increased synchronization of human activities as a form of 'rationalization' typical of the modern state and the capitalist mode of production. In his work, therefore, Thompson (1967:89–90) highlights the bound connection between the political economy of capitalism and the construction of social time. He does so by arguing that, with the advent of the industrial revolution, 'clock time' was established as the hegemonic form of time measurement through a process of propaganda aimed at 'civilizing' the working classes. This process was made possible through institutions such as 'the factory' and 'the school,' which used incentives, fines, and other strategies to transform people's behaviors (Thompson, 1967:90–95).

Influenced by Thompson, Thrift (1990) has therefore argued that between the fourteenth century and the late nineteenth century, especially in England, we have seen the gradual diffusion of a new type of 'time consciousness.' Now, when Thrift was writing, the understanding of 'time consciousness' was not new. In sociology Durkheim ([1912] 2008) had argued that societies share a temporal consciousness, a sense of 'collective time' that individuals internalize and respect. However, in contrast to Durkheim's functionalism, Thrift's (1990) work shows that this sense of 'time consciousness' is not internalized without conflicts within society, but it is often the product of political economic factors and is socially constructed by the institutions and powers of a given epoch. Therefore, Thrift (1990) argues that there is a hegemonic dimension in the construction of time.

Thrift's (1990) analysis is insightful as he traces the way in which the hegemonic capitalist time consciousness was established through the transformation of everyday practices. His account is particularly important to our understanding of the temporality of the internet for two main reasons. First, his analysis shows that the construction of social time is linked to broader political economic factors and the structuring of capitalist society. Second, he shows that the change in time consciousness or, in other words, in the collective understanding of time is made possible through the transformation (and control) of people's behaviors; therefore, he places a particular emphasis on the concept of *practice*.

This particular emphasis on the temporalization of social practices can be found in the sociology of time. Elias (1993), for instance, influenced by Bourdieu (1964), argued that social time – especially in Europe – operated as a form of social *habitus* that was linked to broader processes of 'civilization' and manners, which developed with the rise of the 'merchant' society and the earlier forms of capitalism. According to Elias (1993), social time is tightly connected to forms of self-regulation and is perceived subjectively as part of everyday human experience. His work, with its focus on practice, highlights the fact that through human practices we create a specific hegemonic understanding of time.

Internet Technologies and the Establishment of a New Hegemonic Temporal Context

In the last decades we have seen a major shift in our hegemonic forms of collective time consciousness, which has radically transformed people's everyday practices. This shift was determined by both an economic transformation in forms of production (i.e. the globalization of markets and the reliance on new forms of flexible, casual, and immaterial labor) and a technological transformation (i.e. the development of internet technologies). As Pratt and Gill (2008) have shown, the Autonomous Marxists were perhaps the first to argue that, with the extension of internet technologies, we have witnessed 'a taking over of life by work' (Pratt and Gill, 2008:27), and this claim is largely understood in terms of our changing relationship to time. In fact, the Autonomous Marxists believed that the temporality of life has now become governed by work. This is made possible through internet technologies, which guarantee that working routines under post-Fordism are no longer dictated by 'clock time,' like in the factory, but by a self-regulating flexibility and – as we have seen in the previous chapter – by the deconstruction of the boundary between labor time and leisure time. Such understandings have been developed by a variety of scholars (Hassan, 2007; Leccardi, 2007; Sennett, 2006; Beck, 2005), who are arguing that internet technologies are not only changing our perceptions of notions of intimacy, domesticity, and production (Gregg, 2011) but are also altering our sense of 'temporality' (Adkins, 2009).

The social theorist Hassan argues that this new understanding of time is built on the ideological perception that events are occurring immediately and that the internet offers 'real-time' connection with events and people (Hassan, 2007:44). Also, Tomlinson discusses the role of internet technologies in the rise of a new culture of 'immediacy.' In his argument he draws mostly on the work of Bauman (2005) and argues that 'immediacy' is built on a notion of instantaneous contact and immediate fulfillment (Tomlinson, 2007:91).

The works of both Hassan (2007, 2009) and Tomlinson (2007) on immediacy, I believe, are particularly insightful in the understanding of the temporality of the internet, because they show the fact that the question of internet time is a deeply political one and has much to say about our very Western fascination with 'speed' and 'progress.' In fact in discussing 'immediacy,' Tomlinson (2007) departs from Marinetti and the futurist avant-garde to explore the cultural narratives of 'speed' in the West and highlights how these cultural narratives define people's perception of technologies, including our current perceptions of the internet. Hassan (2007) brings the analysis of the political dimension of immediacy further by drawing on the work of Virilio (1986, 2005).

Virilio (1986, 1995, 2005) developed a consistent body of work on the connection between speed, technologies, and the political. In his earlier writings, Virilio argued that there was a bound relationship between speed and politics because societies are constantly engaged in a race to find new technical means of military innovation. According to Virilio, humans confuse technical superiority with an understanding of general/human superiority over other people (Virilio, 1986:46), and therefore the obsession with speed and acceleration is linked (not only as we have seen above to capitalism) but to the desire of political supremacy. Virilio's understanding of speed, technologies, and politics in the 1980s was very negative as it was linked to an analysis of war. Later, he published an article on new information and communication technologies, where he continued his discussion about speed, technologies, and the political. In this article he argued that globalization had made possible a new 'instantaneity' of time and that – coupled with the extension of new information technologies – created a 'dictatorship of speed' with severe consequences for democratic processes (Virilio, 1995:para 7). Within his article, unfortunately, Virilio does not engage in a thorough exploration of what these consequences are. Yet in his later work on 'the information bomb' he argues that new technologies create a new sense of temporality, a temporality of "incessant telepresence of events" (Virilio, 2005:127), and he contends that this temporality is based on the "relief of instantaneity," which is winning on the depth of historical successivity. A similar argument can be found also in the work of Hassan and Purser (2007) and in Leccardi (2007:27) who argue that contemporary capitalist society is affected by a logic of 'de-temporalized presence' that is reinforced by internet technologies.

Keightley (2012, 2013) has rightly contended that Virilio's approach to time is techno-deterministic and does not take into account the multiple varieties in which people are experiencing temporality through media technologies. She criticizes social theorists like Virilio, who emphasize acceleration, speed, and instantaneity without taking into account the complexities of everyday forms of temporality and how people relate to these forms. A similar problem can be found also in contemporary communication research. In the work of Hassan (2007), Tomlinson (2007), and the other political economy scholars, the emphasis on speed and acceleration is theorized through a focus on structures or cultural narratives without a careful consideration of people's everyday practices.

In contrast to these approaches Leong et al. (2009) discuss the different dimensions of 'internet time' and argue that one of these dimensions is represented by the 'lived experience.' Their contribution is interesting, especially because they explore the multiple times of networks and the merging of the technical and social elements in the construction of internet time. However, the authors draw on Durkheim ([1912] 2008), among others, to contend that the lived experience of time springs from our experience of the social (2008:1277). In doing so, the authors do not consider the incredible variety of 'social times' that define our everyday engagements with internet technologies and do not highlight the fact that the 'lived experience of internet time' is shaped by people's active negotiation with hegemonic temporalities.

In contrast to these approaches, this chapter focuses on everyday internet practices of activists and draws on the anthropology of time to explore how these practices continually reproduce and resist the hegemonic temporality of immediacy.

CONFLICTING TEMPORALITIES: HEGEMONIC TIME AND THE VARIETY OF SOCIAL TIMES

Cultural Varieties, Social Practices, and the Anthropology of Time

The understanding of the complex relationship between temporal perceptions, everyday practices, and the heterogeneity of time systems has been a key area of debate within anthropology. As Munn (1992) and Gell (1992) argued, anthropologists have long been involved in a thorough discussion on how to best understand and define the multiple dimensions of human engagement with time.

Within these debates, anthropologists have discussed the impossibility of understanding time as a 'static' collective representation, as the Durkheimian model suggested. Rather, influenced by Bergson (1908), they spoke about time consciousness as *duration* and they looked at the 'qualitative dimension of time' to argue that there is an incredible variety of social times. Much of earlier works in the anthropology of time looked at these varieties as they explored the connection between the social construction of time and the coordination of human activities. Here particularly influential is Malinowski's work (1927) on lunar and solar calendars in the Trobriand and the one of Evans-Pritchard (1939) on the activities of the Nuer and their structuring of time. Both scholars emphasized the importance of cycles and sequences and the bound connection between 'primitive' time-reckoning and 'nature.' Of course, both of their works were influenced by an implicit functionalism and by a dichotomized understanding of Western versus primitive cultures, which cannot be accepted today. Yet their ethnographic data was rich and was particularly influential in showing how social time is in fact a 'problematic' category.

All the anthropological approaches are sufficiently explored within the work of Munn (1992) and of Gell (1992). Both anthropologists try to make sense of anthropological contributions to time, and they come up with their own theories and understandings. For Munn (1992) time and temporality are necessarily symbolic processes that are linked to everyday temporalizing practices. For Gell (1992) humans will never cognitively grasp the 'real' time, yet their temporal understandings are embedded within this larger ontological category. As Hodges (2008) has argued, there are some fundamental theoretical lacunae in both the work of Gell (1992) and Munn (1992), as they both fail to engage with the philosophical and phenomenological theories. Although I recognize Hodges's argument, in this chapter I do not intend to explore the philosophical meaning of our perceptions of time; rather I am interested in the insights this body of literature offers into the complex relationship between the control and construction of social time, power, and everyday practices.

Anthropological contributions to the study of time, with their emphasis on practice, can highlight the bound connection between the construction of social time, hierarchy, and power. This book is highly influenced by this body of literature and specifically by the anthropological understanding of 'temporalizing practice' or, in other words, the understanding of the fact that it is *through the organization of our everyday human practices that we construct specific temporalities*. Here, however, it is important to highlight the fact that although the anthropology of time can be particularly important in the understanding of the relationship between internet technologies and the social construction of time, there are two weaknesses within this literature that we need to be aware of. In the first place, the relationship between temporalizing practices and hegemonic temporalities has not been sufficiently developed (Munn, 1992:109–111; Postill, 2002), and anthropologists have been often inclined to describe 'other' time systems without considering how these time systems relate to the hegemonic 'clock time' of Western colonialism. In the second place, the anthropology of time often tends to 'simplify' the Western construction of social time (Adam, 1994; Postill, 2002).

Therefore, although this chapter has been inspired by the anthropology of time, it has also been inspired by the understanding that within the so-called 'Western societies,' as Gurevitch (1990) has argued, there is a fundamental difference between the 'macro' temporalities of institutions and the multiple 'micro' temporalities of individuals, communities, and social groups. It is for this reason that in her seminal work on time and social theory, Adam argues that we need to understand the intermingling and clustering of temporal realities (Adam, 1994:38) and appreciate that time is a multilayered, complex fact of life (1994:169) even within industrial and capitalist societies.

This chapter is influenced by anthropological theories on temporality and social practice and by the understanding of the plurality and complexities of social times. It is grounded on the belief that one fascinating aspect of the debate is represented by the fact that if humans through their everyday practices re-create hegemonic understandings of time, they can also resist them. This latter point emerges in the work of Bourdieu (1964). In his account of the Kabyle in Algeria, Bourdieu argues that even though the clock had been introduced for years within the Algerian countryside, it did not regulate the whole life. In everyday practices, the Kabyle were aware of the colonial and hegemonic structuring of time, but they freed themselves from the concern of schedules and showed hostility to the clock, which was at times called the 'devil's mill'[1] (Bourdieu, 1964:58).

Therefore, this chapter draws on the notion of 'temporalizing practice' to explore the way in which activists internalize and reproduce the hegemonic temporality of immediacy through everyday internet practices and to investigate the impacts of these temporalizing practices on political processes.

POLITICAL ACTION, EVERYDAY INTERNET PRACTICES, AND THE SOCIAL PRODUCTION OF IMMEDIACY

On the morning of 22 May 2013, police entered ZAM to evict the premises. For months the activists had been anticipating the evacuation. As mentioned in *Chapter One*, the building was owned by a private landlord but had been abandoned for a period between eight and ten years. When the *Corsari* together with other collectives began to occupy ZAM in January 2011, the building was full of weeds and rats. The two years of 'occupation'[2] had radically transformed the space. The people of ZAM had invested all their resources in building a concert hall, one bar, one exhibition center, and a gym. After two years of relative peace, in early 2013 the police and the council hall announced that they were going to evict ZAM, and for months the activists built a very powerful campaign to save ZAM from the eviction. The campaign was built around a green logo that reproduced the pointer used by Google in *GoogleMaps* as a way to reflect on the notion of space. The pointer was combined with the catchphrase *StayZAM*. For months, activists had been involved in sharing the logo via social networks; they launched a Twitter campaign to organize a series of events to save ZAM; they created a campaign of 'email-bombing,' which was aimed at jamming the mailbox of the mayor of Milan with emails of support for ZAM, and produced T-shirts among other activities.

The morning of 22 May 2013 the people of ZAM were prepared to resist the eviction. They had built barricades and human chains on the road. They choreographed their eviction in very creative and media savvy ways. Groups of activists were involved in a representation of what ZAM had been for them in the last two years. These representations were organized through the following categories: ZAM is Sociality, ZAM is Culture, ZAM is Love, ZAM is Sport, and ZAM is the Students. Another group of activists were prepared for physical resistance and for clashes with the police. They were all wearing bright red overcoats with masks of Spiderman. The reference to Spiderman was not casual at all but was meant to reference the quote used by the superhero in the 2002 film: "From great power comes great responsibility." The reference to the film and to Spiderman was seen as a critique against the Milanese city hall administration. As mentioned in *Chapter One*, in May 2011, Giuliano Pisapia – the left-wing mayor of Milan – was elected after 18 years of ruling from the center-right coalition. At the time of Pisapia's election a large part of the autonomous movement in Milan supported his election and actively campaigned for him. During two years of administration, however, instead of supporting the growth of cultural and social spaces within the city, Pisapia was involved in a politics of repression against the 'social centers.' The quote "From great power comes great responsibility" was ironically directed to him and the city hall administration.

When police approached ZAM, they found themselves confronted with a strikingly visual form of resistance and, as they started making their way through the barricades and into ZAM, on Twitter and Facebook images and calls for solidarity circulated in real time. As an online participant observer, I could follow the events unraveling in front of my eyes and could participate by tweeting to my own networks and friends or texting back messages of support. Throughout the entire day one could also follow the live development of events on the website of *MilanoinMovimento* and could share the numerous calls to action that rose from the eviction. A similar situation reproduced itself in the evening of the eviction, when a demonstration in front of Palazzo Marino[3] culminated in clashes with the police. In the following days the live reportage of actions and events continued. Two days after the eviction, activists occupied an abandoned secondary school, and three days later they organized a 'Reclaim the Space' demonstration against the neo-liberal appropriation of public spaces in Milan.

The above example of the eviction of ZAM and the days that followed is particularly suggestive, I believe, because it highlights how the temporality of immediacy that new web technologies make possible through instantaneous communication is effectively constructed and reproduced by activists' practices. Without activists posting images, comments, and newsfeeds on social media and other online platforms, it would have been impossible for me to follow the eviction of ZAM in real time. Immediacy was thus reproduced through their online practices while they were waiting in anticipation for the arrival of the police, as they watched the blue helmets approaching amidst tear gases and clashes.

This refers back to previous debates, and especially to the work of Bourdieu (1964) and Elias (1993) and other anthropologists interested in the notion of time, that explored how specific understandings of temporality are reproduced through people's practices. During fieldwork within the three organizations, I was confronted with a number of occasions in which the temporality of immediacy was reproduced through everyday internet practices. Messages on social media, emails, and texts were often replied to immediately (or at least as fast as people possibly could), sometimes interrupting face-to-face conversations or activities. As an ethnographer and participant observer, I was also partaking in this process of reproduction of the temporality of immediacy.

What became evident during my research was that the temporality of immediacy, which was reproduced through everyday practices of instantaneous communication, was of fundamental importance to activists. This is because immediacy implied that images and information spread at an incredible pace creating the ground for the establishment of networks of solidarity and affinity. Throughout fieldwork, interviews, and informal chats, I had the confirmation that activists reproduced immediacy, because this temporality enabled them to organize and mobilize action in fast and effective ways.

This understanding emerged particularly well not only within the context of ZAM, as mentioned above, but also within the context of *Ecologistas en Acción* during the 15M movement. In the summer just after the 15M movement I was sitting in a coffee shop near the metro station of Bilbao in Madrid chatting with Javier, the web developer of *Ecologistas en Acción*, whom I introduced in the previous chapters. During our chat, Javier reflected on the role of web 2.0 platforms in the creation and organization of political action. He argued that, during the 15M movement, web 2.0 technologies acted as 'accelerators' and made the organization of the protest much more effective, because activists were able to rapidly establish networks of solidarity and action. A few days later I was talking to Mariola, a freelance journalist and activist, whom I introduced in the previous chapter.

Like Javier had done, during her interview Mariola talked about the 'speed' and 'facility of connection' of the 15M movement and she argued that such facility could not have been possible with the web 1.0.

The reproduction of immediacy, therefore, is important for activists, because it enables them to organize and mobilize action in fast and effective ways. Such an understanding fits well with discussions such as the one of Castells (2012) and the one of Gerbaudo (2012) on social media and the rapid mobilization of collective action through processes of 'emotional contagion.' However, my research revealed that, within the everyday contexts of political activism, immediacy is a double-edged sword. In fact, as the following sections will show, activists felt that – although it was true that web developments have accelerated the possibility to share information and mobilize action in ways not possible before – immediacy challenged political processes in a substantial number of ways, and they felt that they needed to resist the logic of immediacy.

SOCIAL MEDIA AND THE PROBLEM OF IMMEDIACY

Immediacy, Information Overload, and the Conflicting Temporalities of Activism

In spring 2011, a few weeks before the 15M movement exploded with its force, I was sitting in the office of *Ecologistas en Acción* just off Gran Via in Madrid. Like most days, the atmosphere was hectic. In the wake of the Fukushima nuclear disaster, people were organizing direct actions and demonstrations. In addition, everyone was engaged in organizing the political and media action around the different thematic groups of the organization. On the morning of 9 April, I was sharing the office with the group that dealt with the 'climate change' campaign and I was analyzing the content of the *Ecologista* magazine. Hidden behind their computer screens, the people in the office did not pay any attention to me. Phones kept ringing, and the noise of the keyboards combined with the broken conversations over the phone saturated the air. That day I had arranged to sit down for interviews with two part-time staff members, who both had to cancel due to unforeseen commitments. Tired and a bit frustrated with not being able to talk to people, that morning I observed the life in the office. People were coming and going, writing, communicating over the phone, texting, discussing strategies with local groups over Skype, eating an apple in front of the computer screens, combining forces to fix a computer that had just crashed, and answering their mobile phones. The life of the office was dense with human activities. Everyone looked extremely busy.

Arriving in the early afternoon was Rodrigo, who worked for the Madrid local group. He sat down at the same desk where I was sitting, and he started to sort out some mail. At the age of 28, Rodrigo had been involved with the organization for over six years. Having studied architecture at university, he was passionate about urban planning and in 2007 he created a special committee attached to the Madrid local group, which educated local people on how to build resistance against huge, environmentally unfriendly developments and against speculation. Since 2010, Rodrigo had become one of the organizers of the Madrid local group. That day, Rodrigo and I talked about political action, urban planning, and new technologies.

As we were discussing the social role of social media in the organization of collective action, Rodrigo relayed the feeling of tension and distress that he felt towards the use of social media for political participation, because he "simply could not find the time." He explained that for him it was all a matter of choice: Either he spent his time on social media or he dedicated his time to other forms of political action. He concluded that although he had opened different social media accounts he simply "wasn't doing it the right way" and he seemed to imply that 'doing it the right way' meant the reproduction of immediacy. He explained that social media were 'too time consuming' and he could not cope with the pressure of posting information constantly.

During my research within the three political collectives, activists recognized that online technologies were central to their work, yet they also expressed a profound sense of anguish, because many – like Rodrigo – felt that they simply could not respond to the rhythms of technology. As argued elsewhere (Barassi, 2009), the problem of immediacy and instantaneous communication on email and social media is that it produces 'information overload,' and people feel pressured to keep up with the sheer abundance of communication exchanges. As Gregg (2011) has shown with her research on flexible working practices, the anxiety to keep up with email is prevalent among professionals. Similarly to Gregg (2011), my research revealed that this sense of anxiety towards the management of immediacy and information overload was prevalent within all the three ethnographic contexts of fieldwork. Many activists, echoing the insights of post-Fordist critique (Hardt and Negri, 2000; Lazzarato, 1996; Terranova, 2004), believed that new technologies have completely reshaped the classical boundary between labor and free time, making it extremely difficult for one to cope with the pressure of technology.

Although the anguish for managing immediacy – as Gregg's work (2011) shows – can be found in many different social contexts, this anguish is particularly exacerbated in the context of activism, which has historically always been dominated by a tension of conflicting 'times.' This is because people need to manage already quite busy lives and dedicate much of their free time to political action. Therefore, activists experience a great deal of tension between the different 'temporalities' that define their everyday lives, such as the time for labor, the time for leisure, the time for the family and, of course, the time for activism.

The issue of time and of how people manage their conflicting personal times was a central issue within the three different contexts of research. This is because the management of an individual's 'free time' often impacts the activities of the group, and this generates inevitable problems for collective life. In a context like the one of activism where the issue of time is already problematic, the reproduction of immediacy exacerbates the tension between conflicting temporalities and leads activists to actively question whether they can cope with the further pressure of immediacy.

The understanding of the tension between 'immediacy' and the different conflicting times of activists' lives is an important aspect that we need to take into account if we want to understand how the temporality of internet technologies is impacting political action. However, the notion of immediacy is not only problematic for political activists because of the bound connection between immediacy, digital labor, and the management of time but also because of the relationship between immediacy and political processes. In fact, as the next two sections of the paper will show, 'immediacy' challenges democratic processes in two substantial ways. In the first place, instantaneous communication does not guarantee processes of political elaboration and reflection. In the second place, instantaneous communication enables the construction of 'weak ties' (Granovetter, 1973) and generates insurgent networks, which rely on weak affinities and strong emotions but not on shared political projects.

Immediacy and the Time for Political Discussion and Elaboration

In July 2011 I returned to Madrid to continue my fieldwork. The tents of the 15M movement were still up in Puerta del Sol, yet during the daily assembly not many people participated, and the few tents remaining had to struggle with a variety of different day-to-day issues. The majority of the people of the office in Madrid had been involved with the movement on a regular basis and they were still offering their contribution to the many different grassroots initiatives that emerged through the 15M. However, their involvement with the movement was affected by the other commitments that defined their everyday lives. When I arrived in July, most of my conversations and interviews with the people of the Madrid office revolved around the events of the last two months and the 15M. It was during this time that I had the pleasure to sit down and talk to Patricia.[4] She talked about the making of the 15M movement and the central role played by social media in mobilizing the largest mass movement Spain had seen since the end of the dictatorship. During her interview, she also talked about the issue of time.

P: One thing that really surprised me about the 15M was that all the tweeting, all the social media messages, and internet campaigns effectively had a unique effect: they made people come together in a single square, sit on the floor and start to talk [...]. So technologies have made people come together but what made the movement so powerful was the physical space, the process of discussion, and reflection and the availability of the people to sit down and discuss without the pressure of time. [...].

V: It is very interesting that within your interview, one recurrent theme is the theme of time. What do you think about the relationship between new technologies and time?

P: Well the issue of time is central. We can definitely look at it by considering the debates around eco-feminism. It seems to me that the environmental crisis in which we have been embedded is caused by a clash in temporalities: between the temporality that is necessary for life and the temporality of capitalism. The temporality necessary to nature, to 'care,' is slow, cyclical, and this temporality cannot be accelerated. [...] Speed, acceleration is something that challenges the well-being of people and of the planet. Global capitalism, for the contrary, is based on a temporality that is everyday much more accelerated, short-term. Commodities last less in the market and they need to be substituted; every day we extract increasingly more resources; our perception of distance is now no longer measured in kilometers but in time. It is as if time is eating over space. In this framework, new technologies – that in some instances are tools that enable us to save time – lose their instrumental nature for human beings and they are transformed into accelerators. [...]

V: But what do you think are the effects of this acceleration on the political process itself?

P: New technologies have many positive elements for political articulation [...]. Yet, especially Twitter and Facebook are not spaces where it is easy to deconstruct collective ideologies and propose a different alternative. This is because they are based on a different temporality, which is immediate and accelerated. For this reason I believe that new technologies need to coexist with other forms of political action that establish other forms of temporality, such as assemblies, meetings, etc.

The interview with Patricia revealed that the temporality of immediacy is problematic for political processes. This is because political discussion, elaboration, and reflection require time. Her interview also suggested that activists negotiate with this temporality through everyday practices and through the combination of different tactics. When I was listening to Patricia, I could not avoid making a connection back to an earlier interview with Carlotta of the *Corsari*, whom I introduced in the previous chapter. Carlotta's interview shared many similarities with the one of Patricia, especially because she also believed that the problem with social media is a problem of speed and time.

C: [Social media] are good communication and information tools, for instance if you want to launch a campaign to boycott Israeli products, you can use it to inform people about what products not to buy, or you can use Facebook for events or calls for action, but beyond these communicative acts, I don't believe that they are the place for political production and discussion. [...] One issue is the fact that the speed of communication on Facebook is not the same as face-to-face conversation. During our meetings we require a lot of time to decide different elements: Where we are going to meet? How are we going to organize things? This time is necessary to the political process. It is also necessary from one meeting to the next to take time to think, strategize, meet people and test your assumptions. Online communication is not the same; everything is just too fast. On the one hand this is very positive because if I want to communicate something in real-time I have the chance to do it, but [on the other] I feel that you cannot create a real discussion [...]. The communication is too fast, there is no depth. It is also difficult to establish a history of events and thoughts. Clearly the posts I have published six months ago are still there on my wall, but new posts have submerged them and no one really has the time to go and read all past posts.

Different yet interconnected elements emerged in Carlotta's and Patricia's interviews that shed some light on how activists understand the complex relationship between political processes, web 2.0 technologies, and immediacy. One of these elements is the understanding that political processes require time for discussion, elaboration, and thought, and that this is simply not happening on social media platforms. A second issue is that social media do not enable processes of real political reflection and the articulation of alternatives. This is because the cultural practice of immediacy is based on short texts and messages, which are constantly submerged by new ones making it difficult to trace the history of thought or to articulate a coherent argument.

Max,[5] who worked for *Ecologistas en Acción,* highlighted this problem. During the interview, Max talked about the difficulty activists face in getting their message out there.

M: [...] we don't have much space or time to communicate our message, and especially to express a more thorough explanation of our reflections and propositions. To explain a complex message you need more space and time [...]. If we look at the nuclear energy issues, it is not about whether we should have nuclear energy or not, it's much more. It is about how the production of nuclear energy relates to the diminishing of carbon fossils and a life based on consumption. Yet it is also about explaining the importance of our de-growth model and to contextualize it for people, without having people think that we want to return to the caves. We also need to propose our alternatives. The problem is that these complex analyses need to be developed properly; we need time and space to do that.

Similarly to Patricia and Carlotta, Max argued that the time required for political analysis, elaboration, and explanation clashes with our contemporary media practices, which have been completely taken over by a culture of speed and immediacy. It is easy here to trace some analogies between the argument of the three activists and the one of Virilio who contended that the temporality of new media technologies is based on the 'incessant telepresence of events' and on the 'relief of instantaneity,' which is winning on the depth of historical successivity (Virilio, 2005:127). Of course, the argument of the three activists is not as techno-deterministic and absolute as the one of Virilio, as all three of them believed that there were ways to resist this temporality through face-to-face interaction, confrontation, and discussion or by not giving into the rapid production of texts, and instead produce articles based on scientific or investigative journalism. Although there are ways of resisting the temporality of immediacy, there is no doubt that this resistance is negotiated piece by piece in the everyday lives of activists, who are aware of the fact that immediacy can challenge democratic processes rather than reinforce them.

In negotiating with immediacy and the speed of technologies, activists also highlighted a further challenge that they are faced with in their everyday lives: the problem of the temporality of insurgent networks.

Insurgent Networks and the Durability of Weak Ties

As mentioned above, the use of web 2.0 technologies in the organization and mobilization of collective action enables activists to establish networks of affinities and solidarity in very rapid and effective ways. This issue is properly addressed within the work of Castells (2012) who strongly believes that internet technologies enable the construction of insurgent networks based on emotional contagion and the establishment of a shared emotion of outrage and hope. Fieldwork, however, revealed that the situation is far more complex than what Castells (2012) wants us to believe and that one fundamental problem of insurgent networks is precisely their temporality.

What emerged during my research and interviews was that the reproduction of immediacy through social media enabled the coming together of different networked singularities and political realities in fast and effective ways. Yet my research also revealed that the strengthening of these insurgent networks was only conceivable through the process of assembly and face-to-face political elaboration and confrontation. This latter point emerged very vividly in the conversations with Patricia, Mariola, and Max on the 15M. However, as we have seen in the case of the 15M movement, once the moments for collective encounter and assembly ended, and people went back to their everyday lives, the movement lost its force, momentum, and mass participation. Therefore, the temporality of the insurgent networks is a fundamental aspect that movements have to deal with.

This latter aspect emerged very clearly from my research with the *Corsari*. One particularly interesting aspect of the Italian autonomous movement from an anthropological point of view is the way in which, historically, strategic networks of action have been formed, destroyed, and re-formed in a continuous process of renewal and transformation of the movement. When I was doing fieldwork in Milan, this history of strategic alliances and conflicts affected different dimensions of activists' lives from their personal histories to the internal politics of the group. This is because strategic networks were a matter of constant discussion and negotiation within the everyday lives of activists.

However, at the time of fieldwork, the issue of strategic networks of action went well beyond the reality and political fragmentation that we usually find in the autonomous movement. After years of political and media governance, Berlusconi had created a situation of social and cultural deterioration in Italy, where the values of an authoritarian and chauvinist neo-liberalism coexisted with the corrupted political elite that had been in power for more than 20 years. In this context, different grassroots movements, as well as intellectuals, journalists, artists, comedians, actors, and public figures, joined forces to openly criticize not only Berlusconi but also the hegemonic culture based on an uncontrollable sexism and on a constant de-legitimization of the justice system and democratic processes in general. In this social, cultural, and political context, which was also defined by the economic and financial crisis, rising unemployment figures, and the establishment of causalized work, insurgent networks of political critique and action were established well beyond the movement, as different political singularities came together to share their outrage and indignation and to find new ways to trigger change.

During fieldwork, however, it emerged that the creation of these strategic alliances was not an easy matter for the people involved. This latter point emerged really well in a joint interview with Davide and Silvia. Both in their thirties, Davide and Silvia have been together for almost ten years and have been involved with the *Corsari* since the very beginning of the group. In their interview, both of them addressed the problem of insurgent networks of action and strategic alliances.

D: The level of cultural decay has reached a stage in which even those who are of the Left – or who see themselves as communists – find themselves agreeing with people who are very different from them in political terms. Twenty years ago, they would have killed themselves rather than form alliances with these people. [...] Today in Italy we are experiencing a social and cultural civil war, and we are joining forces. I refuse to go against those who are on my side in this war. [...] But it's hard especially in terms of generating social conflict; as my idea is very different from theirs.

S: It is a paradox, but today I can decide to join forces with Rosy Bindi,[6] for example, to fight for women's rights in Italy, such as the right to have a higher percentage of women in public and private administrations. But these are such basic rights. It's crazy that we are still fighting for these, and at present we have to be realistic and understand that if we are fighting for these basic rights, there really is no space for political depth.

D: The truth is that today we end up making strategic alliances, and these strategic alliances are aberrant.

In discussing the problems of strategic alliances, Davide and Silvia did not refer to social media or online technologies, as their aim was to discuss the

Italian situation and the problematic networks that were emerging from a context of crisis, outrage, and indignation. Yet their interview, I believe, was extremely interesting seen in the broader context of my research, and especially if we return to the preceding part on how activists' practices re-create immediacy. In fact as argued above, during fieldwork, among the different collectives, activists believed that one of the advantages of web platforms in the organization of political action was that these tools enabled them to build strategic alliances and for this reason to mobilize a large number of people in very fast and effective ways. Yet, as the interview with Silvia and Davide reveals, strategic alliances can be also extremely problematic in the sense that they are often based on a common reaction/emotion and not on a shared political project or on a shared understanding of social conflict. It is for this reason that scholars need to be aware of the fact that the insurgent networks described by Castells (2009, 2012), more often than not, are 'weak ties' (Granovetter, 1973), which do not translate into long-term political projects. The possibility for translation into stronger ties and concrete political projects comes from the action on the ground, from face-to-face interaction, discussion, deliberation, and confrontation. This was evident within the context of the 15M, as the life of the camps and the discussions gave rise to a variety of different grassroots projects in different neighborhoods in Madrid. Hence, in the understanding of the complex relationship between new web technologies and political action, scholars have to be aware of the temporality of insurgent networks and appreciate how this temporality – grounded on the hegemonic culture of immediacy – often clashes with democratic processes.

In conclusion to this part, it is evident that activists are critically aware of the fact that the temporality of immediacy clashes with democratic processes and that this tension defines not only their understanding of web technologies but also their web uses. However, as Leccardi (2007) has argued and as we shall see in the next part, activists believe that they can challenge the hegemonic temporality of capitalism through their everyday practices of resistance.

THE TIME OF ACTIVISTS: CRITICAL AWARENESS AND ACTIVE RESISTANCE

Resisting Hegemonic Temporalities through Everyday Practice

During fieldwork, I realized that the *Corsari* and *Ecologistas en Acción* used different tactics in order to build an active resistance against the time of capitalism. Within the context of the *Corsari,* such active resistance was expressed mostly through their commitment to create a 'time for the collective.' The first time I had been invited to attend a meeting of the *Corsari,* as mentioned in *Chapter One,* was on a cold November evening in 2010; the meeting took place in the garden of the ARCI Bellezza, a center for social and cultural events in Milan. We were sitting in the dark on bitterly cold, white plastic chairs positioned in a circle, and people started to talk, to discuss various issues that had happened, and strategize future actions. It was cold, and people wanted to end the meeting at a reasonable time in order to avoid the risk of clashes with neo-Nazi groups that could be waiting outside of the center. At the beginning of the meeting there was the shared impression that it would not last long. Yet after four hours, as I felt my fingertips freezing, the activists were still talking, listening to each individual comment, and trying to find a solution through an in-depth analysis of each issue that was on the agenda for the evening. Throughout fieldwork, all weekly meetings that I attended lasted for three or four hours in order to guarantee enough time for political reflection and for collective decision making. As a participant observer to some of these meetings, I realized that through practices of participatory democracy, the activists involved with the *Corsari* were creating a 'time for the collective' and that this form of temporality clashed with the hegemonic temporality of speed and acceleration promoted by the capitalist discourse.

The 'time for the collective' was not only created through meetings but also through the active construction of 'collective spaces' such as ZAM. In fact, I realized during fieldwork that the construction of a shared collective space has much to say about activists' management of time. This is because it is the shared social space that gives them the possibility to organize their everyday lives around the collective with the establishment of the times for sociality, shared experiences, and human exchange.

If within the *Corsari* the active resistance against the time of capitalism translated itself mostly in the construction of the 'time for the collective,' within the context of *Ecologistas en Acción* this active resistance was often linked to the political discourse of *de-growth*. The commitment to de-growth is, of course, a commitment towards the deceleration of modes of production and consumption within capitalism. It cannot be disentangled from a critique against the 'speed' and time of capitalism. Therefore, most of the political activities of the people involved with *Ecologistas en Acción* are linked – in one way or another – to an active resistance to the time of capitalism. This active resistance translates itself into their everyday practices and shapes most discussions about the culture of immediacy and techno-dependency.

During fieldwork and interviews, it emerged that a way in which activists actively resisted the pressure of capitalist acceleration and techno-dependency is through the everyday struggle to defend their 'quality of life.' The shared understanding within the organization is that, in the consumer culture, people spend too much time in traffic or in front of computer screens and that the quality of life has diminished if we consider the quality of spending more time with our children or loved ones, enjoying specific tastes and foods, the pleasure of reading, or contact with nature. Despite struggling to achieve this quality, most of the people involved with *Ecologistas en Acción* actively seek it, defend it, and believe that it is our human right to achieve it. It is for this reason that they are fighting for it.

CONCLUSION

This chapter has argued that web technologies are creating a temporal context that is based on the notion of 'immediacy.' Theoretically this chapter sought to combine the literature on capitalism and hegemonic time consciousness with the one of the anthropology of time, which focuses on the variety of qualitative temporal contexts and on temporalizing practices. In doing so its main concern was to explore how the hegemonic temporal consciousness of immediacy is impacting political and democratic processes and how activists are actively negotiating with these impacts.

My approach was once again grounded on the notion of practice. This is because, as I have discussed in this book, one fascinating aspect of the 'practice' approach is the understanding that human practices simultaneously reproduce hegemonic understandings and resist them. This latter point became very evident in the investigation of the relationship between political activists and the temporal context of immediacy. It is clear that through their everyday web practices activists reproduce immediacy, and this is partly because they believe that the reproduction of immediacy enables them to establish strategic alliances and mobilize action in fast and effective ways. At the same time, however, activists are also critically aware of the negative impacts of immediacy on political processes and believe that immediacy challenges political elaboration, reflection, and actualization. Their critical awareness shapes their everyday practices and transforms itself into active resistance against the time of capitalism. This active resistance is not an easy task as activists struggle to cope with the acceleration of capitalism and the increased pervasiveness of internet technologies in their lives.

Drawing from their testimonies and experiences, this chapter was meant to show that in the analysis of web technologies and social processes, scholars have much to gain if they appreciate that the problem of immediacy is one of the darkest effects of web developments and digital capitalism and needs to be properly addressed and understood. This is because there is a fundamental tension between capitalist time and the 'time for democracy.' This latter point is beautifully expressed in a chapter by Riechmann (2004), which was extracted and edited by Mariola for the spring 2010 issue of the *Ecologista*. The article read:

> [The cult of speed, acceleration] has become in the brave capitalist new world a cultural disease. However, democracy has another temporal dimension: it requires time, much time. The time that is necessary for exchange and confrontation, for collective reasoning; for the free speech, for the creation of consensus, for the revision of the decisions, for the demands arisen by responsibility: the quality of these processes is incompatible with rush. From here [arises] the profound antagonism between capitalism – with its constant acceleration – and democracy. (2004:195)

NOTES

1. Here it is important to understand that, as Adkins (2011) has argued, although Bourdieu's (1964) analysis of the temporalities of practice offers fundamental insights into the making of hegemonic time under capitalism, his own work does not really engage with the connection between industrial capitalism, clock time, and hegemonic temporalities.
2. In this book I have been using the term 'occupation' rather than 'squatting' because this is the term used by the people involved with ZAM.
3. Palazzo Marino is the building in Piazza della Scala in Milan, which hosts the offices of the mayor of Milan.
4. Fictional name due to the informant's will to be anonymous.
5. Fictional name due to the informant's will to be anonymous.
6. Italian politician of the center-left party, the Parito Democratico, former Health Minister under the Prodi Government (1996–2000), who started her political career with the Italian Democratic Christian Party.

6 Activist Magazines in the Digital Age

INTRODUCTION

All the previous chapters explored the social tensions that arise in the encounter between activist cultures and digital capitalism. As it has been shown, while being important tools for political action, web 2.0 technologies can challenge collective and democratic processes of meaning construction, identity formation, and political participation. This chapter draws on the anthropology of material culture and argues that the social tensions experienced by political activists in their uses of web technologies directly impact their relationship with activist magazines and provide these printed media forms with a new social importance.

In the last three decades, questions on the relationship between materiality and immateriality have dominated debates on digital media and cultures. During the 1980s, as political thinkers and economists reflected on the new post-Fordist organization of labor in society (Braverman, 1974; Harvey, 1991), postmodern thinkers like Baudrillard (1983) and Lyotard ([1985] 1996) claimed that our relationship to materiality needed to be re-thought and re-conceptualized. During the 1990s, with the rapid expansion of new information and communication technologies in different areas of social life, debates on the relationship between materiality and immateriality became even more pervasive. In communication studies, scholars started to look at the concept of 'immateriality,' not because they were concerned with the immaterial, simple and pure, but rather with investigating the 'materiality of communication' (Pfeiffer, 1994:2). In fact, in those days, different communication scholars and social theorists argued that the tendency to de-materialization – pointed out by Lyotard ([1985] 1996) – created new forms of materialisms. Hence, they have argued that communication systems and signs were the basis for new material structures (Pfeiffer, 1988; Barck, 1988).

The debates of the 1980s and the 1990s anticipated in many ways the urgency of contemporary debates on the relationship between digital culture and new forms of materialism. Today, in media and cultural studies, scholars are arguing that we must move away from the claims of immateriality and fluidity (Bauman, 2005). On the contrary, as recent works have shown, the concept of materiality and materialism has come to the fore. Particularly fascinating in this regard is the work of Parikka on materialism and media archaeology (Parikka, 2007) and the collection of essays by Coole and Frost (2010) titled *New Materialisms*. The collection of essays argues for the importance of a new focus on 'matter' for social theory and critical thought if scholars want to come to terms with key social issues such as climate change, biotechnologies, and global structures and powers. Although Ahmed (2010) argues that it is important to avoid emphasis on 'novelty' when thinking about the importance of matter today, the collected essays demonstrate how questions on materiality and on our relationship to materiality have not become obsolete in the digital age but have gained a new fundamental significance.

In this chapter, and as argued elsewhere (Barassi, 2013), I wish to explore the relationship between media technologies and materiality, not by looking at the broader sociological and political debates on the role of 'materiality' today, but rather by taking a step back and exploring the anthropological importance of printed media as material objects in contrast to online media. By investigating the material dimension of activist magazines as objects of mediation (Silverstone, 1994), my intention here is to emphasize the tangible nature of printed media forms and to explore how material forms of media, in contrast to online ones, become social objects of collective identification.

In journalism studies, the relationship between online and printed media has become a central focus of academic debate (Li and Chyi, 2013; Chyi and Yang, 2009; De Waal et al., 2005; Thurman and Myllylahti, 2009; Franklin, 2010; Rodrigues Cardoso, 2010; Pimlott, 2011). Within these debates, some scholars have rightly pointed out that printed media continue to be of fundamental importance for their readers, be they leaflets, magazines, or printed newspapers (Chyi and Yang, 2009; Pimlott, 2011). In doing so, these scholars have shown that printed media are not being replaced by online media but rather tend to complement and reinforce their social role. Despite being very interesting, these analyses focus on how new media complement and reinforce the role of print and do not consider the tension between new and old forms of media. Furthermore, for the lack of their ethnographic perspective, these works do not highlight the collective and emotional attachment that renders printed media particularly important and the social reasons behind these forms of emotional attachment. Combining the insights of the anthropology of material culture with ethnographic observations, this chapter highlights the tension between digital and printed forms of media and argues that activists' everyday engagement with online technologies is providing printed media with a new fundamental importance. It will argue that looking at why grassroots political groups remain attached to activist magazines while at the same time developing online ones can raise critical questions on the connection between subjectivity, political association, and new technologies as well as on the difference between individualized and collective forms of communication.

THE SOCIAL LIFE OF ACTIVIST MAGAZINES AND THE CONSTRUCTION OF POLITICAL BELONGING

The Social Importance of Activist Magazines in the Digital Age

For the *Cuba Solidarity Campaign,* 24 October 2007 was not a usual day. Carton-boxes with the latest edition of the *CubaSí* magazine crammed the corridors and rooms of the small office on Seven Sisters Road. It was the 'mail-out day' and volunteers and office workers were all gathered in the communal room, packing the magazines to be sent to members or key figures in the Trade Union Movement and other affiliated organizations. That day people were complaining about the fact that there were too many leaflets to be sent with the magazine and, thus, it would take longer than usual. Overall we must have been around 15 people between office staff and volunteers. Divided into four separate long tables, we constructed chains of 'production' in order to make sure that the 5,000 copies of the *CubaSí* were packed on time. Among sandwiches, coffees, and teas, the *CubaSí* magazine passed from hand to hand while we chatted about Cuba and the work brigade, about the fortieth anniversary of the death of Che Guevara, and about the response article written by CSC's director that had recently been published in *The Guardian.*

The mail-out day in October 2007 was one of the most vivid examples of the way in which the everyday reality of CSC is defined by a strong reliance on printed media, a reliance that is expressed in the resources the campaign dedicated to the production, printing, and distribution of the *CubaSí* magazine and other leaflets. Despite the cost of production being higher than the actual earnings, the people involved with CSC feel a profound emotional attachment to the magazine and believe in the importance of publishing it. As I was carrying out my research, I almost reached a stage of data saturation when I asked whether people were ready to replace the magazine with an online-only version. Almost no one – whatever age group they were – would renounce the *CubaSí* because, according to them, it was the printed magazine that created a real sense of collective belonging to the organization. Throughout fieldwork, expressions of emotional attachment to the magazine accompanied the everyday life within and outside the office. During the mail-out day mentioned above, for instance, a volunteer who had been involved with the solidarity organization since the late 1980s was upset because some copies of the *CubaSí* had been damaged in the delivery. She looked at me and commented, "The problem is that people don't feel for the *CubaSí* like we do."

A few years later, on 31 March 2011, I found myself in a very different ethnographic setting. Together with members of *Ecologistas en Acción,* I participated in a demonstration in Madrid against the neo-liberal policies of the city's administration, which was run mostly by councilors of the Partido Popular (PP).[1] As I was walking down Calle Alcalá in the spring sunset, surrounded by banners, flags, and people pushing their bicycles towards Banco de España, where the demonstration ended and the Critical Mass[2] began, I had the pleasure to chat with a group of activists who were militants within *Ecologistas en Acción* about the importance of the *Ecologista* magazine. That day I discovered that the organization had offered all its members the option to receive only the digital version of the magazine but only 1% decided to give up the material version. There were two reasons why those involved with the organization did not want to replace the printed magazine with an online version. First, many within *Ecologistas en Acción* believed that the environmental impact of online media (which are based on satellite communication systems and electricity) is greater than that of a small printed magazine, which is published using recyclable materials. Second, I was told that people believed that printed media enable specific social processes that online media do not enable, which relate to the construction of a shared collective identity and a feeling of belonging to the group. Therefore, it emerged during fieldwork that despite the difference in ethnographic contexts, the Spanish activists shared many similarities with the people involved with CSC, as they also believed that activist magazines are important media forms that enable political activists to construct political belonging and a feeling of affinity to the group.

The understanding that printed media can create a feeling of belonging to a collective experience is certainly not new and has long been a topic of academic reflection. In *Imagined Communities*, Anderson (1991) contended that the rise of print-capitalism was a major contributor in the construction of the nation-state as an 'imagined community.' This is because newspapers and modern novels were able to confer a sense of *simultaneity*, which permitted different people to imagine themselves as a community (Anderson, 1991:33–46). Furthermore, according to Anderson, the way in which *language* was used in printed practices was a fundamental source of imagination. In fact, through the use of terms of private property (*my, yours*, etc.; Anderson, 1991:68) and terms expressing kinship ties and home (*Heimat, Vaterland, Motherland, Patria*, etc.; Anderson, 1991:143), the nation could be imagined as a united community in newspapers. Tarrow (1998) applied Anderson's insights to the analysis of social movements and suggested that the rise of the popular press in Britain and France at the end of the eighteenth century triggered the creation of new associations that developed around the production and exchange of printed materials. According to Tarrow, therefore, print and association were complementary channels in the development of social movements (1998:45–50). Also Downing (2000) and Atton (2002) have shown how the production of alternative media within social movements and political minorities is embedded in processes of identity construction.

Although insightful, understandings of the relationship between alternative media and identity have often emphasized the way in which, through these media forms, social movements can construct collective imaginaries and ideologies that enable participants to imagine their group as a social unity. The emphasis on imagination and representation, although crucial in shedding light on how printed media enable forms of identity construction, has overshadowed another important dimension of the relationship between alternative media and identity. Here, I am referring to the way in which specific media forms become *collective objects of identification* within political groups.

In order to understand the process whereby printed media become collective objects of identification, it is essential that we turn to the anthropology of material culture. In anthropology, questions on materiality and material culture have long been a focus of debate and attention even during the 1980s (Appadurai, 1986; Kopytoff, 1986), at a time when communication scholars were discussing ideas of de-materialization. Influenced by key contributions in social theory, such as Bourdieu's understanding of practice and habitus (Bourdieu, 1970, 1977), anthropologists started to explore 'the social life of things' (Appadurai, 1986) and the way in which everyday social contexts were built within and around material worlds. What became evident to different anthropologists, who were also heavily influenced by the work of Latour (1986), was that to input all objects with an agency of a sort was a very human process (Gell, 1998). What they also noticed was that the meaning humans attributed to specific objects derived from the human relationships that the objects represented.

As we shall see in the later parts of the chapter, the anthropology of material culture, I believe, can be fundamental in shedding some light on the social importance of printed media at a time of social and mobile media. As we shall see below with reference to the two different examples of the *CubaSí* magazine and the *Ecologista* magazine, printed media become the material accounts of the achievements of a given organization and, hence, they are embedded within its collective history. The fact that these media forms are embedded within the collective history of organizations makes them important social objects to which people feel emotionally attached. The *ownership* and *exchange* of these material objects, as we shall see, are processes of great significance for the people involved in the everyday reality of social movements, because they enable the production and reproduction of social relationships.

MATERIAL MEMORIES AND BIOGRAPHICAL NARRATIVES

The Case of the *CubaSí* Magazine

The *CubaSí* magazine was first published in 1986, as a development of the newsletter of the British Cuba Resource Centre (BCRC) that was first published in 1978. This newsletter was the very heart of the group because it constituted the only means of communication between the organizers and the few hundred members. At the time, a collective of volunteers made the editorial choices for its production. Articles, content, and style were thus negotiated within a group of untrained individuals who produced the newsletter following personal understandings of journalistic practices. In 1986, the group started to produce a glossy magazine.

During interviews and informal conversations, it emerged that throughout the history of the organization, despite the lack of resources, in the most difficult times, the production of the magazine was seen always as a main priority for the people involved. The *CubaSí* magazine has always been central to the campaign; it followed the group in its development as an organization. Members, organizers, and volunteers often attach collective memories to the magazine's production processes and its technological development. More than once I have been asked by people to understand the fact that for them the magazine cannot be detached from an understanding of the organization because it represents the way in which CSC as a campaign has developed. It is by looking at the connection between the history of the magazine, the one of the organization, and personal narratives that we can better appreciate its meaning. In fact, during fieldwork within CSC, it emerged that lived experiences had been turned into collective memories, and the magazine had become the material artifact of these collective memories.

This process became more evident than ever when, on a summer day, I interviewed the director of CSC, Rob, whom I introduced in the previous chapter. That day we went through the old issues of the *CubaSí* together. Rob kept flipping the pages of the magazines that were produced at the end of the 1980s, and he recognized people, pointed out their names, and recalled episodes. A similar situation happened when I went through old issues of the magazine with Kate,[3] whom I mentioned in *Chapter One*. As she looked at past versions of *CubaSí*, she laughed and joked with me on the type of language that was used at the time and on the ways in which 'politics was actually enacted.' As we were reading a 'political report' of Thatcher's Britain, I asked whether she found it amusing that, at the end of the day, what was written there was history. She turned page after page, which reported a reality of strikes and struggle against the policies of the Thatcher government and replied "history? Not really ... this is my life."

During my research at CSC, much data has been gathered on the strong connection between the magazine, the organization, and the collective memory of the group. The relationship between alternative media production and the construction of collective memory has been a topic of academic attention (Downing, 2000; Williams, 2009; Rodriguez, 2011). With reference to the Labor Movement in Britain, Williams (2009) suggested that the production of alternative media acted as 'a force of collective memory' at a time when the British government and dominant media acted 'as forces of erasure' (2009:13–36). In a beautifully written account of the British Left and the media in Britain – which analyzes the representation of left-wing organizations in the British mainstream media between the 1980s and the early 2000s – Curran et al. (2005) showed that during the 1980s tabloids and newspapers constantly assaulted left-wing political groups by picturing them as 'deviant and loony.' According to the scholars, dominant media organizations were particularly fierce against the Greater London Council, which was led by Ken Livingstone and other London-based left-wing organizations that supported it, like the

Cuba Solidarity Campaign (Curran et al., 2005:39–46). At the time, therefore, alternative media such as the *CubaSí* documented the social struggle in which different left-wing organizations in Britain had to engage.

If one picks up the *CubaSí* magazine today, it is possible to find key references to that history of social struggle. This point emerged particularly well in an interview with Luke.[4] Being in his fifties, Luke has always been politically active as a member of the Communist Party, and he has been involved in the campaign since the late 1980s. During his interview, Luke mentioned the importance of the magazine in the history of the campaign and the Labor Movement.

L: Everything the campaign has done is reflected in our magazine, and I wouldn't imagine CSC without the *CubaSí*. I think the magazine is a written version of CSC; it is a written record of what we have done in the years. But perhaps the most important aspect of the magazine goes beyond the focus on Cuba itself, because the *CubaSí* can be perceived as an archive of our movement, and the progression we have made. You know campaigns come and go, and I think keeping track of them is good for the Labor Movement and the progressive politics in the UK. It is of central importance that you understand this.

These ethnographic anecdotes suggest that there is a bound connection between the magazine, activists' understanding of a collective past, and individual experiences and feelings. As emerges from the above discussion, the magazine is seen as the documentation of their achievements and as the construction of the historical narrative of the organization. It is by looking at the relationship between biographical narratives and the production of activist magazines that we can better appreciate the social and political significance of the these printed media forms as material objects that are embedded within the history and the relationships of the group and that acquire a social agency of their own (Appadurai, 1986; Miller, 1997). In fact today the *CubaSí* magazine is seen as the material expression of a collective voice, as their 'printed politics' and the material articulation of their collective effort. For this reason people feel emotionally attached to it.

Throughout the research within CSC, therefore, much data has been gathered on the strong emotional attachment between people and their magazine. One expression of this emotional attachment can be found in an interview with Catriona, who at the time of the interview was only 19 years old. Catriona's family has been involved with the campaign since she was five years old, and during our semi-structured interview, she relayed the meaning the *CubaSí* magazine had for her:

C: I wouldn't imagine the campaign without the magazine. We need it to know what is going on. Without the *CubaSí*, I couldn't imagine how people would keep in touch with the organization. […] If someone did something to the *CubaSí*, I would be very, very angry. You know the *CubaSí* represents the collective effort of people who struggle for what they believe in and you can't destroy it.

Therefore, as can be seen from the above discussion, the magazine has today become a central component in the symbolic construction of the *Cuba Solidarity Campaign*, because it represents the way in which CSC has developed, and the way identity is bestowed upon the organization by its members. Consequently, it has become a collective object of identification.

CREATING HISTORY, CONSTRUCTING A COLLECTIVE IDENTITY

The *Ecologista* Magazine

The history of *Ecologistas en Acción*, as argued in *Chapter One*, is very different from the one of CSC, and this difference is reflected in the relationship activists have with the magazine. *Ecologistas en Acción* was founded in 1998 to counteract the problem of fragmentation affecting the environmental movement in Spain and to bring together different environmental organizations under a unique name. In contrast to CSC, therefore, where people shared a common history and a strong sense of collective identity, when *Ecologistas en Acción* was founded, this common collective history and collective identity needed to be constructed. In this regard, the magazine played a pivotal role. As soon as the organization was established, organizers directed their attention and resources to the creation of a magazine, which – as I have been told by one of the first founders of the organization – needed to be "a space where all the different activities of the autonomous groups were documented, and a reference point for the construction of unity, and of a collective identity of *Ecologistas en Acción*."

In order to make this possible, the magazine needed to express a form of historical continuity and, thus, needed to be linked to the previous organizations that acted as coordinators. For this reason, the first issue of *Ecologista*, which was published in 1999, started from the number 17, because members and organizers wanted to establish a line of continuity with *Gaia*, the official magazine of CODA. Furthermore, the newly published magazine took its name from an old alternative press publication *El Ecologista*,[5] which was published for the first time in 1979 and was produced by an environmental group called Colletivo Tierra. As many have noted, *El Ecologista*, which disappeared during the 1980s for unknown reasons, was an important countercultural magazine that brought together environmental reflections with liberal, feminist, and Marxist ideas, at a historical time of transition from dictatorship to democracy. Despite its short life, *El Ecologista* was heralded as an important document of the environmental movement in Spain. Therefore, when *Ecologistas en Acción* was founded, the choice of calling its internal magazine

Ecologista was motivated by a will of the new organization to emphasize a shared historical memory of the Spanish environmental movement.

During fieldwork, those involved with *Ecologistas en Acción* showed less emotional attachment to their magazine than members and organizers of CSC showed for the *CubaSí*. This is probably due to the short history of the publication as well as to the structure of the organization, which is based on autonomous groups rather than on a centralized system like CSC. However, as it had happened in the context of the British solidarity campaign, the members and organizers of *Ecologistas en Acción* strongly believed in the central role that their activist magazine played in the construction of a sense of belonging and affinity to the organization.

According to Barcia, for instance, the *Ecologista* is published mostly as a response to an internal necessity rather than as a platform to transmit a message to the wider public. One interesting aspect that emerged in his interview was the understanding of the difference between *endogamous* and *exogamous* forms of media. Applying an anthropological concept, Barcia contended that the magazine – in contrast to other media – is a form of *endogamous media*, because it is directed mostly to the members and militants of *Ecologistas en Acción*. Barcia understood the magazine as a form of endogamous media because it works as an internal coordinator and enables its members to imagine that they are part of a collective.

The understanding of the magazine as a form of *endogamous* media can also be found in an interview with Pedro.[6] Like Barcia, Pedro has long been involved with environmental politics since his early teenage years and has been a militant with *Ecologistas en Acción* since it was founded. In discussing the role of the magazine, Pedro expressed his frustration with the internal, endogamous qualities of this media form.

P: You ask me about the magazine. But I am probably the person who has more of a critical perspective. I think there is a certain dependency on printed media, not only among us but also among other movements in Spain. Clearly we must realize that printed media reach only a specific public. The *Ecologista* is a very endogamous form of communication that reaches only our members. It is a very internal form of communication. But, is this really the best way to build our media action? I think we are part of a culture of communicative endogamy; the people who read our magazine are the ones who are most involved. The magazine is not an effective tool for communication outside of *Ecologistas en Acción*. It is a channel of internal collective identification. It is a way of archiving our history, of documenting what we have done. In that regard it is important, but it would be more important for us to develop other channels of communication.

As emerges from the interviews above, there are many lines of similarities between the findings collected within *Ecologistas en Acción* and within the *Cuba Solidarity Campaign*. The two organizations strongly differ in political ideologies and organizational structures; nevertheless, the people involved within both ethnographic contexts believe that their activist magazines are tools for the construction of a feeling of identity and belonging to the group. As the next part of the chapter will show, one important aspect that emerged through this research is the finding that activists believe that the social importance of printed media needs to be found in their material nature, in the fact that people can *own* and *exchange* them. The anthropology of material culture, it will be shown, enables us to shed light on these understandings and to appreciate the fact that online technologies do not enable the same processes of *exchange* and *ownership*, which are central to the construction of political belonging. This will lead us to the realization that the importance of activist magazines as 'social objects' cannot be fully understood without taking into account activists' relationship to online technologies and the social tensions that emerge in the encounter between activist cultures and digital capitalism.

PRINTED MEDIA VERSUS ONLINE MEDIA: EXCHANGE, OWNERSHIP, AND THE CONSTRUCTION OF SOCIAL RELATIONSHIPS

Activist Magazines, the Anthropology of Material Culture, and the Construction of Social Relationships

In order to understand how activist magazines become not only collective objects of identification but also how they come to have a 'social life' of their own, it is essential to turn to the anthropology of material culture. The basic premise of the anthropology of material culture can be found in the understanding that, as Gell (1998) has argued, to input an object with an agency of a sort is a very human process and, thus, that our social worlds are built around and by our objects. The study of material culture is a fascinating field of enquiry for anthropologists, and in the last century we have seen the development of multiple approaches that have looked at the social life of objects through a variety of different angles (Miller, 2002). In this chapter, I am particularly interested in the work of those who have looked at the relationship between the agency of objects and processes of exchange (Appadurai, 1986; Miller, 1997, 2002, 2008, 2013) and have argued that the social importance of objects largely depends on the way in which these objects are exchanged, because it is the process of exchange that enables humans to construct specific types of social relationships. In this framework, material objects become meaningful because they become the material representation of specific types of human relationships.

In order to understand this point we need to consider the classical anthropological distinction between 'commodities' and 'gifts' (Mauss, [1925]

2000). According to Mauss ([1925] 2000), human economies rely on two different forms of exchange. On the one hand, humans exchange commodities, and these forms of exchange are based upon short-lived and distant human relationships. On the other hand, they exchange 'gifts,' and these forms of exchange are defined by long-term human relationships that are based on complex and open-ended processes of human obligation. The first type of exchange is endemic to capitalism, while the latter form of exchange escapes the logic of capitalism.

Mauss's ([1925] 2000) understanding that the meaning of objects largely depends on the ways in which they are exchanged is essential to the argument presented here. However, as many have argued (Bloch and Parry, 1989; Hart, 2007; Graeber, 2007, 2011), it is important to be critical and avoid the classical anthropological dichotomy between gift economies and commodity-based economies, and we must recognize that our Western cultures are largely shaped by both forms of exchange.

During fieldwork, it emerged that the processes of exchange of activist magazines were of central importance in the construction of social and political networks among different organizations as well as among members. In fact, within both organizations – even though the magazines were sold as a commodity in some contexts (e.g. at social events or newsagents) – in the majority of cases the magazines were seen as 'gifts,' as tokens of exchange that symbolized the construction of specific relationships. It is by looking at the social relationships that are embedded in the material objects through processes of exchange that we can better appreciate how printed magazines become the symbols of specific social relationships.

Another fundamental aspect that emerged during fieldwork was that the *ownership* of these objects is of central importance in creating a sense of affinity to the group. In anthropology, the relationship between materiality, ownership, and identity is widely explored (Gosden and Marshall, 1999; Edwards et al., 2004; Miller, 2008, 2013). Throughout my fieldwork, it emerged that my informants made an explicit link between the three and stressed the continuing importance of printed media precisely because they could *own* them. This process of ownership, they argued, made them feel part of the collective life of the group.

As the next part of the chapter will show, and as argued elsewhere (Barassi, 2013), one fascinating aspect that emerged during my research is represented by the fact that activists were convinced that these processes of *ownership* and *exchange*, which are so essential in the construction of political affinity and belonging, are not enabled by online technologies.

The 'Immateriality' of Digital Media and the Importance of Printed Magazines

As mentioned above, during my research I reached a stage of data saturation when a great majority of activists claimed that they would never replace activist magazines with an online version. What emerged from the interviews collected was that people believed that, in contrast to online media forms, the printed magazine conveyed them with a greater emotional attachment and a feeling of belonging to the group, precisely because of its material nature, and the fact that printed media can be *owned* and *exchanged*. This point emerged particularly well in an interview with Rob, the director of CSC, whom I introduced in *Chapter Three*. During his interview, Rob talked about the communication strategies of the campaign, and he emphasized specifically the importance of investing their economic resources in the publication of an activist magazine, despite developing online media platforms:

R: [...] you have to gather people, and make them part of an organization, and to make them part of the organization you have to give them an 'affinity' to the organization, and to do so you have to write to them, and give them something in *exchange* [my emphasis] ....

V: And can't you reach them with the online media?

R: Well the problem is that the online is so hard to associate with a particular 'product.' You just read it because it's online, but you can't really associate it with something. You can't really have an affinity with anything online really. You have got your Websites and your newsletters but then you can easily read something else. You don't stick with it. No one *owns* [my emphasis] the online.

In his interview, Rob mentions the idea of *ownership* and *exchange* when explaining why people build a sense of belonging and affinity to the organization through their printed media. The same understanding can also be found in an interview with Luis, one of the two rotating general secretaries of *Ecologistas en Acción,* whom I introduced in previous chapters. In his interview, Luis argued that the fact that printed media can be owned and exchanged makes them important constructors of a feeling of belonging to the group.

L: The mere fact that there is a magazine that reaches everyone, every group, member, and individual is a way of creating a collectivity, of creating a feeling of commonality.

V: And you can't create that same feeling of commonality with an email newsletter or an online communication?

L: No, it's not the same, because it's not material. You know at the end of the day we come to have relationships with material things, that we can touch, that we can bring with us, you can't really associate the computer with *Ecologistas en Acción*. You associate it with a wide variety of things that you have within it ...

V: What about the website, can't you associate it with *Ecologistas en Acción*?

L: Well yes, but it's not the same. You can't really take it with you, well unless you have an iPhone, but no, you can't really take it with you. I don't know, I can't really explain this, maybe I am telling you this from the perspective of a generation that still values the printed format, because we weren't 'breastfed' with the internet like other generations. I am 36; someone who is 26 or 16 has a totally different relationship with the net. But I am just telling you my personal experience of this, and how I think a great majority of the organization lives it.

In his interview, Luis refers to the issue of age when reflecting on why he believes that printed media still matter and argues that younger generations might feel less attached to forms of printed media. Generational variation may appear to be the issue at stake when reflecting on the continuing importance of activist magazines. Indeed, if we were to base ourselves merely on an average age, the generation issue would seem to be the first reason why people prefer to have a hard copy. Yet I contend that this is a superficial understanding not only because most people I met were extremely familiar with the ICT, but also because the activists in their early twenties whom I had the pleasure to interview emphasized the importance of the printed magazine. Catriona, mentioned above, offers an example of this. During her interview, despite being only 19, she revealed that for her the *CubaSí* magazine had a fundamental importance in creating a feeling of commonality and belonging to the group and that she would never give up the material version because online communication would never feel the gap created by the absence of a printed magazine.

As it emerges from the above interviews, therefore, it is the material nature of printed magazines that is heralded as the fundamental element that enables people to associate with the group, because magazines can be *owned* and *exchanged* in ways that are not possible with online media. In his interview, for instance, Barcia argued that human beings always look for a sensory experience in the construction of their social relationships, and the magazine conveys that experience – it becomes a medium of *cariño* (affection) – between individuals and the organization. It is clear also that digital and visual media can engage the senses in often complex and fascinating ways (Pink, 2006). However, my research revealed that the tangibility of activist magazines makes the experience of these objects in everyday contexts a fundamentally different one, especially if we consider the link between ownership and the construction of identity. Many of my interviewees commented that the experience of owning an online media product is not the equivalent of owning a printed magazine, which can be stored and archived and can be enjoyed, touched, and smelt. In this regard, it is insightful that when I asked Luis of *Ecologistas en Acción* whether a sense of affinity and commonality to the group can be established by online media, he replied that it cannot, because online media are not material and because people come to have relationships with material things, not digital ones.

A similar point can be made also if we look at the issue of *exchange*. In fact my research revealed that the exchange of printed media could not be considered as the equivalent to the exchange of online media. It is important to point out that Kollock (1998) argues that the exchange of digital goods online should be read as the exchange of 'gifts' and suggests that this form of exchange creates an online economy of 'gift-giving' and cooperation. There are two fundamental flaws with his argument. First, he draws on the anthropological literature on 'gift' and 'commodity' exchange without recognizing the work of those who challenge the classical anthropological dichotomy between gift economies and commodity-based economies (Kopytoff, 1986; Appadurai, 1986; Miller, 1997; Bloch and Parry, 1989; Hart, 2007; Graeber, 2006, 2011), and therefore he comes to generalized assumptions about the 'digital economy of cooperation.' Second, Kollock (1998) does not recognize the difference between the exchange of digital and material objects.

In fact, he does not recognize that the relationships and social obligations that are constructed via the exchange of 'digital' gifts are not the same as the ones constructed through the exchange of material gifts. In stating this, I am not suggesting that the exchange of an image, an online video, a file, etc. cannot be perceived 'as a gift,' which in Mauss's ([1925] 2000) terms carries a set of social obligations. What I am suggesting is that the experience of online exchange is different from the experience of the exchange of a material object as it triggers different processes of social obligation. In fact, as it emerged during fieldwork within both organizations, activists highlighted how receiving an email newsletter, although informative, did not trigger the same relational processes as receiving or exchanging a printed magazine.

Therefore, the anthropological literature of material culture enables us to appreciate that processes of exchange and ownership of activist magazines are embedded with social and collective meanings, and that these social and collective meanings cannot be found in online media. As the next and concluding part of the chapter will show, once we appreciate the social importance of activist magazines as material objects of identification, we can take a step forward and consider the fact that it is impossible here to understand the social importance of activist magazines without looking at activists' relationships with online technologies and the social tensions that emerge through activists' everyday web uses. This latter point, as it will be shown next, enables us to expand our analysis and consider the difference between everyday activist use of web technologies, on the one hand, and the use of 'their' alternative media platforms on the other.

WEB 2.0 TECHNOLOGIES, SOCIAL TENSIONS, AND THE ROLE OF ALTERNATIVE MEDIA

The Social Importance of Alternative Media

During fieldwork, it emerged clearly that the continued importance of activist magazines for political groups is strengthened by activists' ambivalent relationship with web technologies. This understanding made me reflect on a broader issue, namely, on the tension between activists' everyday uses of web technologies, on the one hand, and the uses of 'their' alternative media on the other. As we have seen throughout this book, activists believe that web technologies facilitate a form of communication that is individually centered, subjected to corporate power, and subservient to the logic of immediacy. As the following part will show, the activists I worked with believed that their alternative media enabled them to construct completely different communication processes, which were collective in nature, based on in-depth political elaboration and unbound from the logic of capital exploitation. Therefore, I will briefly consider the three ethnographic tensions discussed in this book (the problem of *networked individualism*, the problem of *digital labor,* and the problem of *immediacy*) and will sketch how these ethnographic tensions cannot be found in the relationship between activists and their collective alternative media, such as their printed magazines.

Networked Individualism and the 'Visible Individual' As argued in *Chapter Three*, activists are extremely critical of the individualized and self-centered communication enabled by web 2.0 technologies and, in particular, social media. In contrast to these forms of communication, activists believe that that their alternative media – such as their printed magazine, website, and newsletter – are the spaces for the construction of a 'collective voice.' This is because through the production of these media formats people find themselves collectively involved in the construction of a shared image of the group. Most of the contents that are published on alternative media platforms are in fact produced through collective processes of confrontation, deliberation, and meaning construction. As scholars engaged in the study of social movements or alternative media have shown, these collective processes are central to the social life of political groups (Melucci, 1996; Porta and Diani, 1999; Atton, 2002; Downing, 2000).

Digital Labor and Corporate Surveillance As argued in *Chapter Four,* activists are aware of the problematic tension created by corporate surveillance when using web technologies. As it has been shown, their everyday internet uses are constantly defined by the negotiation with digital capitalism. In contrast to the logic of capitalist accumulation and exploitation, which is intrinsic to web 2.0 platforms and that escapes their control, activists shape their alternative media according to specific ethical principles of capital accumulation. This is particularly true not only if we consider the production processes, but also if we consider their use of advertising. In fact, although using some form of advertising on their printed magazines in order to raise funds, activists publish only the ads of non-profit or commercial entities that share their political and ethical beliefs. In this way they manage to control the relationship between communication processes and the production of economic capital in just and fair ways.

Immediacy As argued in *Chapter Five,* much of online communication is subservient to the logic of immediacy, and this can be extremely problematic for political activists. The logic of immediacy, as we have seen, affects the production of texts, and this is particularly evident if we consider the production of content on social media. However, processes of political reflection and the articulation of alternative ideologies, which are essential to the life of political groups, require the creation of thorough texts that explore issues at length. My research revealed that this depth and thoroughness is often achieved through the production of alternative media and in particular activist magazines.

In conclusion to this part, it seems clear that the social tensions experienced by political activists in their uses of web technologies directly impacts on their relationship with their alternative media and provides these media forms with a fundamental social importance for political action.

CONCLUSION

By highlighting the interplay of different media platforms within the everyday mediation of political action, this chapter raises several questions relating to political participation and contemporary forms of mediation. As the ethnographic contexts of CSC and *Ecologistas en Acción* show, online technologies are not replacing printed media but are transforming people's perception of these media formats by giving materiality a new meaning. In fact, as it has been shown, activists believe that in contrast to online technologies, which are more ephemeral and cannot be associated to a particular group, printed media are embedded with collective values and meanings and are important tools in the construction of a feeling of belonging and affinity to the group. The emphasis on materiality therefore cannot be analyzed without considering people's understanding of web technologies and the social tensions that arise in the encounter between digital capitalism and activist cultures. As this chapter has shown, digital and material, 'new' and 'old' media do not replace one another but enable different, and at times contrasting, communication and social processes. Online media do not play the same role as printed ones, because they create different human processes of socialization, communication, and sensory interaction. Understanding the specificities of media in enabling different processes of identity construction can provide us with important keys of analysis into the multiple complexities of the everyday mediation of political action.

NOTES

1. The Partido Popular (PP) is the conservative political party in Spain, which was the governing party between 1996 and 2004 led by José Maria Aznar. The Party was founded in 1989 by the People's Alliance (Alianza Popular, AP), a party led and funded by the former Minister of Tourism during Francisco Franco's dictatorship, Manuel Fraga Iribarne. The PP holds a strong power in Castilla and

in much of Madrid's administration and in November 2011 won the general elections.
2. Critical Mass is a cycling event typically held on the last Friday of every month in over 300 cities around the world. The ride was originally founded in 1992 in San Francisco as an act of direct action, the appropriation of public spaces for environmental reflection.
3. Fictional name to respect interviewee's choice of anonymity.
4. Fictional name to respect interviewee's choice of anonymity, for the same reason I am not mentioning here the local group he is working for.
5. Although the organization chose the name *El Ecologista* as homage to the magazine that disappeared in the 1980s, *Ecologistas en Acción* chose to drop the article 'el' that indicates a male gender.
6. Fictional name to respect the interviewee's will to remain anonymous.

Conclusion
The Future of the Web, Big Data, and the Power of Critique

INTRODUCTION

In 1999 – just before the dot.com bubble was about to burst – Tim Berners-Lee, the inventor of the World Wide Web, talked about his dream for the future. What he envisaged was a radical transformation in the ways in which we knew and understood the web.

> I have a dream for the Web [...] capable of analyzing all the data on the Web – the content, links, and transactions between people and computers. A 'Semantic Web,' which should make this possible, has yet to emerge, but when it does, the day-to-day mechanisms of trade, machines talking to machines will handle bureaucracy and our daily lives. The 'intelligent agents' people have touted for ages will finally materialize.
>
> (Berners-Lee in Funk, 2008:129)

Berners-Lee, thus, envisaged the creation of new web technologies that were able to process and create meaning from semantic documents and data that would enable societies to organize people's lives and transform the everyday realities from basic health services to local governments. Ten years after Berners-Lee shared 'his vision for the future,' Floridi (2009:28–30) argued that in the future we would see the creation of a new web that would be based on syntax (not meaning, which requires some understanding) and therefore would be more a *Web of Data* or a *Metasyntactic Web* rather than a *Semantic Web,* because it would integrate and combine data producing other data (not semantic information, which is a human capacity, and requires understanding). He also contended that the *Semantic Web* as portrayed by Tim Berners-Lee and the people of the W3C (World Wide Web Consortium) was certainly not feasible either technically (at least not yet) or socially. This is because it would require the construction and success of a specific ontology, an ontology that would have to be created by machines and established globally.

At the time of writing, and five years after Floridi's criticism, we do not know whether he was right that the *Semantic Web*, as described by the W3C, will never be technically or socially feasible or whether it is true that it will be the web of the future, like many seem to suggest. However, we do know that web technologies have been developing well beyond the interactive features of web

2.0 with a new focus on *data*. This last chapter will explore these transformations by looking at some of the rapidly emerging literature on 'big data.' It will argue that, at present, scholars have much to gain if they deconstruct the technological myths around big data (boyd and Crawford, 2012; Crawford, 2013; Boellstorff, 2013) and engage in critical questions about human reflexivity and agency (Couldry and Powell, 2014). This latter aspect, I will argue, is particularly important in the study of digital activism. In fact, activists are critically engaging with the techno-social transformations of their times and are starting to consider the social and political implications of big data. Therefore, the chapter will return to the various debates touched on in the book and will argue that a key step that we need to take in the study of big data is to turn once more to the concept of 'practice' and thus appreciate how people through their everyday practices simultaneously reproduce and resist technological structures.

DECONSTRUCTING TECHNOLOGICAL HYPES: BIG DATA, DEMOCRACY, AND PEOPLE'S AGENCY

Web 3.0, Big Data, and the New Technological Hype

In 2010, I started writing an article together with colleague and friend Emiliano Treré, which brought together the business and the communication literature of the time and contended that significant transformations were taking place in web technologies, because business gurus and computer engineers were faced with a fundamental problem: the problem of data (Barassi and Treré, 2012). The rapid expansion of web 2.0 and mobile technologies created a situation whereby millions and millions of people were producing large amounts of data; yet there was little understanding of the ways in which we could manage and organize these increasingly larger datasets. The transformation in the production of data was radical and unimaginable. According to Floridi (2012), it is estimated that humanity accumulated 180 EB of data between the invention of writing and the year 2006, but that between 2006 and 2011 the total grew by ten times (Floridi, 2012:435).

The question about data was at the very heart of discussions about web developments. At the time, businesses and computer engineers argued for the importance of creating a new evolution of the web, the 'web 3.0,' which was defined by the creation of applications and platforms that managed, organized, and created meaning out of web data. The basic idea was to create databases and connect these databases to offer the possibility to search the web in an intelligent way, not by relying merely on keywords and their connections, as we do now, but by formulating complex sentences (Harris, 2008; Watson, 2011). The model shared some similarity to the Wikipedia model, which unlike Google that works by matching words contextualizes concepts creating new information through users' collaboration (Harris, 2008:29–31; Sheth and Thirunarayan, 2012:5). The concept of the web 3.0, as argued in our article, was entrenched with a profound business rhetoric, which stressed the importance of fostering collaboration among users, integrating data, and making digital identities easily traceable (Tasner, 2010).

In communication research and the social sciences, the concept of web 3.0 was short-lived and received very little attention (Fuchs, 2007; Fuchs et al., 2010; Barassi and Treré, 2012). Part of the reason was that scholars were aware of the fact that terms like *web 1.0*, *web 2.0*, and *web 3.0* were entrenched with a linear and evolutionary understanding that did not reflect the actual technological transformation of the web (Finnemann 2010). In fact, as Everitt and Mills (2009) argued, such concepts apply a version number and a consequent notion of progress 'to cultural shifts that speak more of a complex alliance of social, technological and commercial aims' (Everitt and Mills, 2009:765). Furthermore, the concept of web 3.0 received very little attention because scholars started to focus on a much stronger and all-encompassing concept, which enabled them to study society's changing attitude to data: namely, the concept of 'big data.'

The notion of 'big data' was introduced to start to make sense of the concentration of data in large datasets, which required supercomputers and, hence, the term 'big' data (Manovich, 2011). However, in the last five years it has been used to signify the increasingly larger amounts of data that we have available and the social, cultural, and technological processes that we use to make sense of this data. According to boyd and Crawford (2012), the concept of big data is defined as a *cultural, technological, and scholarly* phenomenon that rests on the interplay of three different yet interconnected dimensions.

First, we have the *technological dimension* that highlights the developments in computer technologies that have brought a maximization of computational power and algorithmic accuracy in the management and organization of large datasets. Second, we have an *analytical dimension*. In fact, in the last five years we have seen a dramatic change in the way in which businesses, research units, and governments draw on large datasets to identify social patterns in order to make economic, social, and legal claims. Third, we have a *mythological dimension*. In fact boyd and Crawford (2012) argue that we are witnessing a cultural turn with the widespread myth that large datasets offer a higher form of intelligence and accurate knowledge not possible before (boyd and Crawford, 2012:663).

The two scholars are right to highlight the different dimensions that the notion of big data entails. Their contribution is particularly interesting because they argue that technological and scientific developments are interconnected to broader cultural changes and the construction of technological discourse. In this book, I have argued that it is essential to understand the power of myth and discourse when we want to analyze the social impacts of technologies. This is because technological discourse enables processes of technological fetishism, whereby humans transform technologies in social agents that have an impact on people's everyday practices and, consequently, on the organization of society.

In this chapter, I want to focus on the mythological dimension of big data, because I believe that 'deconstructing the technological hype' around big data is of central importance if we really want to start to address its social and political implications. In deconstructing the technological hype around big data, I believe, it is essential that we take three fundamental steps. First, we need to critically explore the veracity of the claims about big data accuracy. Second, we need to explore the democratic challenges that big data poses by critically considering the relationship between big data, digital capitalism, and the neo-liberal policies of governments. Third, as Couldry and Powell (2014) have rightly argued, we need to consider issues of agency and reflexivity. This latter point, I will show, is particularly important in the study of digital activism.

Big Data, Raw Data, and Accuracy: Deconstructing Assumptions

As argued above, in order to deconstruct the technological hype around big data we need at first to critically question the claims that are made today about the 'accuracy' and importance of big data in society. Current discourses on big data are largely shaped by two different assumptions: a) The metadata produced by users is 'raw data' or, in other words, is a primary form of data that has not been subjected to processing and manipulation; and b) algorithmic logic and larger datasets offer us a precise and accurate type of knowledge, which enables us to frame individual and social patterns and use this knowledge for different purposes.

Both assumptions, as different scholars have shown (Manovich, 2011; boyd and Crawford, 2012; Crawford, 2013; Gitelman and Jackson, 2013; Boellstorff, 2013), cannot be proven. In the first place, it is clear that there is no such thing as 'raw data.' Gitelman and Jackson's (2013) edited volume, titled "Raw Data Is an Oxymoron," focuses precisely on the fact that all processes of data collection require framing and processing. This is also the case for metadata. In the second place, it is important to critically question the type of data that we have available within big datasets. In fact, as boyd and Crawford have argued: "Too often, Big Data enables the practice of apophenia: seeing patterns where none actually exist, simply because enormous quantities of data can offer connections that radiate in all directions" (boyd and Crawford, 2013:668). In fact, as the scholars rightly argue, the fact that we can trace connections and patterns does not necessarily mean that the knowledge we acquire from these connections and patterns is accurate. Part of the problem lies in the fact that big data is 'thin' data (Boellstorff, 2013), in the sense that it is a type of data that is systematically taken out of context (boyd and Crawford, 2012:670–671). Therefore, it seems clear that one of the first steps that we need to take in order to deconstruct the techno-social hype around big data is to critically consider the type of knowledge big data produces and how we organize and use this knowledge.

Between Discourse and Practice: Big Data and Digital Capitalism

A second step that we need to take when we want to deconstruct the technological hype around big data is to consider the connection between big data and corporate discourse and practice and, therefore, critically evaluate the relationship between big data and digital capitalism. In the introduction to this book, I looked at the work of Boltanski and Chiapello (2007) and argued that one of the principle characteristics of capitalism as an economic system is its ability to constantly renew itself. In my opinion it would be impossible to understand the big data phenomenon without looking at how this is tightly interconnected to a new trend in business that sees data as profit (Ohlhorst, 2013; Minelli et al., 2013; Mayer-Schonberger and Cuckier, 2013). A shared idea at the moment is that big data is good for money and that large corporations and small businesses will have to embrace the 'big data revolution' (Mayer-Schonberger and Cuckier, 2013). Of course, also within the business world, there are those who are critically questioning whether big data is indeed as profitable as it seems and are asking similar questions as the ones asked by critical internet scholars about the accuracy of the data produced (Fader in Gomes, 2012). Despite the few criticisms that are emerging in the business world, overall there is the assumption that big data is rich with profitable opportunities (Davenport, 2014). Observing the way in which the notion of big data has rapidly become established in the business world, Mayer-Schonberger and Cuckier (2013) argued:

> Data was no longer regarded as static or stale, whose usefulness was finished once the purpose for which it was collected, was achieved [...]. Rather data became a raw material of business, a vital economic input, used to create a new form of economic value. In fact with the right mind-set, data can be cleverly reused to become a fountain of innovation and new services.
>
> (Mayer-Schonberger and Cuckier, 2013:5)

It is not my place here to judge whether the new trend in business will in fact be profitable or not. Rather I want to critically reflect on the fact that the relationship between capitalism and big data, although it certainly may be profitable, can represent a real challenge for democratic processes, especially if we consider the issue of surveillance and the way in which big data and corporate interest are transforming the policies of governments.

With the development of web 2.0 technologies and mobile media, it became clear – as we have seen in *Chapter Four* – that user-generated data was being exploited for corporate purposes (Andrejevic, 2005, 2009). However, in the last five years following the Snowden affair, a more complex and dark scenario emerged. What became clear was that governments and web giants as well as mobile corporations had joined forces to surveil every aspect of citizen life (Raley, 2013) with critical implications for our public and legal lives (Ruppert, 2011; Hartzon and Selinger, 2013; Andrejevic, 2013). This has led to a situation whereby, as Dijck (2014) has argued, citizens' trust in institutions is at stake with key consequences for our democratic processes. In addition, the fact that governments are following the corporate trend around big data and finding new ways in which to exploit personal data for profit is raising key questions on individuals' rights to privacy. A prime example is represented by the changes affecting the healthcare system.

Therefore, in understanding the technological hype around big data and expanding our analysis of the socio-technical transformations that are affecting our societies, we need to be aware of the democratic challenges represented by the relationship between digital capitalism, big data, and the new policies of surveillance adopted by governments. At present the situation is extremely worrisome and key critical questions need to be addressed concerning our changing political economies.

Political Activism and Big Data? Reflexivity, Critique, and Negotiation

A third and necessary step that scholars need to take in the deconstruction of the technological hype around big data is to critically consider the way in which people are negotiating with it. In fact, as Couldry and Powell (2014) have argued, not only at present do we have little knowledge about issues of reflexivity and agency when we discuss big data, but also we need to be aware of the fact that:

> the potential disconnect between system and experience, phenomenology and political economy, can be overcome by examining on the ground agents' strategies for building alternative economies of information.
>
> (Couldry and Powell, 2013:4)

This latter point, I believe, is particularly important in the study of digital activism. During fieldwork, it became evident that activists were debating and reflecting on the issue of big data. In a Facebook chat with Javier, the web developer of *Ecologistas en Acción,* whom I have introduced in the previous chapters, he argued that he was starting to think about the problem and that he was worried. According to him, the most worrisome issue for political activists was the problem of safeguarding communicative autonomy and people's right to privacy. Javier believed that activists needed to seriously consider how they can challenge the 'control' over the data and push for the creation of new regulations to protect people's rights.

J: Perhaps we should make the use and processing of specific data illegal, or maybe not. In any way I think it is important to have a strong regulation, which can guarantee transparency [...] Like in other areas [of our lives] (i.e. labor, rights, etc.) what we are missing here is some form of international regulation over such basic human rights like the right to communicative privacy.

During my research, I met other activists who were starting to critically reflect on the fact that the sudden cultural obsession with data is leading to the breach of individual privacy rights and who believed that activists needed to act in order to protect individuals' communicative autonomy. Consequently, I came to the conclusion that activists were critically appraising the challenges of new web developments and foreseeing their implications. Unfortunately, I did not have the time or theoretical preparation for investigating at length the way in which activists were critically negotiating with the issue of big data. Yet I strongly believe that current research should focus on this process of negotiation.

Understanding elements of reflexivity when approaching the study of big data is particularly important because it enables us to appreciate that, as Couldry and Powell argued, activists are engaged in imagining and continuously developing ways to resist the current social and cultural trends brought about by big data by creating 'alternative information economies' (Couldry and Powell, 2013:4). This point was made clear by Blicero[1] from the Autistici/Inventati collective, when during an interview on societies' changing attitude to data, he explained:

B: It is evident that there is no going back, now the importance is to understand the implications of these transformations, and to seriously start reflecting on the issue of identity. Where does your personal/private identity begin? And where does the public one start? [...]. At the moment we should be starting to imagine how to create an infrastructure, similar to the new corporate models, but that is free from corporate power and challenges them. One idea could be to develop a service such as Open ID, which today enables web users to create a digital identity and surf the web with it. But Open ID requires your personal details. My idea is to create a service that gives a digital identity to people, without requiring their personal details. So when you surf the web they will not be able to identify you, and your web practices will no longer linked to your personal/computer ID. [...] You know we are at a difficult point, we know more or less what will happen, and we can predict the next stages of the web, but we don't really know yet what we are going to make of it, and what type of resources we'll have available [...].

As it emerges from Blicero's interview, activists are trying to develop web tactics that challenge the tracking of digital identities. In a fascinating article on the relationship between technological structures and people's practices Orlikowski (2000) argued that we need to be aware of the so-called 'emergent structures' and thus recognize the fact that users often circumvent inscribed ways of using technologies "either ignoring certain properties of the technology, working around them or inventing new ones that may go beyond or even contradict them" (2000:407). This point is particularly important if we want to understand activists' negotiation with big data and the alternative communication economies that these processes of negotiation can construct.

One interesting element that emerged during fieldwork was that although activists were clearly concerned about the fact that current web developments are challenging people's individual rights to privacy, they also believed that there were many margins for resistance and freedom that they could construct through their uses of corporate web platforms. This is not only because they could limit the type of information that they shared on the web, but also because they strongly believed that the 'tracing of digital identities' does not necessarily mean that governments and corporations have the control of personal identities. This latter point emerged particularly well in an interview with Davide, whom I introduced in *Chapter Five*:

D: Of course companies try to appropriate and exploit our information, yet they don't really succeed in framing our personal identities. The problem that companies face is that your individual identity is often different from your digital identity. You can be a friend on Facebook of the PD (Democratic Party in Italy), to monitor their activities but in truth hating them. You could be playing an online game and not being interested in gambling [...] there is no exact correspondence between online activities and real life, although they make you believe that there is.

As Davide highlighted, people's practices can be unpredictable, and thus the construction of metadata does not necessarily translate into a mirror of social reality, especially because metadata does not uncover the human 'intention' or reasoning between specific online choices. This understanding enables us to appreciate the fact that the 'tracking of digital identities' is not always as effective and all-encompassing as the 'panopticon' model of big brother surveillance wants us to believe (Andrejevic, 2009).

The understanding that there is a 'potential disconnect' (Couldry and Powell, 2014) between individuals' online uses and individual identities enables us to ask critical questions on the type of knowledge that big data produces. It seems clear to me that the understanding of digital practices requires a thick contextualization, a type of contextual knowledge that enables us to appreciate the beliefs and intentions whereby specific practices are ordered. This type of contextual knowledge as we have seen above (boyd and Crawford, 2012; Boellstorff, 2013) is missing from metadata analysis. This leads us to the understanding that, as Manovich (2011) has argued, we need to ask fundamental questions about our own research methodologies in the so-called 'big data era.' In particular, I believe, we should critically reflect on the continued importance of the ethnographic method. This is because, if social practices are unpredictable and need appropriate contextualization, with the ethnographic method we can highlight the unplanned, the unpredictable, and the disconnections (Strathern, 2002:309). Knowing how to deal with unpredictability is of central importance for scholars in this particular epoch, because it enables us to understand that if the techno-historical developments of the last decades are transforming social experience, they are doing so in multiple and often contradictory ways.

In this book, I focused on some of the contradictory ways in which web technologies have been transforming the everyday realities of political activists. The next part of the chapter will summarize the main arguments of the book.

ACTIVIST CULTURES AND TECHNOLOGICAL STRUCTURES, UNDERSTANDING ETHNOGRAPHIC TENSION

General Summary and Some Critical Reflections

In this book, I considered the ethnographic tensions that emerged in the encounter between activists' collective and democratic cultures on the one hand and digital capitalism on the other. Although I focused on the concept of digital capitalism, and on the social and cultural tensions that digital capitalism creates especially in the context of political activism, I certainly believe that – as mentioned in the introduction to the book – the cultural experiences witnessed on web platforms cannot be reduced to the tension between capitalism and everyday users. However, in this book I decided to focus on the cultural experiences created by tension between activist cultures and digital capitalism, because I felt that we had little data available on how activists – who have been fighting for years against capitalism – are dealing and negotiating with the bound relationship between web technologies and emerging forms of capitalist accumulation and exploitation.

The book was thus structured as follows. In *Chapter One*, I focused on the cultural variety and richness of the three different activist groups I worked with. I explored the history of the social movements in which they were embedded and described the political projects that shaped their political cultures and information ecologies. In the chapter, I highlighted the importance of the ethnographic method for the study of digital activism, and I argued that it is essential that we gain a 'thick understanding' of activists' political projects and cultures when we analyze their internet uses. It is only by doing so that we can realize that activists' media uses are constantly shaped by their political projects or, in other words, by their *media imaginaries*.

If in *Chapter One* I focused on describing the ethnographic contexts of my research, in *Chapter Two* I discussed the theoretical standpoint on which the research is based by looking at the question of technological agency. I have argued that in order to fully appreciate the way in which digital technologies have redefined political action – and to analyze the tension between activist cultures and digital capitalism – we need to develop a theoretical standpoint that enables us to appreciate the complex relationship between digital discourses and practices and re-frame our understanding of technological agency. The chapter proposed that there are three fundamental theoretical steps that we need to take in the development of this standpoint. The first step is to acknowledge the fact that digital discourses have an impact on everyday practices and, thus, look at how techno-utopian discourses on the democratic power of technologies have transformed activists' priorities and strategies. The second step is to understand the fact that digital discourses have become contested spaces of meaning in our Western societies (e.g. the network); this is because different political cultures imagine internet technologies in different ways and act according to their own imaginations. Therefore, we need to appreciate that web technologies are a contested terrain of imagination and practice. The third step is to look at the difference between the imaginaries and practices of the weak and the ones of power, between activist cultures and digital capitalism.

I have argued that the practices of power have a spatial dimension (De Certeau, 1980) and ultimately define the social environments that we live in. This is evident if we consider the development of the web as user interface. In fact, as different scholars have argued (Schiller, 2000; Curran, 2012), in the last two decades the web was largely shaped according to the imaginations and interest of corporate power. Of course, we need to understand the web as a complex socio-technical environment that is created by a variety of different and often contradicting technical applications, platforms, texts, discourses, cultural, political, and economic processes, practices, stories, lived experiences, and human relations. However, we must also acknowledge the fact that, in this socio-technical environment, like elsewhere in society, the neo-liberal agenda is hegemonic and, therefore, that the web is largely shaped by the cultural and social practices of capitalism.

This book argued that activists are not only critically aware of the fact that the web is largely shaped by the digital discourses and practices of corporate power but their everyday internet uses are largely defined by processes of negotiation with digital capitalism. These processes of negotiation are giving rise to a series of different 'ethnographic tensions' or, in other words, a series of collective experiences defined by the tension between activists' democratic needs on one side and the cultural processes reinforced by digital capitalism on the other. *Chapters Three, Four,* and *Five,* therefore, explored three main ethnographic tensions faced by activists when using web technologies as tools of political action. The tension created by self-centered communication processes and **networked individualism**, the tension created by the exploitation of user **digital labor** and corporate surveillance, and the tension created by the hegemonic temporality of **immediacy**.

Chapter Three argued that the very architecture of social media supports the development of individualized and egocentric forms of communication (Castells, 2007, 2009; Hodkinson, 2007; Fenton and Barassi, 2011), which promote a type of participation that is self-centered, networked, and individualistic. In contrast to those who advocate the benefits of this form of communication for the establishment of communicative and political autonomy (Castells, 2009, 2012), the chapter contended that the networked self creates a great deal of tension among political activists. Not only does mass self-communication enable a type of political participation that challenges collective processes of participation and meaning construction, but also it enhances the visibility of the individual over the collective with critical consequences for democratic deliberation. The chapter has therefore argued that social media enable a form of individualist autonomy, which is profoundly different from the notion of political autonomy as promoted by social movements where the self becomes simultaneously a subjective and collective subject. Unraveling the tension between networked individualism and the political autonomy of social movements, it has been argued, is of central importance if we want to appreciate the impact of social media on collective action. However, this is just one step in our argument. The next step is to understand the fact that different political cultures negotiate differently with the networked self and that this cultural difference defines the very nature of activists' use of social media.

In *Chapter Four,* I moved to the analysis of another ethnographic tension created by everyday web uses. I considered activists' critical awareness of, and negotiation with, the issue of *digital labor*. The chapter departed from an analysis of the different ways in which both the activists involved with *Ecologistas en Acción* and the *Corsari* understood the relationship between internet technologies and new forms of capitalist accumulation and exploitation. I have shown that while the activists in Spain focused on the expansion of 'free labor' within society and on the environmental damages of digital labor, the activists in Italy emphasized the issue of immaterial labor and 'precarization.' Therefore, the chapter argued, both activist cultures were defined by a harsh critique of the relationship between internet technologies and new forms of capitalist exploitation and accumulation. However, it has been shown that, despite activists being aware of the issue of digital labor, they also believe that online production enables them to produce a type of *value* that escapes the logic of capital.

In analyzing activists' relationships to corporate web 2.0 platforms, I thus argued that it is essential that we move away from the understanding of digital production as merely the production of data that can be turned into commodity (Hesmondhalgh, 2010; Khiabany, 2014). A way that we can do so is by learning from the insights of Marxist anthropology and by highlighting the connection between digital production and the production of human relationships. As the work of different Marxist anthropologists (Turner, 2006; Graeber, 2002, 2007) has shown, humans constantly produce social relationships, and these social relationships have an immense value, which is translated not only in material terms but also in representative terms. The chapter has thus argued that the understanding of the intrinsic value of human relationships, of their material and representative dimension, is key to an appreciation of the importance of web 2.0 technologies in the everyday life of political activists and of the many margins of freedom from corporate surveillance that they actively construct through their web 2.0 uses.

If *Chapter Four* focused on the issue of digital labor, *Chapter Five* considered the ethnographic tension created by the temporality of immediacy. The chapter argued that mobile media and web 2.0 technologies are creating a temporal context that is based on the notion of 'immediacy.' Combining the literature on capitalism and hegemonic time consciousness with the one of the anthropology of time, the chapter explored how the hegemonic temporality of immediacy is reproduced through activists' everyday practices. It has been argued that activists are critically aware of the negative impacts of immediacy on political processes and believe that immediacy challenges political elaboration, reflection, and actualization. Drawing from their testimonies and experiences, this chapter was meant to show that in the analysis of web technologies and social processes, scholars have much to gain if they appreciate that the problem of immediacy is one of the darkest effects of web developments and digital capitalism and needs to be properly addressed and understood.

In *Chapters Three, Four,* and *Five,* therefore, I explored the social tensions that arise in the encounter between activist cultures and digital capitalism. I have argued that while being important tools for political action, web 2.0 technologies challenge collective and democratic processes of meaning construction, identity formation, and political participation. In *Chapter Six* I took the argument a bit further. I contended that the social tensions experienced by political activists in their uses of web 2.0 technologies provide alternative media with a new social importance. The chapter focused in particular on printed media and on the relationship between activist magazines and online technologies. By investigating the material dimension of activist magazines as objects of mediation (Silverstone, 1994), the chapter argued that activist magazines – in contrast to online technologies that are more ephemeral and cannot be associated to a particular group – are embedded with collective values and meanings and are important tools in the construction of a feeling of belonging and affinity to the group. As shown, looking at why people – and especially grassroots political organizations – remain attached to printed media, while at the same time developing online ones, can raise critical questions on the connection between subjectivity, political association, and new technologies.

CONCLUSION

In one way or another all the different chapters in this book explored the multiple, contradictory, and fascinating ways in which activists negotiate with the corporate structure of web technologies. Acknowledging these processes of negotiation is of central importance as it enables us to realize that it is in the ways in which people imagine and negotiate with social and technological structures that social change happens. In 2005, as we were witnessing the 'birth' of the web 2.0 (O'Reilly, 2005), the sociologist Zygmunt Bauman published a book titled *Liquid Life*. The book critically reflected on the fact that within contemporary societies everything is not fixed but subjected to a continuous process of transformation, and these transformations occur fast, too fast. Bauman (2005) argued that we live in a world that has been affected by a liquidity of a sort, an acceleration and complication of human experience that has detached people from their sense of humanity. In many respects, his argument is a sound one: The advent of internet technologies and the continuous strengthening and making of online capitalism are transforming the meaning of objects, practices, and social experience. Many individuals within Britain and Western Europe are haunted by the fear of failing to catch up with the latest technologies and the fast moving events; they are often frightened about being left behind; they absorb the social contradictions of our current societies and are affected by a sense of fragility, uncertainty, and inability to cope (Bauman, 2005:15–37). This sense of fragility and powerlessness – this inability of processing and understanding the next 'big' transformation – can also be found today as we try to make sense of the advent of 'big data.'

One way in which we can make sense of the rapidly changing technological transformations and of the social implications that they bring about is to take a step back and critically deconstruct technological hypes by looking at the relationship between new technologies and capitalist discourse and practice and by taking into account the fact that people's negotiation and reaction to contemporary transformations can be extremely complex and creative. Liquidity does not necessarily replace materiality; old forms of political participation are not necessarily replaced by the new. Everything is subjected to social interaction, communication, and negotiation between people. Following Strathern (2002), I believe that from these interactions that are open-ended and complex come much of the creativity and energy of social life. Anthropology looks at these open-ended interactions and the way in which the old and new come together to create something different. To re-use Graeber's formulation, which partly triggered the idea behind this project, anthropology is here to remind us that human possibilities are almost in every way greater than we ordinarily believe (Graeber, 2007:1).

NOTE

1. Online name to protect the activist's anonymity.

Appendix 1
Activism on the Web: A Note on Method

THE TEMPORALITY OF ETHNOGRAPHY AND THE RESEARCH DESIGN

The project presented in this book is a result of five years of research (2006–2011), supported by the Arts and Humanities Research Council (AHRC) and the British Academy Small Research Grant Scheme. In 2006, as scholars discussed the empowering effects of internet technologies in the construction of insurgent networks of action by focusing on the new movements for global justice, I designed a research project that was meant to provide a 'thick' ethnographic analysis of an international solidarity campaign, which was embedded in the reality of the Labor Movement. The research was based on the premise that – although the social movement literature often emphasizes the novelty of global networks of communication and action – political and communication networks between movement organizations at transnational level have always existed, especially if we consider the international solidarity movement (Thorn, 2006). Therefore, rather than concentrating on the *new* movements that were made possible through the extension of internet technologies, my research focused on an 'old' international solidarity organization, the *Cuba Solidarity Campaign* (CSC). Focusing on an 'old' organization, I believed, could enable me to overcome assumptions of novelty and technological determinism, which have often constrained studies on social movement networks, and instead focus on their everyday and ordinary dimension.

For an entire year I volunteered at the offices of the *Cuba Solidarity Campaign* in North London. However, since the very beginning of fieldwork, it became evident that the reality of the organization developed on a variety of different levels and was constructed by the juxtaposition of many networked spaces. Marcus (1998) suggests that there is a variety of ways in which one can do multi-sited ethnographic fieldwork, such as following the thing, the story, the people, or the metaphor (1998:19). For my research I decided to follow the people and the media they produced. During fieldwork, I thus spent an entire year working at the CSC national office on a daily basis; I followed its organizers around Trade Union conferences, I spent days in

Parliament and evenings at social gatherings and events; I interviewed members of networked campaigning organizations and key figures in the Trade Union Movement; I volunteered to work for CSC at the music festival of Glastonbury, and I also traveled to Cuba, to participate in their work brigade at the Julio Antonio Mella International Camp, 40 km from Havana.

My research within the Cuba Solidarity Campaign explored the imaginaries and practices that defined activists' use of different media technologies and especially web technologies. After a yearlong ethnographic research, I reached the conclusion that web technologes have introduced new ways in which to imagine political action and participation. However, I realized that in order to conceptualize these transformations scholars needed to explore the complex interaction between social change and continuity and to take into account the dialectical relationship between the technical and the social. In addition I realized that activists were struggling with the technological constraints of the web as well as with its increased commercialization. Therefore, I came to the conclusion that I needed to critically investigate the processes of negotiation between activists and the political economy of the web.

Between 2010 and 2011 I decided to enrich my findings by looking at the ethnographic contexts of other two organizations in Europe. My hypothesis was that the relationship between internet technologies and political activism varied according to cultural and context-specific political imaginations and so did activists' negotiation with digital capitalism. Therefore, I decided to focus on two organizations, *Ecologistas en Acción* and the *Corsari*, which had two very different political cultures than the one of CSC.

Although as an anthropologist methodologically I have always been committed to long-term ethnographic research, like the one that I had done with CSC, in 2010 the lack of time and resources limited my possibility to carry out long-term fieldwork. However, drawing on Ortner's (1995) critique (see *Chapter One*), which had inspired my research with CSC, I proceeded to design a research project that would enable me to search for a certain degree of ethnographic thickness.

The premise of my research design was grounded on the belief that one of the real strengths of the ethnographic method needs to be found in its *temporality*: in the fact that the ethnographer commits himself or herself to understand another life world over an extensive period of time. It is only through time that the ethnographer resolves issues of access as well as issues of conceptual understanding. It was for this reason that I designed a project that enabled me to 'follow' both organizations for over a year. In order to do so, I alternated three different periods of 15–20 days of fieldwork, which took place in both organizations at different times of the year with a yearlong online ethnography.

Participant observation and informal conversations were key methodologies, which enabled me to actively engage with the social contexts of the different organizations and have a firsthand experience of their internal conflicts, alliances, and beliefs. During fieldwork, I collected a breadth and depth of observations and testimonies – across the different movements – on the meaning of their political practices and on how people responded to and negotiated with web developments.

Ethnography on the Ground/Ethnography Online

Within the three different contexts of research, I integrated real-life ethnographic research work with online ethnography. In contrast to those scholars (Kozinets, 2009) who believe that online ethnography can and should be merely carried only online, for my project I drew on the insights of Miller and Slater (2001) and Hine (2000). Thus, I carried out my research believing that there is a deep interconnection and integration between online and offline ethnographic contexts, and therefore we can only gain an ethnographically thick understanding if we appreciate how online practices, texts, and personal choices are often dictated by the real-life dynamics, beliefs, power relationships, and political imaginations that define the everyday life of the groups studied. Of course, in the last 20 years, we have been confronted with the rise and proliferation of 'social worlds' existing only online (Rheingold, 1993; Hine, 2000; Boellstorff, 2009). Here the most fascinating and ethnographically thick study is certainly the one of Boellstorff (2010) on *Second Life*. His study is brilliant because it challenges our ideas of the meaning of humanity, of social interaction, and of ethnographic practice. However, I approached fieldwork believing that an ethnographic analysis of digital activism needed to rely on a complex methodological approach that enabled me to explore the relationship between activists and web technologies by taking into account the different levels of interaction between online and offline environments.

Overall I structured my online ethnography within three different online environments: a) the web pages of the organizations, b) social media, and c) mailing lists. Within all these different platforms, I acted not only as an 'observer' but also as a 'participant' by sharing the links they shared, by engaging in email exchange and online chats, and by expressing my support for their online petitions and campaigns. In the context of CSC the online ethnography was carried out simultaneously with fieldwork. In the context of the *Corsari* and *Ecologistas*, I had more time to dedicate to the online ethnography, as I spent long periods in which I was not doing research in the field. Although the online ethnography was undertaken mostly in the time of a year, after leaving the field, I continued and I am continuing the practice of online participant observation.

During the years of research and beyond, I documented my online experiences with field notes through the practice of self-reflection. One of the advantages of online ethnography is represented, as Hine (2000) and

Markham (1998) have argued, by the fact that online ethnography is a way of knowing through direct experience. The richness of the ethnographic method in general partly lies in the fact that the ethnographer finds himself or herself immersed in a different world and proceeds to explore it through the self. It is for this reason that it is so important that the ethnographer documents his or her experience, self-reflections, worries, understandings, and breakthroughs in knowledge in field notes. Field notes are essential elements of ethnographic practice; they are essential because they enable the process of self-reflection. During my research, I realized that they are also central to the process of online ethnography.

Textual analysis was a fundamental aspect of my online ethnographic practice. On a daily basis, I analyzed the news items posted on the organizations' websites and social media accounts. Furthermore, I systematically engaged in email or social media exchanges with my informants. In all these research activities, I was required to engage with written and visual media texts. In the analysis of texts I focused on the syntagmatic understanding of meaning, namely on the way in which meaning is constructed by a relation of signs into a narrative sequence (Peterson, 2003; Burgelin, 1974). Although I do not agree with the atomistic and quantitative approach of the content analysis school, my methodological approach also included qualitative content analysis methodologies (Mayring, 2000), which focused upon the presence or absence of a particular content. To enrich my textual analysis, I also considered elements of intertextuality (Peterson, 2003) and explored the interconnected way in which the same message was transmitted by different media across different organizations.

Seeking Historical Depth, Life Narratives, and Interviews

One particular problem with participant observation online and offline is, as DeWalt and DeWalt (2002) have argued, is that with participant observation alone it is unlikely that the anthropologist will understand issues of transformation and change. My ethnographic work was therefore also enriched by two other methodologies, which were aimed at grasping the historical depth. In the first place I focused on the analysis of the printed magazines that acted as historical memory of two of the three organizations. During fieldwork, I analyzed most of the issues of the *CubaSí* magazine published between 1986 and 2008 and the issues of the *Ecologista* magazine that were published between 2008 and 2011. The analysis of magazines depended on the number of copies available in the office. Although CSC kept copies of most of the *CubaSí* issues, the copies available within the office of *Ecologistas en Acción* were quite limited.

My research was also enriched by 87 semi-structured interviews. During the interviews, I concentrated mostly on people's *life histories*. Within people's life accounts, the researcher can grasp issues of social change and historical transformation, and these were vital for addressing the questions of this project. My intention was to understand activists path to political involvement, to explore the way in which they experienced technological change, and to uncover the individual tensions and motivations. The choice of focusing on people's life narratives was motivated by the belief that memory is always shaped by omissions and moral choices and that these omissions and choices are usually defined by both collective and individual understandings (Tilly, 1994; Davis and Hastrup, 1992). In this respect, memory is political, social, and collective as well as personal, emotional, and individual. Following this understanding of memory, the life histories approach can provide the researcher not only with an historical dimension but also with insights concerning the way in which people internalize *collective repertoires* of the past (Tilly, 1994:244). This latter point is fundamental for the understanding of contemporary social movements. Social struggles depend highly on repertoires of contestation (Alleyene, 2000; Tilly, 1994:244). These repertoires of the past are often shaped by the life histories of the people involved in the struggles, being leading figures (e.g. Che Guevara, Malcom X, Martin Luther King) or simple participants. It is perhaps for this reason that Holland and Lave (2001) suggested: "Social struggles become personified, so that their forces assimilate the 'character' of the people from whom they are reproduced. Thus history is made in persons and by persons" (2001:30).

It was through the combination of participant observation, textual analysis, and life narratives that this research project came to life. *Activism on the Web* is the result of this research. Its aim is to offer a critical ethnographic reflection on the human experiences, beliefs, and understandings involved in the use of the web as a tool of political critique.

Ethical Considerations

Throughout its development, this research project respected the ASA Ethical Guidelines and relied on informed consent during its entire process. Fieldwork and interviews were based on my commitment to always protect the confidentiality and privacy of my informants and to develop a straightforward and transparent relationship with them. Many organizers and activists agreed for their name and experiences to be published. When activists chose anonymity, I relied on the use of pseudonyms and on the changing of identifying details. Furthermore, when using recording devices – such as the digital voice recorder – I always made sure that my informant felt free to turn it off at any time.

During both my offline and online research, a series of ethical considerations emerged. In fact I had access to a wide variety of private information, email exchanges, and personal conversations. I did not rely on these sources at any point without asking permission. Furthermore, throughout my fieldwork I had to engage with the already made and diffused self-representations of my informants. My ethnographic analysis, therefore, tried to create a dialogue between activists' own representations and beliefs and my own interpretation. Throughout my research, as much as I could, I discussed my interpretations with the people involved. My anthropological training has taught me that it is only through reflexive practices and negotiation that social researchers can avoid generalized assumptions and understandings. In this framework, I always tried to build on the criticisms and insights of my informants.

Bibliography

Adam, Barbara. 1994. *Time and Social Theory*. New ed. Cambridge: Polity Press.

Adams, Jason M. 2013. *Occupy Time: Technoculture, Immediacy, and Resistance After Occupy Wall Street*. New York, NY: Palgrave Pivot US.

Adkins, Lisa. 2009. "Sociological Futures: From Clock Time to Event Time" 14 (4) (8). https://www.academia.edu/653438/Sociological_Futures_From_Clock_Time_to_Event_Time.

———. 2011. "Practice as Temporalisation: Bordieu and the Economic Crisis." In *The Legacy of Pierre Bourdieu: Critical Essays*, edited by Simon Susen and Bryan S. Turner, 1st ed, 347–65. London; New York: Anthem Press.

Agamben, Giorgio. 1993. *The Coming Community*. Translated by Michael Hardt. Minneapolis: University of Minnesota Press.

Agger, Ben. 1989. *Fast Capitalism: A Critical Theory of Significance*. University of Illinois Press.

———. 2004. *Speeding up Fast Capitalism: Cultures, Jobs, Families, Schools, Bodies*. Paradigm Pub.

———. 2007. "Time Robbers, Time Rebels: Limits to Fast Capital." In *24/7: Time and Temporality in the Network Society*, edited by Robert Hassan and Ronald Purser, 1st ed, 195–219. Stanford, Calif: Stanford Business Books.

Ahmed. 2010. "Orientations Matter." In *New Materialisms: Ontology, Agency, and Politics*, edited by Diana Coole and Samantha Frost, 234–58. Duke University Press.

Ali, Tariq. 2008. *Pirates of the Caribbean: Axis of Hope*. London; New York: Verso.

Alleyne, Brian. 2000. *Personal Narrative & Activism: A Bio-Ethnography of "Life Experience with Britain."* London: Goldsmiths College.

Alvarez, Sonia, Evelyn Dagnino, and Arturo Escobar. 1998. "Introduction: The Cultural and the Political in Latin American Social Movements." In *Cultures of Politics Politics of Cultures: Re-Visioning Latin American Social Movements*, edited by Sonia E. Alvarez, Evelyn Dagnino, and Arturo Escobar, 1–33. Boulder, Colo: Westview Press.

"Amazon.com Link." 2014. Accessed November 19. http://www.amazon.co.uk/The-Culture-Speed-Immediacy-association/dp/1412912024.

Amin, Ash. 1994. *Post-Fordism: A Reader*. Oxford; Cambridge, Mass: Blackwell Pub.

Anderson, Benedict. 1991a. *Imagined Communities: Reflections on the Origin and Spread of Nationalism*. 2nd Revised ed. London; New York: Verso Books.

———. 1991b. *Imagined Communities: Reflections on the Origin and Spread of Nationalism*. 2nd Revised ed. London; New York: Verso Books.

Andreatta, Marco. 2004. "Movimenti E Democrazia Tra Globale E Locale: Il Caso Di Napoli." Presented at the National Conference of the SISP (Società Italiana di Scienza Politica), Padoa.

Andrejevic, Mark. 2003. *Reality TV: The Work of Being Watched*. 1st ed. Lanham, Md: Rowman & Littlefield Publishers, Inc.

———. 2009. *ISpy: Surveillance and Power in the Interactive Era*. Lawrence, Kan.: University Press of Kansas.

———. 2013. *Infoglut: How Too Much Information Is Changing the Way We Think and Know*. New York: Routledge.

Andrejevic, Mark, John Banks, John Edward Campbell, Nick Couldry, Adam Fish, Alison Hearn, and Laurie Ouellette. 2014. "Participations:dialogues on the Participatory Promise of Contemporary Culture and Politics." *International Journal of Communication* 8: 1089–1106.

Ang, Ien. 1995. *Living Room Wars: Rethinking Media Audiences: Rethinking Media Audiences for a Postmodern World*. London; New York: Routledge.

Appadurai, Arjun, ed. 1986. *The Social Life of Things: Commodities in Cultural Perspective*. Cambridge Cambridgeshire; New York: Cambridge University Press.

———. 1990. "Disjuncture and Difference in the Global Cultural Economy." *Theory, Culture & Society* 7 (2): 295–310. doi:10.1177/026327690007002017.

———. 1996. *Modernity at Large: Cultural Dimensions in Globalization*. Minneapolis, Minn: University of Minnesota Press.

Appay, Beatrice. 2010. "Precarization and Flexibility in the Labour Process: A Question of Legitimacy and a Major Challenge for Democracy." In *Globalization and Precarious Forms of Production and Employment: Challenges for Workers and Unions*, edited by Carole Thornley and Steve Jefferys. Cheltenham, UK; Northampton, MA: Edward Elgar Publishing.

Askew, Kelly. 2002. "Introduction to the Anthropology of Media." In *The Anthropology of Media: A Reader*, edited by Richard R. Wilk and Kelly Askew, 1–15. Malden, MA: Wiley-Blackwell.

Askew, Kelly, and Richard R. Wilk, eds. 2002. *The Anthropology of Media: A Reader*. Malden, MA: Wiley-Blackwell.

Atton, Chris. 2002. *Alternative Media*. Thousand Oaks, Calif.: SAGE.

———. 2004. *An Alternative Internet: Radical Media, Politics and Creativity*. Edinburgh: Edinburgh University Press.

Banks, Miranda J. 2010. "The Picket Line Online: Creative Labor, Digital Activism, and the 2007–2008 Writers Guild of America Strike." *Popular Communication* 8 (1): 20–33. doi:10.1080/15405700903502387.

Barassi, Veronica. 2009a. "Mediated Resistance: Alternative Media Imagination and Political Action in Britain." Ph.D., Goldsmiths College (University of London). http://ethos.bl.uk/OrderDetails.do?uin=uk.bl.ethos.514228.

———. 2009b. "Mediated Resistance: Alternative Media Imagination and Political Action in Britain." Ph.D., Goldsmiths College (University of London). http://ethos.bl.uk/OrderDetails.do?uin=uk.bl.ethos.514228.

———. 2012. "Ethnographic Cartographies: Social Movements, Alternative Media and the Spaces of Networks." *Social Movement Studies* 12 (1): 48–62. doi:10.1080/14742837.2012.650951.

———. 2013. "When Materiality Counts: The Social and Political Importance of Activist Magazines in Europe." *Global Media and Communication* 9 (2): 135–51. doi:10.1177/1742766513479717.

Barassi, Veronica, and Emiliano Treré. 2012. "Does Web 3.0 Come after Web 2.0? Deconstructing Theoretical Assumptions through Practice." *New Media & Society* 14 (8): 1269–85. doi:10.1177/1461444812445878.

Barck, Karlheinz. 1988. "Materiality, Materialism, Performance." In *Materialities of Communication*, edited by Hans Ulrich Gumbrecht and Karl Ludwig Pfeiffer, 258–73. Stanford University Press.

Barry, Andrew. 2001. *Political Machines: Governing a Technological Society.* London: A&C Black.

Baudrillard, Jean. 1983. *Simulations.* Paris: Semiotext(e), Inc.

Bauman, Zygmunt. 2005. *Liquid Life.* Cambridge England; Malden MA: Wiley.

Bauwens, Michel. 2008. "The Social Web and Its Social Contracts: Some Notes on Social Antagonism in Netarchical Capitalism." *Re-Public.* http://www.re-public. gr/en/?p=261.

Bayat, Asef. 2009. *Life as Politics: How Ordinary People Change the Middle East.* 1st ed. Stanford, Calif: Stanford University Press.

Beck, Andrew. 2005. *Cultural Work: Understanding the Cultural Industries.* London; New York, N.Y: Routledge.

Benkler, Yochai. 2007. *The Wealth of Networks: How Social Production Transforms Markets and Freedom.* New Haven Conn.: Yale University Press.

Bergson, Henri. 1908. *Essai sur les données immédiates de la conscience.* F. Alcan. http://archive.org/details/essaisurlesdonn00berggoog.

Berners-Lee, Tim. 2005. "Berners-Lee on the Read/write Web." *BBC*, August 9, sec. Technology. http://news.bbc.co.uk/1/hi/technology/4132752.stm.

Beynon, Huw, and Theo Nichols. 2006. *Patterns of Work in the Post-Fordist Era: Fordism And Post-Fordism.* Cheltenham, UK; Northampton, MA: Edward Elgar Pub.

Bird, S. Elizabeth, ed. 2009. *The Anthropology of News & Journalism: Global Perspectives.* Bloomington: Indiana University Press.

Bloch, Maurice, and Maurice Bloch, eds. 2010. "Introduction." In *Marxist Analyses and Social Anthropology*, 1st ed. Routledge.

Bloch, Maurice, and Jonathan Parry. 1989. "Introduction Money and the Morality of Exchange." In *Money and the Morality of Exchange*, edited by Maurice Bloch and Jonathan Parry, 1–33. Cambridge University Press.

Boellstorff, Tom. 2010. *Coming of Age in Second Life: An Anthropologist Explores the Virtually Human.* Princeton: Princeton University Press.

———. 2013. "Making Big Data, in Theory." *First Monday* 18 (10). http://firstmonday. org/ojs/index.php/fm/article/view/4869.

Boltanski, Luc, and Eve Chiapello. 2007. *The New Spirit of Capitalism.* London; New York: Verso.

Borkenau, Franz. 2013. *Socialism National Or International Routledge Library Editions: Political Science.* Routledge.

Bourdieu, Pierre. 1964. "The Attitude of the Algerian Peasant toward Time." In *Mediterranean Countrymen: Essays in the Social Anthropology of the Mediterranean*, edited by Julian Alfred Pitt-Rivers, 55–72. Paris and the Hague: Mouton.

———. 1970. "The Berber House or the World Reversed." *Social Science Information* 9 (2): 151–70. doi:10.1177/053901847000900213.

———. 1977. *Outline of a Theory of Practice.* Edited by Jack Goody. Translated by Richard Nice. Cambridge, U.K.; New York: Cambridge University Press.

boyd, danah, and Kate Crawford. 2012. "Critical Questions for Big Data." *Information, Communication & Society* 15 (5): 662–79. doi:10.1080/1369 118X.2012.678878.

Boyd, D., and J. Heer. 2006. "Profiles as Conversation: Networked Identity Perfor-
mance on Friendster." In *Proceedings of the 39th Annual Hawaii International
Conference on System Sciences, 2006. HICSS '06*, 3:59c – 59c. doi:10.1109/
HICSS.2006.394.

Brauchler, Birgit, and John Postill. 2010. *Theorising Media and Practice*. Oxford;
New York: Berghahn Books.

Braverman, Harry. 1974. *Labor and Monopoly Capitalism: The Degradation of
Work in the Twentieth Century*. New York: Monthly Review Press.

Brophy, Enda. 2006. "System Error: Labour Precarity and Collective Organizing
at Microsoft." *Canadian Journal of Communication* 31 (3). http://cjc-online.ca/
index.php/journal/article/view/1767.

Buchanan, Tom. 1991. *The Spanish Civil War and the British Labour Movement*.
Cambridge University Press.

Bulmer-Thomas, Victor. 1989. *Britain and Latin America: A Changing Relationship*.
Cambridge University Press.

Burgelin, Olivier. 1974. "Structural Analysis and Mass Communication." In *Sociology of Mass Communication*, edited by Denis McQuail, 313–33. Harmond-
sworth: Penguin Books.

Burston, Jonathan, Nick Dyer-Whiteford, and Alison Hearn. 2010. "Digital Labour:
Workers, Authors, Citizens." *Ephemera: Theory & Politics in Organization* 10 (3/4).

Calhoun, Craig. 1995. "New Social Movements of the Early 19th Century." In *Repertoires and Cycles of Collective Action*, edited by Mark Traugott, 173–217. Durham: Duke University Press Books.

Callero, Peter L. 2013. *The Myth of Individualism: How Social Forces Shape Our
Lives*. 2nd ed. Lanham: Rowman & Littlefield Publishers.

Callon, Michel, and Bruno Latour. 1981. "Unscrewing the Big Leviathan: How
Actors Macrostructure Reality and How Sociologists Help Them to Do So'." In
*Advances in Social Theory and Methodology: Toward an Integration of Micro-
and Macro-Sociologies*, edited by Karin Knorr-Cetina and Aaron Victor Cicourel,
277–303. Routledge.

Cammaerts, Bart, Alice Mattoni, and Patrick McCurdy. 2013. *Mediation and Protest
Movements*. Bristol, UK; Wilmington, NC, USA: Intellect.

Carey, James W. 1992. *Communication as Culture: Essays on Media and Society*.
London; New York, N.Y: Routledge.

Caruso, Loris, Alberta Giorgi, Alice Mattoni, and Gianni Piazza. 2010. *Alla ricerca
dell'Onda. I nuovi conflitti nell'istruzione superiore*. Edited by Franco Angeli.
Milano: Franco Angeli.

Castells, Manuel. 1983. *The City and the Grassroots: A Cross-Cultural Theory of
Urban Social Movements*. Berkeley, Calif.: University of California Press.

———. 1996. *The Rise of the Network Society: Information Age: Economy, Society,
and Culture v. 1*. Chichester, West Sussex; Malden, MA: Wiley-Blackwell.

———. 1997. *The Power of Identity: The Information Age - Economy, Society, and
Culture: 2*. Malden, MA: Wiley-Blackwell.

———. 2000. "Materials for an Exploratory Theory of the Network society1." *The
British Journal of Sociology* 51 (1): 5–24. doi:10.1111/j.1468–4446.2000.00005.x.

———. 2001. *The Internet Galaxy: Reflections on the Internet, Business, and Society*.
Oxford: OUP Oxford.

———. 2007. "Communication, Power and Counter-Power in the Network Society."
International Journal of Communication 1 (1): 29.

———. 2009. *Communication Power*. Oxford: Oxford University Press.

———. 2012. *Networks of Outrage and Hope: Social Movements in the Internet Age*. 1st ed. Cambridge, UK; Malden, MA: Polity Press.

Castoriadis, Cornelius. 1991. *Philosophy, Politics, Autonomy: Essays in Political Philosophy*. 1st ed. New York: Oxford University Press.

———. 1998. *The Imaginary Institution of Society*. Translated by Kathleen Blamey. Cambridge: The MIT Press.

Chambers, Deborah. 2013. *Social Media and Personal Relationships: Online Intimacies and Networked Friendship*. Palgrave Macmillan.

Christensen, Henrik Serup. 2011. "Political Activities on the Internet: Slacktivism or Political Participation by Other Means?" *First Monday* 16 (2). http://firstmonday. org/ojs/index.php/fm/article/view/3336.

Chyi, Hsiang Iris, and Mengchieh Jacie Yang. 2009. "Is Online News an Inferior Good? Examining the Economic Nature of Online News among Users." *Journalism & Mass Communication Quarterly* 86 (3): 594–612. doi:10.1177/ 107769900908600309.

Cohen, Anthony. 1994. *Self Consciousness: An Alternative Anthropology of Identity*. London; New York: Routledge.

Cole, G. D. H. 2001. *Short History of the British Working Class Movement: 1900– 1937*. Psychology Press.

Coleman, E. Gabriella. 2012. *Coding Freedom: The Ethics and Aesthetics of Hacking*. Princeton: Princeton University Press.

Coleman, James S. 1988. "Social Capital in the Creation of Human Capital." *American Journal of Sociology [Supplement: Organizations and Institutions: Sociological and Economic Approaches to the Analysis of Social Structure]* 94: 95–120.

Collins, Steven. 1985. "Categories, Concepts or Predicaments? Remarks on Mauss' Use of Philosophical Terminology." In *The Category of the Person: Anthropology, Philosophy, History*, edited by Michael Carrithers, Steven Collins, and Steven Lukes, First Paperback ed, 46–83. Cambridge Cambridgeshire; New York: Cambridge University Press.

Colon Diaz, Manuel. 1987. "Conservacion de La Naturaleza Y Opinion Publica: El Movimiento Ecologista En Andalucia." *Revista de Estudios Andaluces* 9: 1–13.

Coman, Mihai. 2005. "Media Anthropology: An Overview." presented at the European Association of Social Anthroplogy Conference, Debrecen, Hungary.

Coole, Diana, and Samantha Frost. 2010. *New Materialisms: Ontology, Agency, and Politics*. Durham: Duke University Press.

Couldry, Nick. 2003. *Contesting Media Power: Alternative Media in a Networked World: Alternative Media in a Networked World*. Lanham, Md: Rowman & Littlefield Publishers.

———. 2004. "Theorising Media as Practice." *Social Semiotics* 14 (2): 115–32. doi: 10.1080/1035033042000238295.

———. 2008. "Actor Network Theory and Media: Do They Connect and on What Terms?" In *Connectivity, Networks and Flows: Conceptualizing Contemporary Communications*, edited by Andreas Hepp, Friedrich Krotz, Shaun Moores, and Carsten Winter, 93–110. Cresskill, NJ: Hampton Press, Inc. http://www.hamptonpress.com/.

Couldry, Nick, and James Curran. 2003. "The Paradox of Media Power." In *Contesting Media Power: Alternative Media in a Networked World: Alternative*

Media in a Networked World, edited by Nick Couldry and James Curran, 3–17. Lanham, Md: Rowman & Littlefield Publishers.

Couldry, Nick, and Andreas Hepp. 2009. "What Should Comparative Media Research Be Comparing? Towards a Transcultural Approach to Media Cultures." In *Internationalizing Media Studies: Impediments and Imperatives*, edited by Daya Kishan Thussu, 1st ed, 32–47. Routledge.

Couldry, Nick, and Alison Powell. 2014. "Big Data from the Bottom up." *Big Data & Society* 1 (2): 2053951714539277. doi:10.1177/2053951714539277.

Coyer, Kate, Tony Dowmunt, and Alan Fountain. 2007. *The Alternative Media Handbook*. 1st ed. London; New York: Routledge.

Crapanzano, Vincent. 2004. *Imaginative Horizons: An Essay in Literary-Philosophical Anthropology*. Chicago: University of Chicago Press.

Crawford, Kate. 2013. "The Hidden Biases in Big Data." *Harvard Business Review*. https://hbr.org/2013/04/the-hidden-biases-in-big-data.

Critical Art Ensemble. 1994. *Electronic Civil Disobedience: And Other Unpopular Ideas*. Brooklyn, N.Y.: Autonomedia.

Cuba Solidarity Campaign. 1999. "CubaSí Magazine, Winter Issue."

"Cultural Imperialism: A Critical Introduction." 2014. Accessed November 17. http://quod.lib.umich.edu/cgi/t/text/text-idx?c=acls;idno=heb02149.

Curran, James. 2012. "Rethinking Internet History." In *Misunderstanding the Internet*, edited by James Curran, Natalie Fenton, and Des Freedman, 34–67. London New York: Routledge.

Curran, James, Julian Petley, and Ivor Gaber. 2005. *Culture Wars: The Media and the British Left*. Edinburgh University Press.

Dagnino, Evelyn. 1997. "Culture, Citizenship and Democracy: Changing Discourses and Practices of the Latin American Left'." In *Between Resistance and Revolution: Cultural Politics and Social Protest*, edited by Professor Richard G. Fox and Orin Starn, 33–64. New Brunswick, N.J: Rutgers University Press.

Davenport, Thomas H. 2014. *Big Data at Work*. Boston MA Harvard Business Review Press.

Dawson, Michael, and John Bellamy Foster. 2000. "Virtual Capitalism." In *Capitalism and the Information Age: The Political Economy of the Global Communication Revolution*, edited by Ellen Meiksins Wood, John Bellamy Foster, and Robert D. McChesney, 51–67. New York: Monthly Review Press.

Day, Richard J. F. 2005. *Gramsci Is Dead: Anarchist Currents in the Newest Social Movements*. London; Ann Arbor, MI: Toronto: Pluto Press.

De Certeau, Michel. 1980. "On the Oppositional Practices of Everyday Life." Translated by Fredric Jameson and Carl Lovitt. *Social Text*, no. 3: 3. doi:10.2307/466341.

———. 1984. *The Practice of Everyday Life*. Berkeley, Calif.: University of California Press.

Deleuze, Gilles, and Felix Guattari. 1987. *A Thousand Plateaus: Capitalism and Schizophrenia*. New Edition. London: Continuum International Publishing Group Ltd.

Della Porta, Donatella Della, and Gianni Piazza. 2008. *Voices of the Valley, Voices of the Straits: How Protest Creates Community*. New York; Oxford: Berghahn Books.

Della Porta, Donatella, and Mario Diani. 1999. *Social Movements: An Introduction*. Malden, MA: Wiley-Blackwell.

Della Porta, Donatella, and Sidney G. Tarrow, eds. 2004. *Transnational Protest and Global Activism*. Lanham, MD: Rowman & Littlefield Publishers.

DeWaal Ester, Klaus Schönbach, and Edmund Lauf. 2005. "Online Newspapers: A Substitute or Complement for Print Newspapers and Other Information Channels?" *Communications* 30 (1): 55–72. doi:10.1515/comm.2005.30.1.55.

DeWalt, Kathleen Musante, and Billie R. DeWalt. 2002. *Participant Observation: A Guide for Fieldworkers*. Rowman Altamira.

Dorey, Peter. 2006. *Conservative Party and the Trade Unions*. Routledge.

Downing, John. 1995. "Alternative Media and the Boston Tea Party." In *Questioning the Media: A Critical Introduction*, edited by John D. H. Downing, Ali Mohammadi, and Annabelle Sreberny, 2nd Revised ed, 238–53. Thousand Oaks, Calif: SAGE Publications, Inc.

———. 2000. *Radical Media: Rebellious Communication and Social Movements*. 1st ed. Thousand Oaks, Calif: Sage Publications, Inc.

———. 2003. "Audiences and Readers of Alternative Media: The Absent Lure of the Virtually Unknown." *Media, Culture & Society* 25 (5): 625–45. doi:10.1177/01634437030255004.

Dumont, Louis. 1992. *Essays on Individualism: Modern Ideology in Anthropological Perspective*. Chicago: University of Chicago Press.

Dunlop, John T., Karl Marx, Friedrich Engels, Richard Hyman, A. Lozovsky, Vladimir Ilyich Lenin, Thomas Taylor Hammond, et al. 1987. *Theories of the Labor Movement*. Edited by Bruce Nissen and Simeon Larson. Detroit, Mich: Wayne State University Press.

Durkheim, Émile. 2008. *The Elementary Forms of Religious Life*. Edited by Mark S. Cladis. Translated by Carol Cosman. Oxford, England: Oxford Paperbacks.

Dyer-Whiteford, Nick. 1999. *Cyber-Marx: Cycles and Circuits of Struggle in High-Technology Capitalism*. Champaign, Ill.: University of Illinois Press.

———. 2001. "Empire, Immaterial Labor, the New Combinations, and the Global Worker." *Rethinking Marxism* 13 (3–4): 70–80. doi:10.1080/089356901101242009.

Earl, Jennifer, and Katrina Kimport. 2011. *Digitally Enabled Social Change: Activism in the Internet Age*. Cambridge, Mass.: MIT Press.

Edgar Gómez Cruz, Elisenda Ardèvol. 2013. "Some Ethnographic Notes on a Flickr Group." *Photographies* 6 (1). doi:10.1080/17540763.2013.788836.

Edwards, David B. 2004. "Print Islam: Media and Religious Revolution in Afghanistan." In *Social Movements: An Anthropological Reader*, edited by June Nash, 1st ed, 99–117. Malden, MA: Wiley-Blackwell.

Edwards, Elizabeth, Janice Hart, Elizabeth Edwards, and Janice Hart, eds. 2004. "'Photographs as Objects.'" In *Photographs Objects Histories: On the Materiality of Images*, 1–16. London; New York: Routledge.

Edwards, Jeanette, Penny Harvey, and Peter Wade. 2008. "Introduction: Epistemologies in Practice." In *Anthropology and Science: Epistemologies in Practice*, edited by Jeanette Edwards, Penny Harvey, and Peter Wade, 1–19. Oxford; New York: Berg Publishers.

Elias, Norbert. 1993. *Time: An Essay*. Translated by Edmund Jephcott. Reprint ed. Oxford: Blackwell Pub.

Elliott, Anthony. 2003. *Critical Visions: New Directions in Social Theory*. Rowman & Littlefield.

Ellison, N.B., C. Lampe, and C. Steinfield. 2009. "Social Network Sites and Society: Current Trends and Future Possibilities." *Interactions Magazine* 16 (1): 6–9.

Ellison, Nicole B., Charles Steinfield, and Cliff Lampe. 2007. "The Benefits of Facebook 'Friends:' Social Capital and College Students' Use of Online Social Network Sites." *Journal of Computer-Mediated Communication* 12 (4): 1143–68. doi:10.1111/j.1083–6101.2007.00367.x.

Engels, Friedrich. 2010. *The Origin of the Family, Private Property and the State.* Penguin UK.

Evans-Pritchard, E. E. 1939. "Nuer Time-Reckoning." *Africa* 12 (02): 189–216. doi:10.2307/1155085.

Everitt, Dave, and Simon Mills. 2009. "Cultural Anxiety 2.0." *Media, Culture & Society* 31 (5): 749–68. doi:10.1177/0163443709339463.

Feigenbaum, Anna, Fabian Frenzel, and Patrick McCurdy. 2013. *Protest Camps.* London: Zed Books.

Fenton, Natalie, and Veronica Barassi. 2011. "Alternative Media and Social Networking Sites: The Politics of Individuation and Political Participation." *The Communication Review* 14 (3): 179–96. doi:10.1080/10714421.2011.597245.

Fernandez Duran, Ramon. 2008. *El crepúsculo de la era trágica del petróleo: pico del oro negro y colapso financiero (y ecológico) mundial.* Madrid: Ecologistas en Accion.

Finnemann, Niels Ole. 2010. "Christian Fuchs: Internet and Society – Social Theory in the Information Age. London: Routledge. 2008." *MedieKultur. Journal of Media and Communication Research* 26 (48): 4.

Fisher, Eran. 2010. *Media and New Capitalism in the Digital Age: The Spirit of Networks.* Basingstoke and New York, NY: Palgrave Macmillan.

Floridi, Luciano. 2009. "Web 2.0 vs. the Semantic Web: A Philosophical Assessment." *Episteme* 6 (01): 25–37. doi:10.3366/E174236000800052X.

———. 2012. "Big Data and Their Epistemological Challenge." *Philosophy and Technology* 25 (4): 435–37.

Fox, Professor Richard G., Orin Starn, and Sonia Alvarez, eds. 1997. "Reweaving the Fabric of Collective Action: Social Movements and the Challenges of the 'Actually Existing Democracy' in Brazil'." In *Between Resistance and Revolution: Cultural Politics and Social Protest,* 83–118. New Brunswick, N.J: Rutgers University Press.

Franklin, Bob. 2010. "Introduction." *Journalism Studies* 11 (4): 442–63. doi:10.1080/14616701003802535.

Friedman, Jonathan. 2000. *Cultural Identity and Global Process.* London; Thousand Oaks, Calif: Sage Publications UK.

Fuchs, Christian. 2007. *Internet and Society: Social Theory in the Information Age.* London and New York: Routledge.

———. 2010. "studiVZ: Social Networking in the Surveillance Society." *Ethics and Inf. Technol.* 12 (2): 171–85. doi:10.1007/s10676–010–9220–z.

———. 2013a. "Class and Exploitation on the Internet." In *Digital Labor: The Internet as Playground and Factory,* edited by Trebor Scholz, 211–25. New York, NY: Routledge.

———. 2013b. "Digital Prosumption Labour on Social Media in the Context of the Capitalist Regime of Time." *Time & Society,* October, 0961463X13502117. doi:10.1177/0961463X13502117.

———. 2014. *Digital Labour and Karl Marx.* London; New York, N.Y: Routledge.

Fuchs, Christian, Wolfgang Hofkirchner, Matthias Schafranek, Celina Raffl, Marisol Sandoval, and Robert Bichler. 2010. "Theoretical Foundations of the Web: Cognition, Communication, and Co-Operation. Towards an Understanding of Web 1.0, 2.0, 3.0." *Future Internet* 2 (1): 41–59. doi:10.3390/fi2010041.

Fuchs, Christian, and Sebastian Sevignani. 2013. "What Is Digital Labour? What Is Digital Work? What's Their Difference? And Why Do These Questions Matter for Understanding Social Media?" *tripleC: Communication, Capitalism & Critique. Open Access Journal for a Global Sustainable Information Society* 11 (2): 237–93.

Funk, Tom. 2008. *Web 2.0 and Beyond: Understanding the New Online Business Models, Trends, and Technologies.* Westport, Conn: Greenwood Press.

Gauntlett, David. 2011. *Making Is Connecting: The Social Meaning of Creativity, from DIY and Knitting to YouTube and Web 2.0.* 1st ed. Cambridge, UK; Malden, MA: Polity Press.

Gell, Alfred. 1992. *The Anthropology of Time: Cultural Constructions of Temporal Maps and Images.* Oxford; Providence: Berg 3PL.

———. 1998. *Art and Agency: An Anthropological Theory.* Oxford; New York: Clarendon Press.

Georgescu-Roegen, Nicolas. 2011. *From Bioeconomics to Degrowth: Georgescu-Roegen's "New Economics" in Eight Essays.* Edited by Mauro Bonaiuti. London; New York, NY: Routledge.

Gerbaudo, Paolo. 2012. *Tweets and the Streets: Social Media and Contemporary Activism.* London: Pluto Press.

Giddens, Anthony. 1991. *The Consequences of Modernity.* 1st ed. Stanford, Calif.: Stanford University Press.

Gillmor, Dan. 2006. *We the Media: Grassroots Journalism By the People, For the People.* 1st ed. Beijing; Sebastopol, CA: O'Reilly Media.

Gill, Rosalind, and Andy Pratt. 2008. "In the Social Factory? Immaterial Labour, Precariousness and Cultural Work." *Theory, Culture & Society* 25 (7–8): 1–30. doi:10.1177/0263276408097794.

Ginsburg, Faye. 1994. "Culture/Media: A (Mild) Polemic." *Anthropology Today* 10 (2): 5. doi:10.2307/2783305.

Ginsburg, Faye D., Lila Abu-Lughold, and Brian Larkin, eds. 2002. *Media Worlds: Anthropology on New Terrain.* Berkeley: University of California Press.

Gitelman, Lisa. 2013. *"Raw Data" Is an Oxymoron.* Cambridge, MA London, England: MIT Press.

Gitelman, Lisa, and Virgina Jackson. 2013. "Introduction: Raw Data Is an Oxymoron." In *Raw Data Is an Oxymoron*, edited by Lisa Gitelman and Jackson, 1–15. Cambridge; London: MIT Press.

Gomes, Lee. 2012. "Is There Big Money in Big Data?" *MIT Technology Review.* May 3. http://www.technologyreview.com/news/427786/is-there-big-money-in-big-data/.

Goody, Jack. 2013. *Capitalism and Modernity: The Great Debate.* John Wiley & Sons.

Gosden, Chris, and Yvonne Marshall. 1999. "The Cultural Biography of Objects." *World Archaeology* 31 (2): 169–78. doi:10.1080/00438243.1999.9980439.

Graeber, David. 2002a. "The New Anarchists." *New Left Review*, II, , no. 13 (February): 61–73.

———. 2002b. *Towards an Anthropological Theory of Value: The False Coin of Our Own Dreams.* New York: Palgrave Macmillan.

———. 2007. *Possibilities: Essays on Hierarchy, Rebellion, and Desire.* Oakland, CA: AK Press.

———. 2011. *Debt: The First 5,000 Years.* BROOKLYN, NY: Melville House.

———. 2013. "It Is Value That Brings Universes into Being." *HAU: Journal of Ethnographic Theory* 3 (2): 219–43. doi:10.14318/hau3.2.012.

Granovetter, Mark S. 1973. "The Strength of Weak Ties." *American Journal of Sociology* 78 (6): 1360–80.

Green, Sarah, Penny Harvey, and Hannah Knox. 2005. "Scales of Place and Networks: An Ethnography of the Imperative to Connect through Information and Communications Technologies." *Current Anthropology* 46 (5): 805–26. doi:10.1086/432649.

Gregg, Melissa. 2011. *Work's Intimacy.* 1st ed. Cambridge, UK; Malden, MA: Polity Press.

Gupta, Akhil, and James Ferguson. 1992. "Beyond 'Culture': Space, Identity, and the Politics of Difference." *Cultural Anthropology* 7 (1): 6–23.

Gurevitch, G. 1990. "Varieties of Social Time." In *Sociology of Time,* edited by Hassard. Basingstoke: Palgrave Schol, Print UK.

Hall, Gary. 2008. *Digitize This Book!: The Politics of New Media, Or Why We Need Open Access Now.* Minneapolis: University of Minnesota Press.

Hallin, Daniel C., and Paolo Mancini. 2004. *Comparing Media Systems: Three Models of Media and Politics.* Cambridge University Press.

Hands, Joss. 2010. *@ Is for Activism: Dissent, Resistance and Rebellion in a Digital Culture.* 1st ed. London; New York: Pluto Press.

Hannerz, Ulf. 2004. *Foreign News: Exploring the World of Foreign Correspondents.* Chicago: University of Chicago Press.

Hardt, Michael, and Antonio Negri. 2000. *Multitude: War and Democracy in the Age of Empire.* New York: Penguin.

———. 2001. *Empire.* Cambridge, Mass.: Harvard University Press.

Harris, Daniel. 2008. *Web 2.0 Evolution into The Intelligent Web 3.0: 100 Most Asked Questions on Transformation, Ubiquitous Connectivity, Network Computing, Open ... Databases and Intelligent Applications.* Australia: Emereo Pty Ltd.

Hart, Keith. 2007. "Marcel Mauss: In Pursuit of the Whole. A Review Essay." *Comparative Studies in Society and History* 49 (02): 473–85. doi:10.1017/S0010417507000564.

Hartzog, Woodrow, and Evan Selinger. 2013. "Big Data in Small Hands." *Stanford Law Review Online* 66 (September): 81.

Harvey, David. 1991. *The Condition of Postmodernity: An Enquiry into the Origins of Cultural Change.* Oxford England; Cambridge, Mass.: Wiley-Blackwell.

———. 2003. "The Fetish of Technology: Causes and Consequences." *Macalester International* 13 (1). http://digitalcommons.macalester.edu/macintl/vol13/iss1/7.

Hassan, Robert. 2003. "Network Time and the New Knowledge Epoch." *Time & Society* 12 (2–3): 225–41. doi:10.1177/0961463X030122004.

———. 2007. "Network Time." In *24/7: Time and Temporality in the Network Society,* edited by Robert Hassan and Roland Purser, 1st ed, 37–62. Stanford, Calif: Stanford Business Books.

———. 2009. *Empires of Speed: Time and the Acceleration of Politics and Society.* BRILL.

———. 2014. "A Temporalized Internet." *The Political Economy of Communication* 2 (1). http://polecom.org/index.php/polecom/article/view/27.

Hassard, John. 1990. *The Sociology of Time*. Macmillan.

Hastrup, Kirsten, and John Davis. 1992. "History and the People without Europe." In *Other Histories*, 1–14. London; New York, N.Y: Routledge.

Herzfeld, Michael. 2000. *Anthropology: Theoretical Practice in Culture and Society*. Malden, Mass: Wiley-Blackwell.

Hesmondhalgh, David. 2010. "User-Generated Content, Free Labour and the Cultural Industires." *Ephemera: Theory & Politics in Organization* 10 (3/4).

Hindman, Matthew. 2008. *The Myth of Digital Democracy*. Princeton: Princeton University Press.

Hine, Christine. 2000. *Virtual Ethnography*. Thousand Oaks, Calif.: SAGE.

Hodges, Matt. 2008. "Rethinking Time's Arrow Bergson, Deleuze and the Anthropology of Time." *Anthropological Theory* 8 (4): 399–429. doi:10.1177/1463499608096646.

Hodkinson, Paul. 2007. "Interactive Online Journals and Individualization." *New Media & Society* 9 (4): 625–50. doi:10.1177/1461444807076972.

Holland, Dorothy, and Jean Lave. 2001. *History in Person: Enduring Struggles, Contentious Practice, Intimate Identities*. Santa Fe, N.M.; Oxford: James Currey: SAR Press.

Holloway, John. 2002. *Change the World without Taking Power: The Meaning of Revolution Today*. London; Sterling, Va: Pluto Press.

Hollowell, Jonathan. 2008. *Britain Since 1945*. John Wiley & Sons.

Hornborg, Alf. 1992. "Machine Fetishism, Value, and the Image of Unlimited Good: Towards a Thermodynamics of Imperialism." *Man* 27 (1): 1. doi:10.2307/2803592.

Horst, Heather A. 2012. *Digital Anthropology*. Edited by Daniel Miller. London; New York: Berg Publishers.

Howley, Kevin. 2005. *Community Media: People, Places, and Communication Technologies*. Cambridge University Press.

Huws, Ursula. 2003. *The Making of a Cybertariat: Virtual Work in a Real World*. Monthly Review Press.

Ingold, Tim. 2000. *The Perception of the Environment: Essays on Livelihood, Dwelling and Skill*. Reissue ed. London; New York: Routledge.

Jakobsson, Peter, and Fredrik Stiernstedt. 2010. "Pirates of Silicon Valley: State of Exception and Dispossession in Web 2.0." *First Monday* 15 (7). doi:10.5210/fm.v15i7.2799.

Jarrett, Kylie. 2008. "Interactivity Is Evil! A Critical Investigation of Web 2.0." *First Monday* 13 (3). http://firstmonday.org/ojs/index.php/fm/article/view/2140.

Jenkins, Henry. 2008. *Convergence Culture: Where Old and New Media Collide*. 2nd Revised ed. New York: New York University Press.

Jordan, Tim. 2004. *Activism!: Direct Action, Hacktivism and the Future of Society*. Reaktion Books.

Joyce, Mary. 2010. *Digital Activism Decoded: The New Mechanism of Change*. 1st ed. New York: Central European University Press.

Juris, Jeffrey S. 2008. *Networking Futures: The Movements against Corporate Globalization*. Durham, N.C: Duke University Press Books.

———. 2012. "Reflections on #Occupy Everywhere: Social Media, Public Space, and Emerging Logics of Aggregation." *American Ethnologist* 39 (2): 259–79. doi:10.1111/j.1548-1425.2012.01362.x.

Juris, Jeffrey S., and Alexander Khasnabish, eds. 2013. *Insurgent Encounters: Transnational Activism, Ethnography, and the Political*. Durham; London: Duke University Press.

Kaun, Anne, and Fredrik Stiernstedt. 2014. "Facebook Time: Technological and Institutional Affordances for Media Memories." *New Media & Society* 16 (7): 1154–68. doi:10.1177/1461444814544001.

Kearney, M. 1995. "The Local and the Global: The Anthropology of Globalization and Transnationalism." *Annual Review of Anthropology* 24 (1): 547–65. doi:10.1146/annurev.an.24.100195.002555.

Keightley, Emily. 2012. "Introduction: Time, Media and Modernity." In *Time, Media and Modernity*, edited by Emily Keightley, 1–25. Palgrave Macmillan.

———. 2013. "From Immediacy to Intermediacy: The Mediation of Lived Time." *Time & Society* 22 (1): 55–75. doi:10.1177/0961463X11402045.

Kellner, Douglas. 2002. "Theorizing Globalization." *Sociological Theory* 20 (3): 285–305. doi:10.1111/0735-2751.00165.

Kelty, Christopher. 2012. "Geeks, Social Imaginaries, and Recursive Publics." *Cultural Anthropology* 20 (2): 185–214.

Khasnabish, Alex. 2008. *Zapatismo Beyond Borders: New Imaginations of Political Possibility*. Toronto: University of Toronto Press, Scholarly Publishing Division.

Khiabany, Gholam. 2014. "Uneven and Combined Independence of Social Media in the Middle East: Technology, Symbolic Production and Unproductive Labor." In *Media Independence: Working with Freedom or Working for Free?*, edited by James Bennett and Niki Strange, 1st ed, 261–81. New York: Routledge.

Klein, Naomi. 2001. *No LOGO*. Barcelona; Buenos Aires; México: Paidos Iberica, Ediciones S. A.

Knox, Hannah, Mike Savage, and Penny Harvey. 2006. "Social Networks and the Study of Relations: Networks as Method, Metaphor and Form." *Economy and Society* 35 (1): 113–40. doi:10.1080/03085140500465899.

Kollock, Peter. 1998. "The Economies of Online Cooperation: Gifts and Public Goods in Cyberspace." In *Communities in Cyberspace*, edited by Peter Kollock and Marc Smith, 220–42. London; New York: Routledge.

Kopytoff, Igor. 1986. "The Cultural Biography of Things: Commodization as Process." In *The Social Life of Things: Commodities in Cultural Perspective*, edited by Arjun Appadurai, 64–95. Cambridge Cambridgeshire; New York: Cambridge University Press.

Kowal, Donna. 2002. "Digitizing and Globalizing Indigenous Voices: The Zapatista Movement." In *Critical Perspectives on the Internet*, edited by Greg Elmer. Lanham, Md.: Rowman & Littlefield.

Kozinets, Robert V. 2009. *Netnography: Doing Ethnographic Research Online*. Thousand Oaks, Calif.: SAGE.

La Calle Dominguez, Juan J., Manuel Ortiz Heras, David Ruiz Gonzalez, and Isidro Sanchez Sanchez. 2001. "Movimientos ecologistas en Espana del siglo XX." In *Movimientos sociales y Estado en la España contemporánea*. Univ de Castilla La Mancha.

Laclau, Ernesto. 1996. *Emancipation(s)*. London; New York: Verso.

Laclau, Ernesto, and Chantal Mouffe. 2001. *Hegemony and Socialist Strategy: Towards a Radical Democratic Politics*. London; New York: Verso.

Langlois, Andrea, and Frédéric Dubois. 2005. *Autonomous Media: Activating Resistance & Dissent*. Montreal, CA: Cumulus Press.

Langlois, Ganaele, Fenwick McKelvey, Greg Elmer, and Kenneth Werbin. 2009. "FCJ-095 Mapping Commercial Web 2.0 Worlds: Towards a New Critical Ontogenesis." http://fourteen.fibreculturejournal.org/fcj-095-mapping-commercial-web-2-0-worlds-towards-a-new-critical-ontogenesis/.

Latouche, Serge. 2009. *Farewell to Growth*. Polity.

Latour, Bruno. 2005. *Reassembling the Social: An Introduction to Actor-Network-Theory*. Oxford; New York: OUP Oxford.

Latour, Bruno, and Steve Woolgar. 1986. *Laboratory Life: The Construction of Scientific Facts*. Edited by Jonas Salk. Reprint ed. Princeton, N.J: Princeton University Press.

Laux, Henning. 2011. "The Time of Politics: Pathological Effects of Social Differentiation." *Time & Society* 20 (2): 224–40. doi:10.1177/0961463X11402439.

Lazzarato, Maurizio. 1996. "Immaterial Labor." In *Radical Thought in Italy: A Potential Politics,* edited by Virno, Paolo, 133–51. Minneapolis: University of Minnesota Press,.

Leccardi, Carmen. 2007. "New Temporal Perspectives in the 'High-Speed Society.'" In *24/7: Time and Temporality in the Network Society*, edited by Robert Hassan and Ronald Purser, 1st ed, 25–37. Stanford, Calif: Stanford Business Books.

Leong, Susan, Teodor Mitew, Marta Celletti, and Erika Pearson. 2009a. "The Question Concerning (Internet) Time." *New Media & Society*, November. doi:10.1177/1461444809349159.

———. 2009b. "The Question Concerning (Internet) Time." *New Media & Society*, November. doi:10.1177/1461444809349159.

———. 2009c. "The Question Concerning (Internet) Time." *New Media & Society*, November. doi:10.1177/1461444809349159.

Li, Xigen, and Hsiang Iris Chyi. 2013. "Re-Examining the Market Relation between Online and Print Newspapers: The Case of Hong Kong." In *Internet Newspapers: The Making of a Mainstream Medium*, 193–205. Routledge.

Lievrouw, Leah. 2011. *Alternative and Activist New Media*. 1st ed. Cambridge, UK; Malden, MA: Polity Press.

Livingstone, Sonia. 2003. "On the Challenges of Cross-National Comparative Media Research." *European Journal of Communication* 18 (4): 477–500.

Lovink, Geert. 2007a. "Indifference of the Networked Presence: On Time Management of the Self." In *24/7: Time and Temporality in the Network Society*, edited by Robert Hassan and Ronald Purser, 1st ed, 161–73. Stanford, Calif: Stanford Business Books.

———. 2007b. *Zero Comments: Blogging and Critical Internet Culture*. New ed. New York: Routledge.

Lyotard, J F. 1996. "Les Immatériaux." In *Thinking about Exhibitions*, edited by Reesa Greenberg, Bruce W. Ferguson, and Sandy Nairne, 159–75. London: Psychology Press.

Macpherson, Crawford Brough. 2011. *The Political Theory of Possessive Individualism: Hobbes to Locke*. Oxford University Press.

Malinowski, Bronislaw. 1927. "Lunar and Seasonal Calendar in the Trobriands." *The Journal of the Royal Anthropological Institute of Great Britain and Ireland* 57 (January): 203. doi:10.2307/2843682.

Manovich, Lev. 2012. "Trending: The Promises and Challenges of Big Social Data." In *Debates in the Digital Humanities*, edited by Matthew K. Gold, 460–75. U of Minnesota Press.

Marcus, George E., ed. 1996. *Connected: Engagements with Media!*. Chicago: University of Chicago Press.

———. 1998. *Ethnography Through Thick and Thin*. Princeton, N.J.: Princeton University Press.

Markham, Annette N. 1998. *Life Online: Researching Real Experience in Virtual Space*. Lanham, Md.: Rowman Altamira.

Marsden, Christopher T. 2010. *Net Neutrality: Towards a Co-Regulatory Solution*. A&C Black.

Marwick, Alice. 2005. "'I'm a Lot More Interesting than a Friendster Profile': Identity Presentation, Authenticity and Power in Social Networking Services." Presented at the Association of Internet Researchers 6.0: Internet Generations, Chicago, May 9.

Marx, Karl. 1990. *Capital: Critique of Political Economy v. 1*. Edited by Ernest Mandel. Translated by Ben Fowkes. New ed. London; New York: Penguin Classics.

Marx, Karl, and Friedrich Engels. 2012. *The Communist Manifesto: A Modern Edition*. Verso Books.

Mattelart, Armand. 1996. *The Invention of Communication*. U of Minnesota Press.

Mattoni, Alice. 2012. *Media Practices and Protest Politics How Precarious Workers Mobilise by Mattoni, Alice (AUTHOR) Jun-28-2012 Hardback*. Ashgate Publishing Group.

Mauss, Marcel. 1985. "A Category of the Human Mind: The Notion of Person and the Notion of Self." In *The Category of the Person: Anthropology, Philosophy, History*, edited by Michael Carrithers, Steven Collins, and Steven Lukes, First Paperback ed, 1–26. Cambridge Cambridgeshire; New York: Cambridge University Press.

———. 2000. *The Gift: The Form and Reason for Exchange in Archaic Societies*. Translated by W. D. Halls. New York: W. W. Norton & Company.

Mayer-Schonberger, Viktor, and Kenneth Cukier. 2013. *Big Data: A Revolution That Will Transform How We Live, Work and Think*. London: John Murray.

Mayo, Marjorie. 2005. *Global Citizens: Social Movements and the Challenge of Globalization*. London: Zed Books.

Mayring, Philipp. 2000. "Qualitative Content Analysis." *Forum Qualitative Sozialforschung / Forum: Qualitative Social Research* 1 (2). http://www.qualitative-research.net/index.php/fqs/article/view/1089.

McCaughey, Martha, and Michael D. Ayers, eds. 2003. *Cyberactivism: Online Activism in Theory and Practice*. New York: Routledge.

McChesney, Robert D., Ellen Meiksins Wood, and John Bellamy Foster, eds. 1998. *Capitalism and the Information Age: The Political Economy of the Global Communication Revolution*. New York: Monthly Review Press.

McChesney, Robert W. 2013. *Digital Disconnect*. New York: THE NEW PRESS.

McChesney, Robert W., and John Nichols. 2002. *Our Media, Not Theirs: The Democratic Struggle against Corporate Media*. New York: Seven Stories Press.

McCurdy, Patrick. 2011. "Theorizing 'Lay Theories of Media': A Case Study of the Dissent! Network at the 2005 Gleneagles G8 Summit." *International Journal of Communication* 5 (0): 20.

McDowell, Linda, and Susan Christopherson. 2009. "Transforming Work: New Forms of Employment and Their Regulation." *Cambridge Journal of Regions, Economy and Society* 2 (3): 335–42. doi:10.1093/cjres/rsp024.

Meikle, Graham. 2003. *Future Active: Media Activism and the Internet*. Annandale, N.S.W.; New York: Routledge.

Melucci, Alberto. 1996. *Challenging Codes: Collective Action in the Information Age*. Cambridge England; New York: Cambridge University Press.

Miller, Daniel. 1997. *Material Culture and Mass Consumption*. 1st ed. Oxford, UK; New York: Wiley-Blackwell.

———. 2001. *Home Possessions: Material Culture Behind Closed Doors*. London: Bloomsbury Academic.

———. 2008. *The Comfort of Things*. Cambridge, UK; Malden, MA: Polity Press.

———. 2011. *Tales from Facebook*. 1st ed. Cambridge, UK; Malden, MA: Polity Press.

———. 2013. *Stuff*. Hoboken, N.J.: John Wiley & Sons.

Miller, Daniel, and Don Slater. 2001. *The Internet: An Ethnographic Approach*. Oxford; New York: Berg 3PL.

Minelli, Michael, Michele Chambers, and Ambiga Dhiraj. 2013. *Big Data, Big Analytics: Emerging Business Intelligence and Analytic Trends for Today's Businesses*. 1st ed. Hoboken, N.J.: John Wiley & Sons.

Montagna, Nicola. 2006. "The De-commodification of Urban Space and the Occupied Social Centres in Italy [1]." *City* 10 (3): 295–304. doi:10.1080/13604810600980663.

———. n.d. "The de-Commodification of Urban Space and the Occupied Social Centres in Italy'." *City* 10 (3): 295–304.

Morley, David. 1992. *Television, Audiences and Cultural Studies*. London; New York: Routledge.

———. 2006. *Media, Modernity, Technology: The Geography of the New*. New ed. New York: Routledge.

Moroni, Primo. n.d. "Origine Dei Centri Sociali Autogestiti a Milano. Appunti per Una Storia Possibile." In *Comunità Virtuali. I Centri Sociali in Italia*, edited by VV AA, x–xx.

Morozov, Evgeny. 2011. *The Net Delusion: How Not to Liberate the World*. London: Penguin.

Morris, Brian. 1994. *Anthropology of the Self: The Individual in Cultural Perspective*. Pluto Press.

Morrison, Kenneth. 2006. *Marx, Durkheim, Weber: Formations of Modern Social Thought*. 2nd ed. London; Thousand Oaks, Calif.: SAGE Publications Ltd.

Mosco, Vincent. 2004. *The Digital Sublime: Myth, Power and Cyberspace*. Cambridge, Mass.; London: MIT Press.

Mosco, Vincent, and Dan Schiller. 2001. *Continental Order?: Integrating North America for Cybercapitalism*. Lanham, Md.: Rowman & Littlefield.

Munn, Nancy D. 1992. "The Cultural Anthropology of Time: A Critical Essay." *Annual Review of Anthropology* 21 (1): 93–123. doi:10.1146/annurev.an.21.100192.000521.

Nardi, Bonnie, and Vicki O'Day. 1999. "Information Ecologies: Using Technology with Heart: Chapter Four: Information Ecologies." *First Monday* 4 (5). http://firstmonday.org/ojs/index.php/fm/article/view/672.

Negroponte, Nicholas. 1996. *Being Digital*. New ed. London: Coronet Books.

Neilson, Brett, and Ned Rossiter. 2008. "Precarity as a Political Concept, Or, Fordism as Exception." *Theory, Culture & Society* 25 (7–8): 51–72. doi:10.1177/0263276408097796.

Nugent, Stephen. 1997. "Anthropology and Cultural Studies." In , edited by Stephen Nugent and Cris Shore, 1–11. London: Pluto Press.

Nunziato, Dawn C. 2009. *Virtual Freedom: Net Neutrality and Free Speech in the Internet Age*. Stanford Law Books.

Nyland, C. 1990. "Capitalism and the History of Work-Time Thought." In *The Sociology of Time*, edited by John Hassard. Palgrave Macmillan. http://www.palgrave.com%2Fpage%2Fdetail%2Fthe-sociology-of-time-john-hassard%2F%3FK%3D9780333440926.

Ohlhorst, Frank J. 2013. *Big Data Analytics: Turning Big Data into Big Money.* 1st ed. Hoboken, N.J: John Wiley & Sons.

O'Reilly, Tim. 2005. *What Is Web 2.0: Design Patterns and Business Models for the Next Generation of Software.* 1st ed. O'Reilly Media.

Orlikowski, Wanda J. 2000. "Using Technology and Constituting Structures: A Practice Lens for Studying Technology in Organizations." *Organization Science* 11 (4): 404–28. doi:10.1287/orsc.11.4.404.14600.

Orlikowski, Wanda J. (Wanda Janina), and Sloan School of Management. Center for Information Systems Research. 1991. *The Duality of Technology: Rethinking the Concept of Technology in Organizations.* Cambridge, Mass.: Center for Information Systems Research, Sloan School of Management, Massachusetts Institute of Technology. http://archive.org/details/dualityoftechnol00orli.

Ortner, Sherry B. 1995. "Resistance and the Problem of Ethnographic Refusal." *Comparative Studies in Society and History* 37 (01): 173–93. doi:10.1017/S0010417500019587.

Parikka, Jussi. 2007. *Digital Contagions: A Media Archaeology of Computer Viruses.* Bern, Switzerland: Peter Lang.

Peterson, M. A. 2003. *Anthropology & Mass Communication: Media and Myth in the New Millennium.* New York; Oxford: Berghahn Books.

Petranker, Jack. 2007. "The Presence of Others: Network Experience as an Antidote to the Subjectivity of 'Time." In *24/7: Time and Temporality in the Network Society*, edited by Robert Hassan and Ronald Purser, 1 edition, 173–95. Stanford, Calif: Stanford Business Books.

Pfaffenberger, B. 1988. "Fetished Objects and Humanised Nature: Towards an Anthropology of Technology." *Man* 23 (2). doi:10.2307/2802804.

Pfeiffer, Karl Ludwig. 1988. "The Materiality of Communication." In *Materialities of Communication*, edited by Hans Ulrich Gumbrecht and Karl Ludwig Pfeiffer, 1–15. Stanford University Press.

Pimlott, Herbert. 2011. "'Eternal Ephemera' or the Durability of 'disposable Literature': The Power and Persistence of Print in an Electronic World." *Media, Culture & Society* 33 (4): 515–30. doi:10.1177/0163443711398690.

Pink, Sarah. 2006. *The Future of Visual Anthropology: Engaging the Senses.* Taylor & Francis.

Pollard, Sidney. 1999. *Labour History and the Labour Movement in Britain.* Farnham, Surrey, UK: Ashgate.

Postill, John. 2002. "Clock and Calendar Time A Missing Anthropological Problem." *Time & Society* 11 (2–3): 251–70. doi:10.1177/0961463X02011002005.

———. 2014. "Democracy in an Age of Viral Reality: A Media Epidemiography of Spain's Indignados Movement." *Ethnography* 15 (1): 51–69. doi:10.1177/1466138113502513.

Powdermaker, Hortense. 1950. *Hollywood the Dream Factory.* 1st ed. London: Little, Brown and Company.

Putnam, Robert. 2001. *Bowling Alone: The Collapse and Revival of American Community.* New ed. New York: Simon & Schuster Ltd.

Raley, Rita. 2013. "Datavaillance and Counterveilance." In *Raw Data Is an Oxymoron*, edited by Lisa Gitelman and Virgina Jackson, 121–47. Cambridge, Mass.: MIT Press.

Rash, Wayne. 1997. *Politics on the Nets: Wiring the Political Process.* New York: W.H. Freeman & Company.

Recio, Albert. 1992. "Los problemas del movimiento ecologista en el estado Espa-nol." In *Ecología política: cuadernos de debate internacional*. Barcelona: FUHEM ICARIA.

Reynolds, Glenn. 2007. *An Army of Davids: How Markets and Technology Empower Ordinary People to Beat Big Media, Big Government, and Other Goliaths*. anno-tated ed. Nashville, Tenn.: Thomas Nelson.

Rheingold, Howard. 1993. *The Virtual Community: Homesteading on the Elec-tronic Frontier*. Cambridge, Mass.: MIT Press.

———. 2003. *Smart Mobs: The Next Social Revolution*. New ed. Cambridge, MA: Perseus Books.

Ribeiro, Gustavo L. 1998. "Cybercultural Politics: Political Activism at a Distance in a Transnational World." In *Cultures of Politics Politics of Cultures: Re-Visioning Latin American Social Movements*, edited by Sonia E. Alvarez, Evelyn Dagnino, and Arturo Escobar, 325–53. Boulder, Colo: Westview Press.

Richardson, John. 1986. "The Forms of Capital." In *Handbook of Theory and Research for the Sociology of Education*, 241–61. New York: Greenwood.

Richardson, John G., and Pierre Bourdieu, eds. 1986. "The Forms of Capital." In *Handbook of Theory and Research for the Sociology of Education*, 242–58. New York: Greenwood.

Riechmann, Jorge. 2004. *Gente que no quiere viajar a Marte: ensayos sobre ecología, ética y autolimitación*. Los Libros de la Catarata.

Rockmore, Tom. 2002. *Marx After Marxism: The Philosophy of Karl Marx*. Oxford; Malden, MA: Wiley-Blackwell.

Rodrigues Cardoso, Carla. 2010. "The Future of Newsmagazines." *Journalism Studies* 11 (4): 577–86. doi:10.1080/14616701003638467.

Rodriguez, Clemencia. 2000. "Civil Society and Citizens' Media: Peace Architects for the New Millennium." In *Redeveloping Communication for Social Change: Theory, Practice, and Power*, edited by Karin Gwinn Wilkins, 147–60. Lanham, Md: Rowman & Littlefield Publishers.

———. 2011. *Citizens' Media Against Armed Conflict: Disrupting Violence in Colombia*. University of Minnesota Press.

Rodriguez, Clemencia, Dorothy Kidd, and Laura Stein, eds. 2009. *Making Our Media: Global Initiatives Toward a Democratic Public Sphere: v.1: Creating New Communication Spaces*. Cresskill, NJ: Hampton Press.

Roig, Antoni, and Gemma San Cornelio. 2013. "The Fruits of My Own Labour: A Case Study on Clashing Models of Co-Creativity in the New Media Land-scape." *International Journal of Cultural Studies*, 1367877913503828. doi:10.1177/1367877913503828.

Rootes, Christopher. 1999. "Environmental Movements: From Local to Global." In *Environmental Movements: Local, National and Global*, edited by Christopher Rootes, 1–13. London: Routledge.

Rosa, Hartmut. 2013. *Social Acceleration: A New Theory of Modernity*. Columbia University Press.

Rosa, Hartmut, and William E. Scheuerman. 2009a. *High-Speed Society: Social Acceleration, Power, and Modernity*. Edited by Hartmut Rosa and William E. Scheuerman. Penn State Press.

———. 2009b. *High-Speed Society: Social Acceleration, Power, and Modernity*. Penn State Press.

Rosenberg, Howard, and Charles S. Feldman. 2008. *No Time To Think: The Menace of Media Speed and the 24-Hour News Cycle*. A&C Black.

Rossiter, Brett Neilson and Ned. 2014. "FCJ-022 From Precarity to Precariousness and Back Again: Labour, Life and Unstable Networks." Accessed November 28. http://five.fibreculturejournal.org/fcj-022-from-precarity-to-precariousness-and-back-again-labour-life-and-unstable-networks/.

Rothenbuhler, Eric W., and Mihai Coman. 2005. *Media Anthropology*. Thousand Oaks, Calif.: SAGE Publications.

Ruggiero, Vincenzo. 2000. "New Social Movements and the 'Centri Sociali' in Milan." *The Sociological Review* 48 (2): 167–85. doi:10.1111/1467-954X.00210.

Ruppert, E. 2011. "Population Objects: Interpassive Subjects." *Sociology* 45 (2): 218–33. doi:10.1177/0038038510394027.

Rushe, Dominic. 2015. "Large US Tech Firms Plan 'Go Slow' Day in Protest over Net Neutrality Rules." *The Guardian*. Accessed January 19. http://www.theguardian.com/technology/2014/sep/04/etsy-mozilla-reddit-protest-net-neutrality.

Sahlins, Marshall. 2005. *Culture in Practice: Selected Essays*. 2nd ed. New York: Zone Books.

Sánchez, Manuel Jiménez. 2005. *El impacto político de los movimientos sociales: un estudio de la protesta ambiental en España*. CIS.

Sandoval, Marisol, and Christian Fuchs. 2010. "Towards a Critical Theory of Alternative Media." *Telemat. Inf.* 27 (2): 141–50. doi:10.1016/j.tele.2009.06.011.

Sayers, Janet, Mary Evans, and Nanneke Redclift. 2010. *Engels Revisited: Feminist Essays*. Routledge.

Scannell, Paddy. 1996. *Radio, Television and Modern Life*. Oxford, UK; Cambridge, Mass., USA: Blackwell Publishers.

Scheuerman, William E. 2004. *Liberal Democracy and the Social Acceleration of Time*. Baltimore, Md: Johns Hopkins University Press.

Schiller, Dan. 2000. *Digital Capitalism: Networking the Global Market System*. New ed. Cambridge, Mass.: MIT Press.

Scholz, Trebor. 2013. *Digital Labor: The Internet as Playground and Factory*. New York, Routledge.

Segal, Howard P. 1985. *Technological Utopianism in American Culture*. Syracuse, N.Y.: Syracuse University Press.

Sennett, Richard. 2007. *The Culture of the New Capitalism*. 1st ed. New Haven, Conn: Yale University Press.

Sheth, Amit, and Krishnaprasad Thirunarayan. 2012. *Semantics Empowered Web 3.0: Managing Enterprise, Social, Sensor, and Cloud-Based Data and Services for Advanced Applications*. San Rafael, Calif.: Morgan & Claypool Publishers.

Shirky, Clay. 2008. *Here Comes Everybody: The Power of Organizing Without Organizations*. New York: Penguin Books.

Silverstone, Roger. 1994. *Television and Everyday Life*. London; New York: Routledge.

Slater, David. 1998. "Rethinking the Spatialities of Social Movements: Questions of (B)orders, Culture and Politics in Global Times." In *Cultures of Politics Politics of Cultures: Re-Visioning Latin American Social Movements*, edited by Sonia E. Alvarez, Evelyn Dagnino, and Arturo Escobar, 380–405. Boulder, Colo: Westview Press.

Sneath, David, Martin Holbraad, and Morten Axel Pedersen. 2009. "Technologies of the Imagination: An Introduction." *Ethnos* 74 (1): 5–30. doi:10.1080/00141840902751147.

Spitulnik, Debra. 1993. "Anthropology and Mass Media." *Annual Review of Anthropology* 22 (1): 293–315. doi:10.1146/annurev.an.22.100193.001453.

Sreberny, A., and G. Khiabany. 2010. *Blogistan: The Internet and Politics in Iran.* London; New York: I. B. Tauris.

Stalder, Felix. 2006. *Manuel Castells: The Theory of the Network Society.* Somerset, NJ: Wiley-Blackwell.

Starr, Amory. 2005. *Global Revolt: A Guide to the Movements Against Globalization.* London: Zed Books.

Stein, Laura. 2011. "Environmental Website Production: A Structuration Approach." *Media, Culture & Society* 33 (3): 363–84. doi:10.1177/0163443710394898.

Steinfield, Charles, Nicole B. Ellison, and Cliff Lampe. 2008. "Social Capital, Self-Esteem, and Use of Online Social Network Sites: A Longitudinal Analysis." *Journal of Applied Developmental Psychology*, Social Networking on the Internet Developmental Implications, 29 (6): 434–45. doi:10.1016/j.appdev.2008.07.002.

Stiegler, Bernard. 2009. "Teleologics of the Snail The Errant Self Wired to a WiMax Network." *Theory, Culture & Society* 26 (2–3): 33–45. doi:10.1177/0263276409103105.

Strathern, Marylin. 2002. "Abstraction and Decontextualization: An Anthropological Comment." In *Virtual Society?: Technology, Cyberbole, Reality*, edited by Steve Woolgar, 302–14. Oxford; New York: OUP Oxford.

Tapscott, Don, and Anthony D. Williams. 2006. *Wikinomics: How Mass Collaboration Changes Everything.* New York: Portfolio Trade.

Tari, Ilaria, and Marcello Vanni. 2006. "FCJ-023 On the Life and Deeds of San Precario, Patron Saint of Precarious Workers and Lives." http://five.fibreculturejournal.org/fcj-023-on-the-life-and-deeds-of-san-precario-patron-saint-of-precarious-workers-and-lives/.

Tarrow, Sidney G. 1998. *Power in Movement: Social Movements and Contentious Politics.* Cambridge; New York: Cambridge University Press.

Tasner, Michael. 2010. *Marketing in the Moment: The Practical Guide to Using Web 3.0 Marketing to Reach Your Customers First.* FT Press.

Taylor, Charles. 2003. *Modern Social Imaginaries.* Durham, NC: Duke University Press Books.

Taylor, Rupert. 2004. *Creating a Better World: Interpreting Global Civil Society.* Kumarian Press.

Terranova, Tiziana. 2000. "Free Labor: Producing Culture for the Digital Economy." *Social Text* 18 (2): 33–58.

———. 2004. *Network Culture: Politics For the Information Age.* London; Ann Arbor, MI: Pluto Press.

———. 2013. "Free Labor." In *Digital Labor: The Internet as Playground and Factory*, edited by Trebor Scholz, 33–54. New York: Routledge.

Thompson, E. P. 1967. "Time, Work-Discipline, and Industrial Capitalism." *Past & Present*, no. 38 (December): 56–97.

Thörn, Håkan. 2006. *Anti-Apartheid and the Emergence of a Global Civil Society.* London: Palgrave Macmillan.

Thrift, Nigel. 1990. "The Making of a Capitalist Time Consciousness." In *The Sociology of Time*, edited by John Hassard. London: Palgrave Macmillan.

Thurman, Neil, and Merja Myllylahti. 2009. "Taking the Paper Out of News." *Journalism Studies* 10 (5): 691–708. doi:10.1080/14616700902812959.

Tilly, Charles. 1994. "Afterward: Political Memories in Space and Time." In *Remapping Memory: The Politics of TimeSpace*, edited by Jonathan Boyarin, Minnesota Archive ed, 241–57. Minneapolis: University of Minnesota Press.

Toffler, Alvin. 1995. *Creating a New Civilization*. 1st ed. Atlanta: Kansas City, Mo: Titles Distributed by Macmillan Australia.

Tomlinson, John. 1991. *Cultural Imperialism: A Critical Introduction*. London; New York, NY: Continuum International Publishing Group Ltd.

———. 2007. *The Culture of Speed: The Coming of Immediacy*. Los Angeles; London: SAGE Publications Ltd.

Touraine, Alain. 1985. *Actores sociales y sistemas políticos en América Latina*. PREALC.

Trebilcock, Michael J. 1997. *The Limits of Freedom of Contract*. Boston Massachusetts: Harvard University Press.

Treré, Emiliano. 2012. "Social Movements as Information Ecologies: Exploring the Coevolution of Multiple Internet Technologies for Activism." *International Journal of Communication* 6 (0): 19.

Turner, Terrance. 2002. "Representation, Politics, and Cultural Imagination in Indigenous Video: General Points and Kayapo Examples." In *Media Worlds: Anthropology on New Terrain*, edited by Faye D. Ginsburg, Lila Abu-Lughold, and Brian Larkin, 75–90. Berkeley: University of California Press.

———. 2006. "'Kayapo Values: An Application of Marxian Value Theory to a Non-Commodity Based System of Production.'" Paper contributed to the panel, "Values of Value", 100th Annual Meeting of the American Anthropological Association, New Orleans.

Valenzuela, Sebastián, Namsu Park, and Kerk F. Kee. 2009. "Is There Social Capital in a Social Network Site?: Facebook Use and College Students' Life Satisfaction, Trust, and Participation1." *Journal of Computer-Mediated Communication* 14 (4): 875–901. doi:10.1111/j.1083-6101.2009.01474.x.

Van Dijck, José van. 2013. *The Culture of Connectivity: A Critical History of Social Media*. Oxford: Oxford University Press.

———. 2014. "Datafication, Dataism and Dataveillance: Big Data between Scientific Paradigm and Ideology." *Surveillance & Society* 12 (2): 197–208.

Van Dijck, José, and David Nieborg. 2009. "Wikinomics and Its Discontents: A Critical Analysis of Web 2.0 Business Manifestos." *New Media & Society* 11 (5): 855–74. doi:10.1177/1461444809105356.

Virilio, Paul. 1986. *Speed and Politics*. Los Angeles, CA: MIT Press.

———. 1995. "Speed and Information:Cyberspace Alarm!" Edited by Arthur Kroker and Marilouise Koker. *Ctheory.net*. http://www.ctheory.net/articles.aspx?id=72.

———. 2005. *The Information Bomb*. Verso.

Virno, Paolo. 2004. *A Grammar of the Multitude*. Cambridge, Mass; London: Semiotext[e].

Vosko, Leah F. 2006. *Precarious Employment: Understanding Labour Market Insecurity in Canada*. McGill-Queen's Press - MQUP.

Wallerstein, Immanuel. 1980. *The Modern World-System II: Mercantilism and the Consolidation of the European World-Economy, 1600–1750*. Revised ed. New York: Academic Press.

Waltz, Mitzi. 2005. *Alternative and Activist Media*. Edinburgh: Edinburgh University Press.

Waterman, Peter, and Jane Wills. 2001. *Place, Space and the New Labour Internationalisms*. John Wiley & Sons.

Watson, Mark. 2011. *Scripting Intelligence: Web 3.0 Information, Gathering and Processing.* 2009 edition. Berkeley, Calif: Springer.

Webb, Sidney, and Beatrice Potter Webb. 1919. *The History of Trade Unionism, 1666–1920.* [London] Printed by the authors for the Trade Unionists of the United Kingdom. http://archive.org/details/historyoftradeu00pass.

Weber, Max. 1978. *Economy and Society: An Outline of Interpretive Sociology.* University of California Press.

Wellman, Barry. 2001. "Physical Place and Cyberplace: The Rise of Personalized Networking." *International Journal of Urban and Regional Research* 25 (227–252).

Wheeler, Mark. 2000. "Dan Schiller, Digital Capitalism: Networking the Global Market System, (Cambridge, Mass.: MIT Press, 1999) 294 Pp. ISBN 0 262 19417 1." *Convergence: The International Journal of Research into New Media Technologies* 6 (2): 126–28. doi:10.1177/135485650000600211.

Williams, Granville. 2009. *Shafted: The Media, the Miner's Strike & the Aftermath.* Campaign for Press and Broadcasting Freedom.

Wolfson, Todd. 2014. *Digital Rebellion: The Birth of the Cyber Left.* Urbana: University of Illinois Press.

Woolgar, Steve. 2002. *Virtual Society?: Technology, Cyberbole, Reality.* Oxford; New York: OUP Oxford.

Wrigley, Chris. 1997. *British Trade Unions, 1945–1995.* Mancheser, UK: Manchester University Press.

York, Dominic Rushe in New. 2015a. "Large US Tech Firms Plan 'Go Slow' Day in Protest over Net Neutrality Rules." *The Guardian.* Accessed January 19. http://www.theguardian.com/technology/2014/sep/04/etsy-mozilla-reddit-protest-net-neutrality.

———. 2015b. "Large US Tech Firms Plan 'Go Slow' Day in Protest over Net Neutrality Rules." *The Guardian.* Accessed January 19. http://www.theguardian.com/technology/2014/sep/04/etsy-mozilla-reddit-protest-net-neutrality.

Zimmer, Michael. 2008. "The Externalities of Search 2.0: The Emerging Privacy Threats When the Drive for the Perfect Search Engine Meets Web 2.0." *First Monday* 13 (3). doi:10.5210/fm.v13i3.2136.

Index